AF664072

SEED TREATMENT, PLANT HEALTH AND AGRO-TECHNOLOGY

ENV BOOKS SERIES

SEED TREATMENT PLANT HEALTH AND AGRO-TECHNOLOGY

Editors

Dr. Avnish Chauhan
Assistant Professor
Phonics Group of Institutions
Roorkee (Uttarakhand)
(India)

&

Dr. Pawan Kumar 'Bharti'
Vice President
Society for Environment, Health, Awareness of Nutrition & Toxicology (SEHAT)
1775, Sohan Ganj, Near Clock Tower
Delhi - 110 007 (India)
E-mail: *gurupawanbharti@rediffmail.com*

DPH

DISCOVERY PUBLISHING HOUSE PVT. LTD.
NEW DELHI-110 002

Published by:
Namit Wasan
DISCOVERY PUBLISHING HOUSE PVT. LTD.
4383/4B, Ansari Road, Darya Ganj
New Delhi-110 002 (India)
Phone : +91-11-23279245, 43596064-65
Fax : +91-11-23253475
E-mail : discoverypublishinghouse@gmail.com
namitwasan9@gmail.com
sales@discoverypublishinggroup.com
web : www.discoverypublishinggroup.com

First Edition: **2016**

ISBN: 978-93-5056-810-1

Seed Treatment, Plant Health and Agro-Technology

© Editors

All rights reserved. No part of this publication should be reproduced, stored in a retrieval system, or transmitted in any form or by any means: electronic, mechanical, photocopying, recording or otherwise, without the prior written permission of the author and the publisher.

This book has been published in good faith that the material provided by authors is original. Every effort is made to ensure accuracy of material, but the editor, publisher and printer will not be held responsible for any inadvertent error(s). In case of any dispute, all legal matters are to be settled under Delhi jurisdiction only.

Printed at:
Infinity Imaging Systems
Delhi

ENV Books Series, India

Calls lengthy and error free chapters for further volumes of books on various environmental issues. (Send your manuscripts to envbooks@gmail.com)

Founding Editor (Editor-in-Chief)

Dr. Pawan Kumar 'Bharti'
Society for Environment, Health, Awareness of Nutrition & Toxicology (SEHAT-India)
1775, Sohanganj, Near Clock Tower, Delhi-7, (India)
E-mail:*gurupawanbharti@rediffmail.com*

Other Titles by Editor-in-Chief:

1. **Advances in Biotechnology and Ecological Sciences (2013)**
   Bharti, P.K., Chauhan, A. and Ray, J. (eds.)
   (ISBN: 978-93-5056-358-8).
2. **Advances in Agriculture and Ecology (2013)**
   Bharti, P.K.; Chauhan, A. and Ezeaku Peter Ikemefuna (eds.)
   (ISBN: 978-93-5056-362-5).
3. **Agriculture and Environmental Biotechnology (2014)**
   Bharti, P.K. and Chauhan, A. (eds.)
   (ISBN: 978-93-5056-479-0).
4. **Agriculture Development and Sustainable Environment (2015)**
   Ray, J. and Bharti, P. K. (eds.)
   (ISBN: 978-93-5056-759-3)
5. **Agriculture Ecology and Environment (2014)**
   Bharti, P.K. and Olubukola O. Babalola (eds.)
   (ISBN: 978-93-5056-480-6).
6. **Agriculture, Environment and Nano-science (2015)**
   Bharti, Pawan K. (ed.)
   (ISBN: 978-93-5056-760-5)
7. **Agro-biodiversity: *Conservation & Sustainable Development* (2016)**
   Sharma, Pankaj; Singh, Narayan; and Bharti, P.K. (eds.)
   (ISBN: 978-93-505-782-1)
8. **Agro-forestry and Climate Change (2014)**
   Bharti, Pawan K. and Singh, Narayan (eds.)
   (ISBN: 978-93-5056-514-8).

9. **Agro-forestry and Sustainable Agriculture (2016)**
Sharma, Pankaj; Bharti, P.K. (eds.)
(ISBN: 978-93-5056-786-9).
10. **Aquaculture and Fisheries Environment (2014)**
Gupta, S.K. and Pawan K. Bharti (eds.)
(ISBN: 978-93-5056-408-0).
11. **Aquatic Biodiversity and Pollution (2013)**
Bharti, P.K.; Chauhan, A. and Kaoud, H.A.H. (eds.)
(ISBN: 978-93-5056-359-5).
12. **Aquatic Ecology and Biotechnology (2014)**
Bharti, P.K. and Zaki, M.S.A. (eds.)
(ISBN: 978-93-5056-451-6).
13. **Aquatic Environment and Toxicology (2013)**
Bharti, Pawan K. (ed.)
(ISBN: 978-93-5056-236-9).
14. **Biodiversity, Biotechnology and Environmental Conservation (2015)**
Bharti, P.K. and Bhandari, G. (eds.)
(ISBN: 978-93-5056-750-0).
15. **Biodiversity of Aquatic Ecosystem:** ***Significance, Threat and Conservation*** **(2013)**
Bharti, P.K. and Kaoud, H.A.H. (eds.)
(ISBN: 978-93-5056-297-0).
16. **Biological Diversity and Ecology (2016)**
Arya, M.K.; Bharti, P.K. and Ritesh Joshi (eds.)
(ISBN: 978-93-5056-785-2).
17. **Bioremediation and Microbial Biotechnology (2016)**
Gupta, Sandeep; and Bharti, P.K. (eds.)
(ISBN: 978-93-5056-783-8)
18. **Biotechnological Approaches & Water Ecosystem (2016)**
Zaki, M.S.A.; and Bharti, P.K. (eds.)
(ISBN: 978-93-5056-779-1)
19. **Biotechnology, Agro-ecology and Environment (2015)**
Chauhan, Avnish and Bharti, P.K. (eds.)
(ISBN: 978-93-5056-757-9).
20. **Clean Technologies and Environmental Protection (2015)**
Chauhan, A.; Sharma, S. and Bharti, P.K. (eds.)
(ISBN: 978-93-5056-731-9).
21. **Climate Change and Agriculture (2012)**
Bharti, P.K. and Chauhan, Avnish (eds.)
(ISBN: 978-93-5056-148-5).
22. **Climate Change and Biodiversity (2013)**
Bharti, P.K. and Chauhan, Avnish (eds.)
(ISBN: 978-93-5056-360-1).

23. **Climate Change, Disaster Management and Environment (2016)**
Chauhan, Alka; Bharti, P.K. (eds.)
(ISBN: 978-93-5056-784-5).

24. **Conservation and Cultivation of Medicinal Plants (2015)**
Bharti, P.K. and Singh Narayan (eds.)
(ISBN: 978-93-5056-740-1).

25. **Crop Productivity and Plant Disease Management (2016)**
Chauhan, Alka; Bharti, P.K. and Sadana, Deepti (eds.)
(ISBN: 978-93-5056-791-3)

26. **Eco-toxicology and Eco-technology (2013)**
Bharti, P.K. and Zaki, M. (eds.)
(ISBN: 978-93-5056-313-7).

27. **Environmental Biotechnology and Application (2013)**
Bharti, P.K. and Chauhan, Avnish (eds.)
(ISBN: 978-93-5056-262-8).

28. **Environmental Conservation and Biotechnology (2014)**
Chauhan, A. and P.K. Bharti (eds.)
(ISBN: 978-93-5056-512-4).

29. **Environmental Health and Problems (2013)**
Bharti, P.K. and Gajananda, Kh. (eds.)
(ISBN: 978-93-5056-263-5).

30. **Environmental Pollution and Biodiversity (2012)**
Bharti, P.K.; Chauhan, Avnish and Kumar, P. (eds.)
(ISBN: 978-93-5056-149-2).

31. **Fisheries and Toxicology (2014)**
Zaki, M.S.A.; Bharti, P.K. and Chauhan, A. (eds.)
(ISBN: 978-93-5056-452-3).

32. **Fish Habitat and Aquaculture (2015)**
Bharti, P.K.; Gupta Kr. Sanjay (eds.)
(ISBN: 978-93-5056-744-9).

33. **Food Processing, Management and Nanotechnology (2016)**
Chauhan, Avnish; Bharti, P.K. (eds.)
(ISBN: 978-93-5056-796-8).

34. **Freshwater Ecosystem and Xenobiotics (2013)**
Bharti, P.K.; Zaki, M. and Chauhan, A. (eds.)
(ISBN: 978-93-5056-299-4).

35. **Limnology and Aquatic Science (2015)**
Sharma, S. and Bharti, P.K. (eds.)
(ISBN: 978-93-5056-735-7).

36. **Medicinal Plants:** ***Distribution, Utilization and Significance*** **(2015)**
Sharma, P.; Bharti, P.K. and Narayan Singh (eds.)
(ISBN: 978-93-5056-734-0).

37. **Microbial Applications and Environment (2014)**
Bharti, Pawan K. (ed.)
(ISBN: 978-93-5056-515-5).

38. **Microbial Ecology and Habitat (2014)**
Bharti, Pawan K. (ed.)
(ISBN: 978-93-5056-514-8).

39. **Natural Ecosystem and Climate Change (2015)**
Bharti, P.K., and Kh. Gajananda (ed.)
(ISBN: 978-93-5056-745-6).

40. **Pest Management and Agro-Techniques (2016)**
Biswas, Asim; Bharti, P.K., Chauhan, Avnish (eds.)
(ISBN: 978-93-5056-794-4).

41. **Prakriti me Aushadhi (*in Hindi*) (2012)**
Singh, J.R.; Bharti, P.K. and Bharti, B.
(ISBN: 978-93-5056-200-0).

42. **Seed Technology, Plant Growth and Cropping System (2015)**
Tyagi, P.K. and Bharti, P.K. (eds.)
(ISBN: 978-93-5056-738-8).

43. **Soil Characteristics and Agro-ecology (2015)**
Avnish Chauhan and Bharti, P.K. (eds.)
(ISBN: 978-93-5056-758-6)

44. **Soil Contamination and Conservation (2015)**
Ezeaku, P.I. and Bharti, P.K. (eds.)
(ISBN: 978-93-5056-737-1).

45. **Soil Quality and Contamination (2013)**
Bharti, P.K. and Chauhan, Avnish (eds.)
(ISBN: 978-93-5056-361-8).

46. **Sustainable Aquaculture Management (2016)**
Gupta, S.K.; Bharti, P.K (eds.)
(ISBN: 978-93-5056-797-5).

47. **Waste Disposal and Management (2015)**
Bharti, P.K.; Tabassum, B. and Bajaj, P. (eds.)
(ISBN: 978-93-5056-729-6).

48. **Waste Generation and Utilization (2016)**
Bajaj Priya; Tabassum, B., and Bharti, P.K. (eds.)
(ISBN: 978-93-5056-792-0).

49. **Waste Management and Environmental Health (2016)**
Tabassum, B., Bajaj Priya, and Bharti, P.K. (eds.)
(ISBN: 978-93-5056-777-7).

50. **Water Resources and Agriculture (2014)**
Bharti, P.K. and Ezeaku Peter Ikemefuna (eds.)
(ISBN: 978-93-5056-481-3).

51. **Waste Resources Management: *Monitoring and Assessment* (2016)**
Gupta, Sandeep and Bharti, P.K. (eds.)
(ISBN: 978-93-5056-799-9).

Preface

In agriculture and horticulture, seed treatment or seed dressing is a chemical, typically antimicrobial or fungidal, with which seeds are treated or dressed prior to planting. Less frequently insecticides are added. Seed treatments can be an environmentally more friendly way of using pesticides as the amounts used can be very small. It is usual to add colour to make treated seed less attractive to birds if spilt and easier to see and clean up in the case of an accidental spillage. Seed coating is a thicker form of covering of seed and may contain fertilizer, growth promoters and or seed treatment as well as an inert carrier and a polymer outer shell. Seed dressing is also used to refer to the process of removing chaff, weed seeds and straw from a seed stock.

The concept of seed treatment is the use and application of biological and chemical agents that control or contain primary soil and seed borne infestation of insects and diseases which pose devastating consequences to crop production and improving crop safety leading to good establishment of healthy and vigorous plants resulting better yields. Presently, 70% requirement of seed is met from the farmer's own stock, which goes for sowing without seed treatment. Even if seed is sourced from the private or public sector agencies, except hybrid seeds, large percentage of such seed is untreated. The estimates reveal that on an average, 80% of the seed sown in the country is untreated, as against the 100% seed treatment practice in developed countries. Seed treatment not only protects the seeds from seed and soil borne diseases but also gives protection to the emerged seedlings from sucking insect pests affecting crop emergence and its early growth. However, many farmers in the country are neither familiar with the practice nor follow it. The practice of seed treatment is also IPM compatible. However, seed treatments should not be considered as a cure for all maladies for the selection of poor/unhealthy seed lots. For example, treatment of seeds with excessive mechanical damage or other damages or seeds kept in poor storage conditions, or genetic differences in a variety will not increase seed germination.

Agriculture is the cultivation of animals, plants, fungi, and other life forms for food, fiber, biofuel, medicinal and other products used to sustain and enhance human life. Agriculture was the key development in the rise of sedentary human civilization, whereby farming of domesticated species created food surpluses that nurtured the development of civilization. The study of agriculture is known as agricultural science. The history of agriculture dates back thousands of years, and its development has been driven and defined by greatly different climates, cultures, and technologies. However, all farming generally relies on techniques to expand and maintain the lands that are suitable for raising domesticated species.

This book updates the subject matter and issues related to Seed treatment technology, plant health issues, agro-technology and sustainable development. Thanks are due to contributors from various institutions and publisher for their interest in this book. The book will definitely provide a multidisciplinary forum to explore emerging areas in the field of seed technology, plant health, agro-biodiversity, biotechnology, environmental conservation and agro-technology.

–Editors

(envbooks@gmail.com)

Contents

Pages: 1-13

SEED TREATMENT, PLANT HEALTH AND AGRO-TECHNOLOGY

Edited by: Dr. Avnish Chauhan and Dr. Pawan Kumar 'Bharti'

ISBN: 978-93-5056-810-1

***Edition:* 2016**

***Published by:* Discovery Publishing House Pvt. Ltd., New Delhi (India)**

1

Seed Treatment Methods in Vegetable Crops

Chandan Singh Ahirwar[1] and D.K. Singh[2]

Introduction

Seed treatment practices Seed treatment practices offer three approaches through biological or chemical control of pests. Treatment of vegetable seeds to kill disease-causing organisms (pathogens) carried within or on the seed has repeatedly been shown to prevent plant disease epidemics (epiphytotics). Chemical seed treatments also protect the seed or seedling from the common soil-inhabiting fungi that cause seed rots and dampingoff diseases. When seed is planted in cold wet soil or is slow to germinate, it may be necessary to treat seed in order to obtain satisfactory plant stands. Seed treatment can be useful in reducing the amount of pesticide required to manage a disease, because an effective seed treatment can eliminate the need to make foliar applications of fungicides or bactericides later in the season. This reduction in pesticide use is both economically and environmentally beneficial. Treatments may disinfect (kill pathogens borne within the seed), disinfest (kill externally born pathogens), or protect the seed.

Raising seedlings for transplanting is extensively practiced around the world for most horticultural crops except certain root vegetables such as radishes, carrots, beets etc. Transplanting is also increasingly being practiced with field crops such as rice and sweet corn in many parts of the world.

[1] Ph.D. Scholar, Department of Vegetable Science, College of Agriculture, Govind Ballabh Pant University of Agriculture and Technology, Pantnagar, Uttarakhand - 263 145 (India)

[2] Professor, Department of Vegetable Science, College of Agriculture, Govind Ballabh Pant University of Agriculture and Technology, Pantnagar, Uttarakhand - 263 145 (India)

Even though a large proportion of the transplants are raised by individual growers on their own farms, commercial production of seedlings has been rapidly increasing in many countries. The reasons for raising transplants are that they:

- Provide intimate protection of seedlings from climatic and biological stresses
- Allow early harvest and yield increases
- Make it possible to grow warm-season crops in regions too cold for direct seeding
- Allow plants to develop better root systems
- Promote or prevent flower bud differentiation and germination rate
- Facilitate grafting and increase grafting operations
- Reduce labour and management expenses during the early stage
- Increase land-use efficiency.

Seed Protectants

Fungicide label registrations are always changing, thus the information provided in this publication may become invalid at anytime. Always read the entire, most recent label carefully and follow all directions and restrictions before using one of the recommended seed protectants.

- **Protectant** – protection of the health of the host plant
- **Eradicant** – curative therapy of an infested host plant
- **Disinfectant** – destruction of a phase in the life cycle of the pest

The earliest reported use of a seed treatment dates back to 60 A.D., when wine and crushed cypress leaves were used to protect seed from storage insects. The active component in this mixture was likely hydrogen cyanide.

Fungicide seed treatment had a serendipitous beginning in the 17th century, when wheat seed salvaged from a shipwreck near the United Kingdom grew very well.

Improvement in shelf life of the seed, protection of seed during germination, seedling establishment and improvement in the vigour of seedling and plant with chemical or physical treatment of seed.

In 1948, a fungicide named captan was discovered, and in 1950 was introduced as a seed treatment. Captan was a broad-spectrum contact fungicide, and was rapidly introduced to a number of crops, including field corn

Vegetable crops are grown worldwide as a source of nu-trients and fiber in the human diet. Fungal plant pathogens can cause devastation in these crops under appropriate en-vironmental conditions. Vegetable producers confronted with the challenges of managing fungal pathogens have the opportunity to use fungi, bacteria and yeasts as biological control agents. Several commercially available products have shown significant disease reduction through various mechanisms to reduce pathogen development and disease. Plant diseases need to be controlled to maintain the quality and abundance of food, feed, and fiber produced by growers around the world. Different approaches may be used to prevent, mitigate or control plant diseases. Beyond good agronomic and horticultural practices, growers often rely heavily on chemical fertilizers and pesticides.

A fairly large number of pathogens are carried externally or internally in the seed. The pathogen associated with the seed also becomes active when the seed germination takes place resulting in seed rot, seedling decay/ deformities or produces disease at a later crop growth stage. Use of healthy seed, free from seed- borne pathogens is ideal for management of seed borne diseases. However, it is very difficult to obtain seed free from pathogens particularly in the tropical climate of India. The next choice remains to treat the seed with chemicals, use of physical factors or bio-control agents. Recently several novel methods have been developed to manage seed borne diseases by seed treatment.

The purpose of any seed treatment is to improve seed performance in one or more of the following ways:

1. Eradicate seed borne pathogens or protect from soil borne pathogens.
2. Optimize ease of handling and accuracy of planting (reduce gaps in stand or the need for thinning of seedlings, particularly when mechanical planters are used).
3. Improve germination rates. In conventional production, seed is often treated with chemical fungicides which reduce seed and seedling losses due to seed borne and soil borne disease.
4. Most seed protestants are not an option for organic growers, however, there are some seed treatments, such as priming, pelletizing, and the use of hot water can be used by organic farmers to improve seed performance.
5. Certain crops are better candidates for seed treatment due to the nature of the seed (small or irregularly shaped) or the intended production regime. For example, pelleted seed is useful in head lettuce production because of the need for precision seeding, but is less advantageous for thick sowings of loose-leaf lettuce in bed production.

Type of Seed treatment:

1. Chemical Treatment
2. Physical Treatment
3. Biological Treatment

1. Chemical Treatment

The chemical may be a fungicide (to kill fungus) or antibiotic (to kill bacteria) or nematocide (to kill nematodes) with different formulations including, water dispersible powder (WP), dust or slurries are used to control specific pathogen. Based on the mode of action the chemical may be a protectant i.e., the chemical that becomes effective when applied prior to infection e.g., captan, thiram, organo-mercurial, dithane M-45, ziram, ferbam etc., and herapeutant i.e., the chemical that is capable of eradicating the pathogen after it has caused infection and there by cure the plant e.g., carbandazim (bavistin, derosol), oxathin (vitavax), benzidmiazole (benomyl) etc. The chemicals those act by entering into the system of the plant are known as systemic e.g., therapeutant chemicals, whereas, the other chemicals, which do not act systemically are called non-systemic e.g., protectant chemicals.

Seed treatment with chemicals: Seeds can be treated with following methods.

1. **Rotary seed dresser**: Small quantity of seed is treated by rotary seed dresser.
2. **Slurry treater:** Large quantity of seed in seed processing plant is treated by slurry treater. The required quantity of the chemical is automatically mixed with the specified quantity of seed before bagging. In a seed processing plant it is a continuous process and is more efficient than rotary seed dresser.
3. **Seed dip method:** It involves the dipping of seed or propagating material in a chemical (Fungicide and antibiotic etc.) solution for a specified period prior to sowing. Seed soaking with organo-mercurial (for potato scab), Dithane M-45 or ridomil (for potato late blight), streptomycin sulphate (for cabbage, cauliflower or mustard bacterial and fungal diseases) have been found effective. Hot water treatment followed by seed dip in streptomycin sulphate has given very effective results against bacterial diseases of cabbage and cauliflower. Seed soaking of cluster and Indian bean in antibiotics like streptocycline and aureofungin controls Xanthomonas spp. Seed dip and treatment with 20 percent trisodium phosphate solution dilute the tobacco mosaic virus (TMV) concentration.
4. **Seed seeping in botanicals:** Soaking of loose smut infected wheat seeds in 3 per cent onion or 4 percent garlic extract at 300C for 29 hours bring down the infection, however, soaked seeds cannot be stored for more than 10 months. With the development of systemic fungicides for loose smut pathogen the rest of the methods have only academic significance. Hopper box treatment: Requisite quantity of the chemical (dust formulation) is mixed in the hopper box of a seed drill before sowing.

5. **Vacuum infiltration:** Soaking of seed in captafol or benomyl (lg a.i./1 water plus 0.1 ml Tween-20) solution for seven days with change of solution every day or as a vacuum infiltration treatment keeping the seed in a vacuum pump/chamber has been reported' most effective for controlling deep seated *Fusarium oxusporium* f.sp. *elacidies* in oil palm.
6. **Osmotic priming:** Aqueous solution of polyethylene glycol (PEG) provides an osmotic environment. Immersion of seed in PEG solution followed by drying and storage does not impair germination and the method is called osmotic priming. Immersing rice seed' 20% PEG containing 0.1% carboxin reduces seed-borne infection of *Drechslera oryzae.*
7. **Solid matrix priming:** Pre sown hydration in a solid based medium is called solid matrix priming. It increases the efficiency of the fungicide in contrile of seed born infection. Seed treatment with standard fungicides (Thiram, Captan, Metalaxyle etc.) plus priming agent effectively control the seed and soil borne pathogens and increase the stand od maize in field whereas, seed treatment only with fungicide is ineffective.

Fungicides with major target seed borne diseases:

Fungicide	Disease
Metalaxyl	Downy mildew of sunflower and pearl millet, late blight of potato
Benomyl	Dry rot of potato, wilt of sweet potato, *Ascochyta* blight of French bean, cluster bean and Indian bean, *Phomopsis* blight of brinjal, ashy stem of cowpea, *Allthrac1lose* of cowpea, Indian bean, French bean, *Cercospora* leaf spot of sesame
Carboxin	Loose smut of wheat, barley etc.
Thiram plus carbendazim	*Anthracnose* of French bean, cluster bean, cowpea, fruit rot of brinjal, tomato leaf spot, ashy stem of cowpea and potato *Phoma* rot
Mancozeb, Ziram (as foliar application)	Protective fungicide for major diseases (bean anthracnose, Alternaria leaf spot, Phomopsis fruit rot), Fusarial wilt, chilli-ripe fruit rot and ergot of sorghum and pearl millet early and late blight of tomato, potato, chilli, and anthracnose.
Propiconazole (as foliar application)	Bunt of rice, wheat and triticale

2. Physical Treatment:

1. **Seed dip in water:** Soaking of seed in plain water at 20°C for 41 hours reduces the loose smut infection without damage to wheat seed. Soaking in water at 28°C for 41 hours or 30°C for 28 hours eliminate the fungus from wheat seed effectively.

2. **Hot water treatment:** The seeds are dipped for specific period of time in hot water to a particular temperature safe to the seed embryo and deleterious to the associated pathogen. This method is useful for low volume high value seed. The method is effective for internally associated fungi and bacterial pathogens. Hot water (52°C) treatment for 30 minutes ensures effective control of black leg of cabbage and black rot of cabbage and cauliflower.

After treatment, dip bags in cold water to stop heating action, spread seeds to dry Recommends applying protective seed tx fungicide to hot-water treated seed old seed can be severely damaged by this treatment. A small sample of any seed lot over 1 year old should be treated and tested for germination to determine amount of injury that may occurThiram is most frequently suggested seed-protectant.

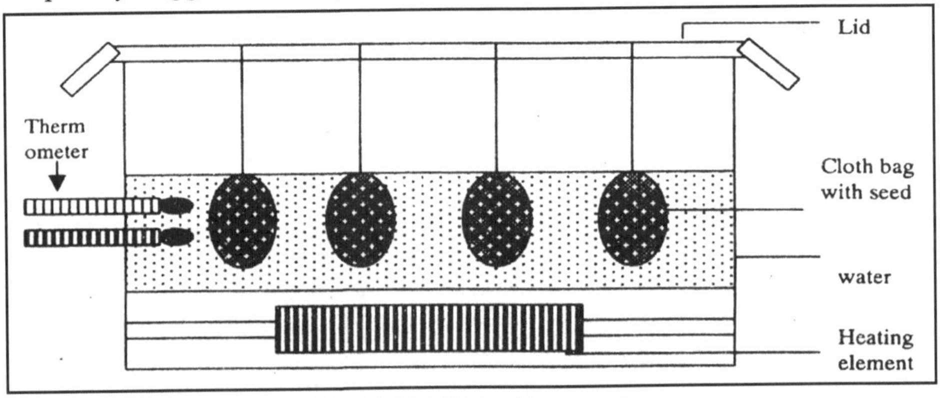

Fig.1.1: **Hot Water Treatment**

3. **Hot air treatment**: The seed material is exposed to hot air stream for a specific period, which is safe for viability of seed. The method is more effective for the Pathogens associated on to the seed surface. Treatment of set with hot air currents ensures effective control of smut pathogen.

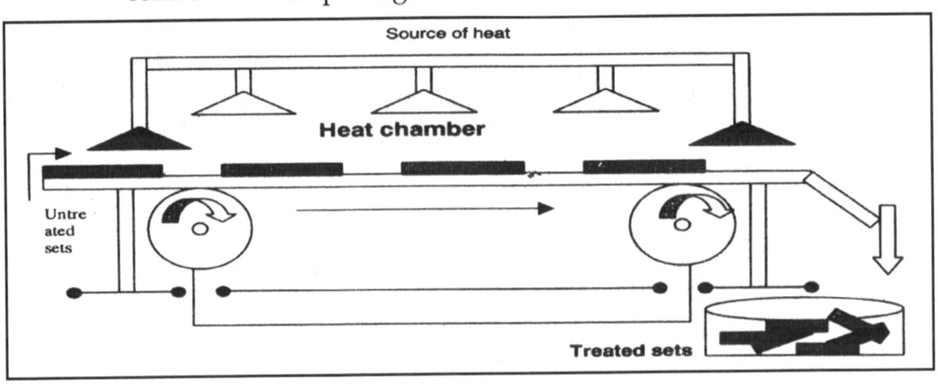

Fig. 1.2: **Hot Air Treatment**

Table 1.1: Recommended Temperatures and Treatment Times for Hot Water Disinfestations of Vegetable Seed

M. L. Lewis Ivey, Plant Pathologist, Louisiana State University, LSU Ag Center		
Vegetable Crop	**Water Temperature (°F°/°C)**	**Soaking Time**
Broccoli	122/50	20 to 25
Brussel sprouts	122/50	25
Cabbage	122/50	25
Carrot	122/50	15 to 20
Cauliflower	122/50	20
Celery	122/50	25
Chinese cabbage	122/50	20
Collard	122/50	20
Cucumber	122/50	20
Eggplant	122/50	25
Garlic	120/49	20
Kale, Kohlrabi	122/50	20
Lettuce	118/48	30
Mint	112/44	10
Mustard, Cress, Radish	122/50	15
Onion	115/46	60
Pepper	125/51	30
Rape, Rutabaga	122/50	20
Shallot	115/46	60
Spinach	122/50	25
Tomato	122/50	25
Turnip	122/50	20

Note: Cucurbits other than cucumbers can be severely damaged by hot water treatment and should be disinfested using chlorine bleach.

4. **Solar energy treatment**: The seeds are soaked in water for 6-8 hours thereby activating the dormant mycelium present in the embryo and subsequently exposing the seed lot to solar heat. As a result of the solar heat the activated mycelium is destroyed without damaging the seeds. Soaking of seed for 4 hours in cold water on a bright summer day and then spread over a hard cemented floor or on galvanized iron sheet exposing the seeds to direct sun light for: 4-6 hours controls the-disease

5. **Seed seeping:** Seed seeping in 20 percent commercial salt (common salt) efficiently eliminate the lighter, chaffy, karnal bunt infected seeds and nematode galls from seed and seed of *Cichorium intybus.*

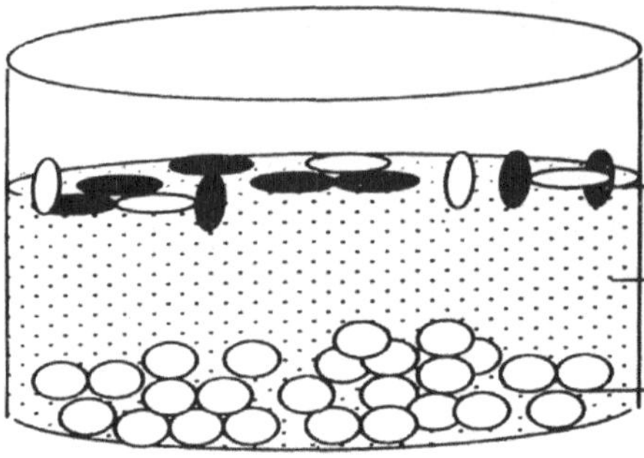

Fig. 1.3: **Seed Seeping in Brine Solution**

3. Biological Treatment

Micro-organisms have also been successfully used as seed treatment. Seed treatment with of *Brassicca* seed with Gilcoladium roseum and *Trichoderma harzianum* reduced infection of *alternaria brassicola* and increases the seedling emergence. Several formulations of biological control agents are available in the marker. Solid matrix priming alongwith addition of a biological control agent is called bio-priming effectively controls various seed and soil borne diseases and also improves the emergence.

Products of seed treatment developed from Pantnagar:

1. **Biocontrol agent-1** for plant disease control
2. **Biocontrol agent-2** for plant disease control
3. **Biocontrol agent-3** for plant disease control
4. **Biocontrol agent-4** for plant disease control
5. **Beauveria bassiana** for insect control

Products for the industry: Effective strains of following bioagents along with bioefficacy data available.

1. *Trichoderma harzianum*
2. *Pseudomonas fluorescens*
3. Mixed formulation of compatible strains of *T. harzianum* + *P. fluorescens*
4. *Beauveria bassiana*

The Some important seed borne fungal diseases not designated as objectionable.

Recommendation of Seed Treatment for Vegetable Crops

Sl.No.	Name of Crop	Pest/Disease	Seed Treatment	Remarks
1	**Chillies**	Anthracnose spp. Damping off	Seed treatment with *Trichoderma viride* 4g/kg, Carbandazim @ 1g/100 gm seed.	For seed dressing metal seed dresser/ earthern pots or polythene bags are used.
		Soil borne infection of fungal disease, Jassid, aphid, thrips	*Trichoderma viride* @ 2 gm/kg. seed and *Pseudomonas flourescens,* @ 10gm/kg. Captan 75 WS @ 1.5 to 2.5 gm a.i./litre for soil drenching. *Imidacloprid* 70 WS @ 10-15 gm a.i./kg seed	-do-
2	**Pea**	Root rot White rot	- *Bacillus subtilis* - *Pseudomonas fluorescens* Soil application @ 2.5-5 kg in 100kg FYM or - *Carbendazim* or *Captan* 2 gm/kg. seed -*Thiram+Carbendazim* 2gm/kg seed -*Carbendazim* or *Captan* 2gm/kg seed	For seed dressing metal seed dresser/ earthern pots or polythene bags are used.
3	**Bhindi**	Root knot nematode	*Paecilomyces lilacinus* and *Pseudomonas fluorescens* @ 10 gm/kg as seed dresser.	-do-

(Contd...)

Sl.No.	Name of Crop	Pest/Disease	Seed Treatment	Remarks
4	**Tomato**	Soil borne infection of fungal disease Early blight, Damping off and Wilt	*T. viride* @ 2 gm/100gm seed. Captan 75 WS @ 1.5 to 2.0 gm a.i./litre for soil drenching. *Pseudomonas fluorescens* and *V. clamydosporium* @ 10gm/kg as seed dresser.	For seed dressing metal seed dresser/earthern pots or polythene bags are used.
5	**Coriander**	Wilt	*Trichoderma viride* @ 4 gm./kg seed.	-do-
6	**Brinjal**	Bacterial wilt	*Pseudomonas fluorescens* @ 10gm/kg.	-do-
7	**Leguminous Vegetables**	Soil borne infection, Nematode	*Trichoderma viride* @ 2 gm/100gms. seed. Carbofuran/Carbosulfan 3% (w/w)	-do-
8	**Cruciferous vegetables (Cabbage, Cauliflower, Broccoli, Knol-khol, radish)**	Soil/Seed borne diseases (Damping off) Root knot nematode	*Trichoderma viridi* @ 2 g/100 g seeds Captan 75% WS @ 1.5 to 2.5 gm a.i./litre for soil drenching. *Pseudomonas fluorescens* and *Verlicillium* clamydosporium @ 10gm/kg seed as seed dresser.	For seed dressing metal seed dresser/earthern pots or polythene bags are used

(Contd...)

Sl.No.	Name of Crop	Pest/Disease	Seed Treatment	Remarks
9	**Potato**	Soil and Tuber borne diseases	Seed treatment with MEMC 3% WS @ 0.25% or boric acid 3% for 20 minuts before storage.	
10	**Capsicum**	Root knot nematode	*Pseudomonas fluorescens* 1% WP, Paecilomyces *lilacirius* and *Verticillium chlamydosporium* 1% WP @ 10g/kg as seed dresser.	For seed dressing metal seed dresser/ earthern pots or polythene bags are used

Seed Coating

Seed coating is one of the most useful and handy means of seed treatment. Seed handling and placement can be greatly simplified by altering seed shape. Placement of agrochemicals in seed-coating materials that regulate and improve germination greatly enhances seedling growth.

Seed Coat Removal

Partial removal of the seed coat, either by chemicals such as sulphuric acid or by using a sharp knife or sandpaper, can significantly increase germination and seedling establishment. Seeds of triploid watermelons are frequently processed this way, and nail clippers are frequently used by growers for seeds of triploid watermelons and some hard-seeded rootstock seeds such as star cucumbers. The removal of spines or beards from carrot seeds greatly enhances early seed germination. Elaborated removal of the pericarp from spinach seeds, botanically fruit, greatly enhances the germination of spinach, thus resulting in an early harvest of uniform produce.

Benefits of Seed Processing Treatments

Some seed treatments such as heat and scarification are familiar practices and have been used by growers at sowing time. Some recently developed treatments are still being researched. The benefits of seed treatments vary with crops and cultural practices.

1. Reduction or inactivation of seed-borne pathogens such as viruses, bacteria and fungi.
2. Control and/or prevention of soil-borne diseases.
3. Enhancement of seed and seedling vigour.
4. Facilitation of handling and mechanical sowing.
5. Efficient and accurate addition of agrochemicals, nutrients, plant bio-regulators etc.
6. A supply of useful micro-organisms.
7. Reduction of labour needed for pest management.
8. An increase in the tolerance in seedlings of adverse environmental conditions.
9. Reduction of the total amount of agrochemicals required for crop protection.

Conclusion

Seed treatment techniques have been developed mainly by large seed companies that produce and distribute seeds. Producing high-quality seeds and applying proper fungicide treatments have been the most common treatments. However, due to increasing concern about the chemicals that are added to various seeds and the possible residual effects, more sophisticated and safer methods of seed treatment are required. Upgraded seeds of high quality, which have been proven to provide higher and uniform germination as well as vigorous and uniform seedling growth, have become vital pre-requisites for some cultural practices, especially direct seeding in the field as well as machine sowing in cell trays under greenhouse conditions.

REFERENCES

Cantliffe, D.J., 1997. "Industrial Processing of Vegetable Seeds", *Journ. Kor. Soc. Hort. Sci.* 38; pp. 441-455.

Cantliffe, D.J., 1993. "Pre- and Postharvest Practices for Improved Vegetable Transparent Quality", *Horttechnology* 3: 415-418.

Copeland, L. O. And M. B. Mcdonald. 1995. Principles of Seed Science and Technology. Kluwer Academic Publishers.

C. Life Foundation 2013. The Role of Seed Treatment in Modern U.S. Seed Production. 1156: 15. St NW, Suite 400 Washington.

Chaube H.S, Pundhir VA. 2005. Crop Diseases and Their Management. PHI Learning Pvt. Ltd. Http://books.google.com/books?Id=rgaded3dstec&source=gbs_navlinks_s

Desai, B.B., P.M. Kotecha and D.K. Salunkhe, 1997. *Seeds Handbook: Biology, Production, Processing and Storage*, Marcel Dekker; pp. 503-520.

George, R.A.T., 1999. *Vegetable Seed Production*, CABI Publishing, Oxon, Wallingford, United Kingdom.

Greathead, A.S., 2003. "Prevention and Management of Disease on Vegetable Transplants", *Hort. Technology* 13; pp. 55-57.

ISTA, 2003. International Rules for Seed Testing, Annex to Chapter 7, Seed Health Testing Methods: 7-002a/b Blotter and Malt Agar Method for the Detection of *Alternaria radicina* on *Daucus carota*.

Jalink, H., R. Van der Schoor, A. Frandas, J.G. van Pijlen & R.J. Bino (1998). Chlorophyll Fluorescence of *Brassica oleracea* Seeds as a Non-destructive Marker for Seed Maturity and Seed Performance. Seed Science Research 8: 437-443.

Konstantinova, P., R. Van der Schoor, R. Van den Bulk and H. Jalink (2002). Chlorophyll Fluorescence Sorting as a Method for Improvement of Barley (*Hordeum vulgare* L.) Seed Health and Germination. Seed Sci. Technol. 30: 411-421.

Khan, A.A., (1992). "Pre-plant Physiological Seed Conditioning", *Hort. Rev.* 13; pp. 131-181.

Khan, A.A., A. Szafirowska, I. Satriyas and W. Ptasznik. (1995). "Pre-sowing Seed Conditioning to Improve Stand Establishment and Yield of Vegetables", *Journ. Kor. Soc. Hort. Sci.* 36; pp. 438-451.

Prior, B.M., R.M. Davis and R.L. Gilbertson, (1994). Detection and Eradication of *Alternaria radicina* on Carrot Seed. Plant Disease 78: 452-456.

Pages: 14-32

SEEDTREATMENT, PLANT HEALTH AND AGRO-TECHNOLOGY

Edited by: Dr. Avnish Chauhan and Dr. Pawan Kumar 'Bharti'

ISBN: 978-93-5056-810-1

Edition: 2016

Published by: Discovery Publishing House Pvt. Ltd., New Delhi (India)

2

Isolation and Identification of Pathogens (Fungi) from Sorghum Seeds and Their Effect on Germination of Seeds

Shashi Kant*, Manisha Gautam and **Bhawna Bajpai**

ABSTRACT

Sorghum has multiple uses as grain, forage, fodder, and more recently as bioenergy crop. In Asia and Africa, sorghum grains are consumed by humen or as animal feed; stalks are used as animal fodder, or as housing material. It is a major staple food crop of Africa and in Asia and especially in India. The crop has been suffered from various types of diseases majority of them are known to be caused by fungi, which are mostly seed born. An experiment was conducted at the department of botany in c.c.s. university Meerut (U.P.) to assess the incidence of seed born fungi and their effects on seed germination on Sorghum bicolor. Two varieties (Kanpuri Jowar and Desi Jowar) were collected from different locations of Meerut and Baghpat distt. fungi associated with sorghum genotype were detected by using standard blotter method and studied the fungal colony characters after isolation. About seven different seed borne pathogens were identified in order of the infection.

Key words: Sorghum bicolor, pathogens, diseases.

INTRODUCTION

Sorghum is a tropical plant belonging to the family poacea. Several improved varieties are released every year by sorghum breeders. More than 7000 sorghum varieties have been identified (Knudsen *et al.*, 1988). It is

Department of Botany, C.C.S. University, Meerut (U.P.) (India).

popularly known as "Jowar" in India. Sorghum plant is a potentially attractive raw material for food, feed, fuel and industry (Hallgreen *et al.*,1992). Grain sorghum is the most commonly cultivated agronomic type of sorghum worldwide (Banerjee and Dahlberg, 2004).

Sorghum grain has 95 to 98% of the nutritional value of maize; vitamin content for corn and sorghum is similar but sorghum has a higher mineral content than maize (Balota, 2012 ,Jacob *et al.* 2013). Sorghum grain has a lot of nutritional benefits due to its rich antioxidant properties (Green, 2012). It is higher in protein (11.5 to 16.5%) and calories than several other grains (Martin and MacMasters, 1950).

Sorghum contains the following vitamins and minerals: vitamins B1, B2 and B3, calcium (Ca), potassium (K), iron (Fe), phosphorous (P), and sodium (Na). 100g (one cup serving) would provide 55% Recommended Dietary Allowance (RDA) of phosphorus, 19% RDA of potassium, 47% RDA of iron, 5.4% RDA of calcium and 0.5% RDA of sodium.

Protein is one of the major components of sorghum; the primary function of dietaryprotein is to satisfy the body's need for nitrogen and essential amino acid (FAO, 1995). The average starch content of sorghum is 69.5% (Jambunathan and Subramanian, 1988), and the crude fat content is 3% which is higher than wheat and rice (FAO, 1995). It contains no cholesterol, and like all other grains, has a fairly good amount of carbohydrates that could meet a good deal of recommended daily intake (Thompson, 2010).

Sorghum is cultivated during both rainy (kharif) and postrainy (rabi) seasons. All cultivated sorghum belongs to Sorghum bicolor subsp.bicolor. when conditions are congenial for the seed infection by large number of fungi, some of them are seed transmitted, resulting into poor seed germination and plant stand in the field affecting the quality and yield. The most destructive Sorghum diseases reported are fungal diseases.

Seed is a basic input for the production of crops. The Government of India has taken steps for the production and distribution of good quality seeds of high-yielding cultivars through the National Seed Programme. In addition, several agencies in the private sector have also ta~en up the task of producing and distributing high-quality seeds to farmers. So far only the germination and purity of seed were thought to be the main criteria for quality. In recent years, however, with the increasing incidence of seed-borne diseases like Karnal bunt and loose smut of wheat, bunt and bacterial leaf blight of paddy, and ergot and downy mildew of pearlmillet, there is better appreciation of the need of producing disease-free seed. Seed production personnel and the farmers make anxious inquiries about the seed-borne diseases and about the ways and means of controlling them.

Sorghum is an important grain and forage crop of semiarid regions due to its high adaptability and suitability to rain-fed low input agriculture. It has substantial popularity amongst farmers due to its greater adaptability and various forms of utilization like green fodder, stover, silage and hay to suit the diverse needs of farming system, besides its grain.

Grain mold is most commonly caused by *Fusarium moniliforme* J. Sheld. and *Curvularialunata* (Wakk.) Boedjin, although many other fungal species are also associated with the mold complex. (Esele *et al.*, 1993). (Navi *et al.*, 1999).

The literature on brief account of sorghum seed borne fungi on various aspects has reviewed which is given belo.

Symptoms and Signs of Pathogens

Sorghum is known to suffer from more than 30 fungal diseases (USDA, 1960). Important seed borne fungal diseases recorded on sorghum are stalk rot (*Aspergillus niger*), target spot (*Bipolaris sorghicola*), stalk rot/anthracnose/ red leaf (*Colletotrichum graminicola*), seed rot/stalk rot (*Fusarium verticillioides*), seedling blight/charcoal rot (*Macrophomina phaseolina*) and covered smut/ grain smut (*Sphacelotheca sorghi*) (Richardson, 1990). Seed is the most important input for crop production. Pathogen free healthy seed is urgently needed for desired plant populations and good harvest. Many plant pathogens are seed borne and can cause enormous crop losses. Besides, the mold fungi growing on the seed substratum produce mycotoxins which are hazardous to man and animals (Halt, 1994).

The major constraints of sorghum production are insects, birds and diseases. Fungi and bacteria are important sorghum disease pathogens. Anthracnose is a seed, soil and trash borne fungal disease of sorghum caused by *Colletotrichum sublineolum* (formerly called *Colletotrichum graminicola*). It is the most destructive foliar disease of sorghum, most prevalent in warm humid regions. Anthracnose affects all plant parts including the, stem, leaf, peduncle, inflorescence and grain (Gwary *et al.*, 2003). Various reports have shown yield losses of up to 67% (Pande *et al.*, 1991; Marley, 1996; Gwary *et al.*, 2002).

Curvularia species have been reported as causal agents of leaf spots, leaf blights, kernel rot, root rot, seedling blights, grain discoloration, grain lesions and rice grain deformation (Rashid, 2001; Parimelazhagan and Francis, 1999; Kim- Jisoo and Lee-DuHyung, 1998; Sisterna and Bello, 1998).

Some *Curvularia* species have been more extensively studied since they are known as cellulase producers (Banerjee, 1990; Banerjee, 1992; Freire, 1995; Jyoti and Sing, 1985; Nitharwal *et al.*, 1991).*Curvularia. verruculosa* has a haloperoxidase enzyme system, which has been found to cause reductions in counts of some bacteria, yeasts and filamentous fungi. Hence, it has been shown to have an effective disinfectant property on contact lenses (Eva etal., 2003). 3 different species of *Curvularia* [(*C. affinis Boedijn, C. clavata B.L. Jain and C. penniseti* (M. Mitra) Boedijn] have been reported on Eichhornia crassipes in the United State of America and India (Evans and Reeder, 2001).

Bonzi, S., 2007 and Zida *et al* 2008 told that *Phoma sorghina* is one of the seed-borne fungi most frequently detected on sorghum samples collected in farmers' yards in Burkina Faso. It is one of the fungi responsible of sorghum seed mould.

Thakur *et al.* (2006) described symptoms produced by each fungus on the sorghum grains as white to pinkish white by *Fusarium spp.*, shiny velvety black by *Curvularialunata*, grayish black by *Altenaria alternata* and pin-head black pycnidia by *Phoma sorghina* while *Colletotrichum graminicola* produces small, black, enlarged acervuli studded with clusters of setae forming concentric rings on the grain.

Isolation of Pathogen

Isolation of pathogen is necessary for diagnosis of a particular disease. It provides information regarding on the surface and inside the seed. It is most reliable method to find out about seed health , their further use as seed.

Fusarium moniliforme, Fusarium oxysporum, Curvularialunata, Fusarium semitectum from mouldy grains of sorghum was isolated by Bhagwat and Pedgaonkar (1973). Seventeen fungal species belonging to eleven genera from field-collected molded sorghum grain in England isolated by Rao and Williams (1978). The fungi isolated included *Alternaria triticina, Cladosporium tenniussimum*, Cohiliobolus spicifer, *Colletotrichum sp., Curvularialunata, Curvularia* verruculosa, Drechslera halodes, Drechslera sp., *Fusarium semitectum,Fusarium moniliforme, Fusarium acuminatum, Fusarium lateritium, Olpitrichum sp., Penicillium oxalicum, Phoma sorghina* and *Trichothecium roseum*. The most frequently isolated genera were *Fusarium, Curvularia, Phoma* and *Trichothecium.*

Grain Molds Effect on Seed Germination of Sorghum

Grain mold, caused by a complex of fungi, is a serious problem of sorghum (Sorghum bicolor) that affects its grain yield, quality and market value. The annual economic loss in Asia and Africa as a result of grain mold is more than US$130 million (Chandrashekar *et al.* 2000). Early-maturing, short-statured, high-yielding hybrids that flower and mature during wet weather are particularly vulnerable to attack by mold fungi. Among the fungi involved in the mold complex, species of *Fusarium, Curvularia* and *Alternaria* are more abundant than others (Girish *et al.* 2004). *Fusarium spp.* was noticed by Tarr (1962). Tripathi (1974) reported 56 per cent seed germination of molded sorghum seeds as against 76 per cent germination in apparently healthy seeds. Hiremath *et al.* (1993) observed 26 per cent reduction in germination of sorghum seed due to infection of *Phoma sorghina*. Navi *et al.* (2005) reported infected sorghum grains suffer breakdown of grain structure, loss of viability, increased chalkiness of endosperm and contamination with mycotoxins. Narnaware *et al.* (2006) reported that *Fusarium* and *Curvularia* are the two most important fungal genera causing grain discoloration and reduction in viability of seed.

MATERIAL AND METHOD

Collection of Sorghum Grains

The infected and healthy grain samples of sorghum bicolor varieties viz., Kanpuri and Desi Jowar were collected in Kharif season in brown paper bags during grain development stages and after harvest from farmer's fields. Then variety wise grains were manually separated carefully from each . All the grains separated from earheads, irrespective of location of earhead collection, were thoroughly mixed together taking variety into consideration in order to have a composite grain sample.

Various Pathogens Symptoms and Signs Observed on Grains of Sorghum

The symptoms was examined by microscopic and visually of infected grain samples.. To study the symptoms and signs present with the different diseased (infected) grains, critical visual observations were carried out followed by separation of grains from healthy and diseased sorghum earheads.The different infected grain lots of similar symptoms and signs were made by means of magnifying hand lens under artificial light. The symptoms and signs appeared in field condition and microscopic examination of such infected grains each was carried out and presence of pathogen was recorded.

Isolation of Pathogen

Isolation of fungi associated with sorghum grains was carried out from randomly collected 100 grains of the composite grain samples by standard blotter method (ISTA, 1976).

Isolation of Ectophytic Mycoflora

The infected sorghum grains having similar symptoms and signs of each variety were separated and different grain lots of similar symptoms and signs were prepared. From these lots repeated isolation were carried out by using 10 grains of each symptom lot. In each petriplate 10 grains having similar symptoms and signs were kept aseptically by maintaining equidistance from each other on three layers of properly moistened sterilized blotters. The plated petriplates were then incubated at room temperature (24±20C). The fungal hyphae developing from the infected grains were sub cultured in Potato Dextrose Agar (PDA) slants. The different isolates obtained from different grain lots were labelled by numbering. They were purified by employing single spore and hyphal tip isolation technique.

Isolation of Endophytic Mycoflora

The infected sorghum grain lots or their infected tissues of endosperm having similar symptoms and signs were disinfected by dipping in 1: 1000 mercuric chloride (HgCl2) solution for 2 minutes followed by three washings with sterile water to remove the HgCl2 from each grain or their tissues used for isolation. Such 10 grains per petriplate were kept aseptically by maintaining equidistance from each other in petriplate containing three layers of properly moistened and sterilized blotters. The plated petriplates were then incubated at room temperature (24 ± 20C). The fungal hyphae developing from the infected grains were sub cultured on PDA slant.

Identification of Pathogens

The pure cultures of different fungal isolates were grown on PDA medium. They were visually observed to record their cultural characters and under microscope to know their morphological characters. The fungal characters observed were compared with the characters described in literature.

Pathogenicity Test

Isolated from sorghum grains were tested in the laboratory by adopting standard methods of pathogenicity test (Joi and Ahmed, 1976 and Bora and Gogoi, 1992). The pathogenicity test was carried out for *Fusarium moniliforme, Alternaria alternata, Macrophomina phaseolina*and *Colletotrichum graminicola.*

Pathogenicity Test in *in vitro*

The high quality transparent plastic petriplates were disinfected using alcohol. Three white sterile blotting papers moistened with sufficient quantity of sterilized water were kept in each petriplate. Ten inoculated seeds were then placed in each petriplates containing sterilized moist blotting papers for each test pathogen seperately. The petriplates plated with uninoculated seeds served as a control treatment. These petriplates were incubated at room temperature (24±20C) for five days and when the seeds started germinating the lid of petriplates were opened in aseptic condition. The petriplates were watered with sterilized water as and when required. Observations were recorded on seed germination after 7 days, discoloration of radical and plumule, seedling mortality if any and seedling length after 10 and 15 days of incubation at room temperature. Healthy emergence of the seedlings from seeds was considered as successful germination.

Physiological Investigation

The five major grain molds isolated viz., *Fusarium moniliforme,* Alternaria alternata, *Macrophomina phaseolina* and *Colletotrichum graminicola* were studied.

Semi-Synthetic Media

Potato Dextrose Agar (PDA)

Peeled potatoes: 200.0 g

Dextrose (C6H12O6): 20.00 g

Agar agar: 20.00 g

Distilled water: 1000ml

The Agar medium was sterilized and 20 ml medium was poured into previously sterilized petriplates and allowed them to cool at room temperature (24 ± 20). The culture block (5mm diameter) of test pathogens were cut aseptically with the help of sterilized cork borer (5mm) from 10 days old culture of *Fusarium moniliforme*, *Alternaria alternata*, *Mcrophomina phaseolina* and *Curvularia graminicola*. The petriplates were inoculated aseptically by placing culture block in the centre of petriplate separately for each test pathogen and labelled. The petriplates were incubated at room temperature (24 ± 20).

Grain Molds Effect on Seed Germination of Sorghum

Impact of grain infecting fungi on seed germination and seedling vigour was studied by seed inoculation with fungi isolated from naturally infected sorghum grains. Seed germination was carried out by Paper towel method (Sahu and Agarwal, 2003).

$$\text{Seed Germination (\%)} = \frac{\text{Number of Germinated Seeds 14 Days}}{\text{Total Number of Seeds}} \times 100$$

RESULTS AND DISCUSSION

The results and discussion of present investigation on various aspects of ear-infecting fungi of sorghum are as follows.

Pathological Investigations

The presence of pathogens was confirmed by microscopic examination of discolored and infected grains part. The natural symptoms and signs on infected grains were observed visually and are recorded as under.

Symptoms and signs observed on grains in nature due to infection of various pathogens

The various discolored and infected grain samples collected were associate visually and by means of magnifying hand lens on the basis of typical color symptoms *viz.*, pink to pinkish yellow discoloration, brown to blackish discoloration, dark brown spots on grain, abnormal grain development, grain filling and growth of fungus on the grain surface. The symptoms and signs expressed by different pathogens on sorghum grains are described below.

Symptoms produced on grains due to natural infection of *Fusarium* sp.

The *Fusarium* infected sorghum grains were pink to pinkish yellow and pinkish white fungal growth was seen on the infected sorghum grains.

Grains were shrivelled and white mycelial growth was observed during the early grain filling period. Microscopic examination of such infected grains indicate the presence of *Fusarium*. Similarly, white to pinkish white discoloration was described by Thakur *et al.* (2006).

Symptoms produced on grains due to natural infection of *Colletotrichum* sp.

Dark brown to blackish discoloration with small raised black pycnidial bodies were noticed in *Colletotrichum* infected sorghum grains. Microscopic examination revealed the presence of *Colletotrichum* sp. and black color pycnidia scattered throughout the surface of dry grains.

Symptoms produced on grains due to natural infection of *Alternaria* sp.

The *Alternaria* infected sorghum grains showed light to dark brown and ashy gray to blackish discoloration. The infected grains were shrivelled. Microscopic examination of such infected grains revealed the presence of *Alternaria* sp. The similar symptoms were recorded by Anon. (1980). They reported gray discoloration in sorghum grains infected with *Alternaria* sp. Thakur *et al* . (2006) reported grayish black discoloration in sorghum grains infected with *Alternaria* sp.

Symptoms produced on grains due to natural infection of *Macrophomina* sp.

Light to dark brown spots and blackish discoloration was seen in *Macrophomina* infected sorghum grains. The microscopic examination of such infected grains revealed the presence of *Macrophomina* sp. Thedevelopment of symptoms of *Macrophomina* sp. on grains correlated exactly with thesymptoms described by Kotgire (2009). They observed blackish discolored grains ininfection with *Macrophomina* sp.

Symptoms produced on grains due to natural infection of *Phoma* sp.

Majority of *Phoma* infected sorghum grains were with dark brown to blackish discoloration and black pin head size pycnidial bodies present. Microscopic examination revealed the presence of *Phoma* sp. and black color pycnidia scattered throughout the surface of dry grains.

Symptoms produced on grains due to natural infection of *Aspergillus* sp.

The sorghum grains infected with *Aspergillus* sp. exhibited light to dark brown spots, yellow, black and bluish green to blackish green discoloration. The microscopic examination of such grains revealed the presence of various fruiting structures, yellow to green and black in color consisting of fungal spore mass of *Aspergillus* sp. The symptoms observed during the present study tallied with those reported by Kotgire (2009). They found dark brown spots and pink to blackish discolored sorghum grains infected with *Aspergillus* sp.

Symptoms produced on grains due to natural infection of *Curvularia* sp.

The *Curvularia* infected sorghum grains showed brown to chocolate brownish spots and extensive brown to blackish discoloration. Microscopic examination of such infected grains revealed the presence of *Curvularia* sp. The symptoms observed during the present study tallied with those described by Gallegos and Castro (1977), Anon. (1980), and Thakur *et al.* (2006) They reported black discoloration on sorghum grains infected with *Curvularia* sp.

Isolation of Pathogens

Symptoms and signs of different infected and discolored grains were recorded and the presence of pathogens was confirmed by microscopic examination. The different isolated ectophytic and endophytic fungal flora from sorghum grains of different varieties are presented in Table 2.1.

Table 2.1: The Different Isolates Obtained from Discolored Sorghum Grains and Their Tentative Identification

Genra of Fungi	Name of Variety	Ectophytic/ Endophytic	Symptoms on Discolored Seed
Colletotrichum *Alternaria*	Kanpuri jowar' Kanpuri jowar	Endophytic Endophytic	Brown to black discoloration Blackish discoloration
Fusarium	Kanpuri jowar	Ectophytic	Pikish yellow
Macrophomina	Kanpuri jowar	Ectophytic	Dark brown spota
Phoma	Desi jowar"	Ectophytic	Black dots
Aspergillus	Kanpuri jowar	Ectophytic	Dark brown blotch
Curvularia	Desi jowar	Ectophytic	Brown to chocolate brownish
Colletotrichum	Desi jowar	Ectophytic	Brown to chocolate brownish spota
Alternaria	Desi jowar	Ectophytic	Light to dark brown discoloration
Fusarium	Desi jowar	Endophytic	Plae yellow discolored seed
Macrophomina	Desi jowar	Ectophytic	Dark brown spots

'UP CHARI 1

"PCH 10

Identification of Pathogens

The identification of isolated fungus was done by studying the cultural, morphological characters and by microscopic examination of the each isolate. The observations recorded as under.

Isolate Number-1

The fungus *Fusarium* sp. produced white to light orange fungal hyphae, later on became pinkish with powdery growth apperance. The dirty white fungal growth covers the entire petriplate (90 mm) in seven days (24 ± 20) of incubation. The colonies of isolate were initially white with a little dark purple reverse. The mycelial growth consisting of aggregated or loose with scattered chains of microconidia. They were slightly hooked at the tip, thin walled with the apical cell slightly curved and tapering to both the end point .The cultural and morphological characters of vegetative and reproductive structures of the fungal isolate indicated its close identity with *Fusarium moniliforme*.

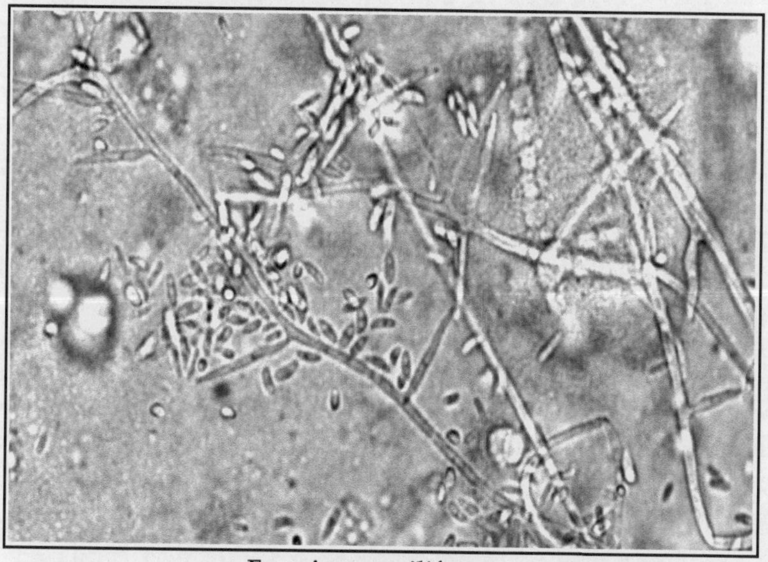

Fusarium moniliforme

Isolate Number-2

The mycelium of fungus *Colletotrichum* sp. grew fairly quick on PDA covering whole petriplate within seven days of incubation at room temperature (24 ± 20 C). Initially the fungus produced white cottony mycelial growth, which turned into light pink and finally dirty brown when acervulus was produced after 21 days of incubation at room temperature (24 ± 20). The hyphae were thin, branched, hyaline and septate. Conidia were hyaline, thin walled, straight, oblong, slightly depressed in the middle with rounded ends.

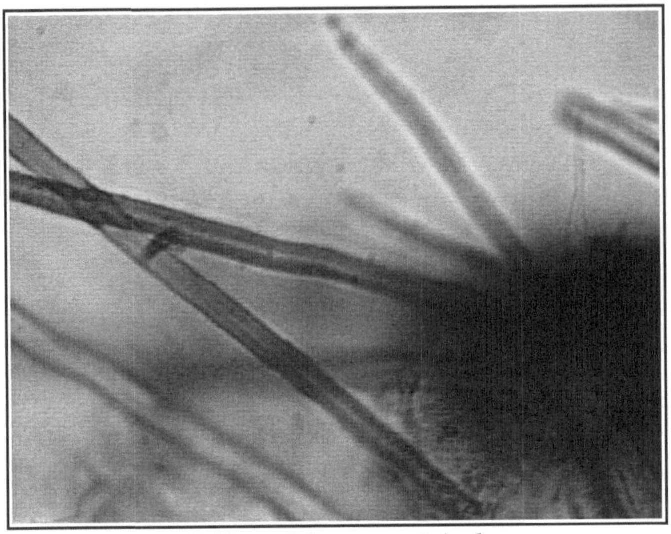

Colletotrichum graminicola

Isolate Number-3

The fungus *Alternaria* sp. produced olive brown to dark brown mycelial growth and cover 90 mm growth in seven days (24 ± 20) of incubation. The mycelium was abundant, usually light olive, green to brown. The hyphae were dark brown, thick and septate. Conidiophores were simple, erect, geniculate and often clustered. They produced darkly pigmented conidia in an acropetal succession of simple or branched chains. Conidia appeared quite broader at base as compared to tip portion. The cultural and morphological characters of vegetative and reproductive structures of the fungal isolate indicated its close identity with *Alternaria alternata*

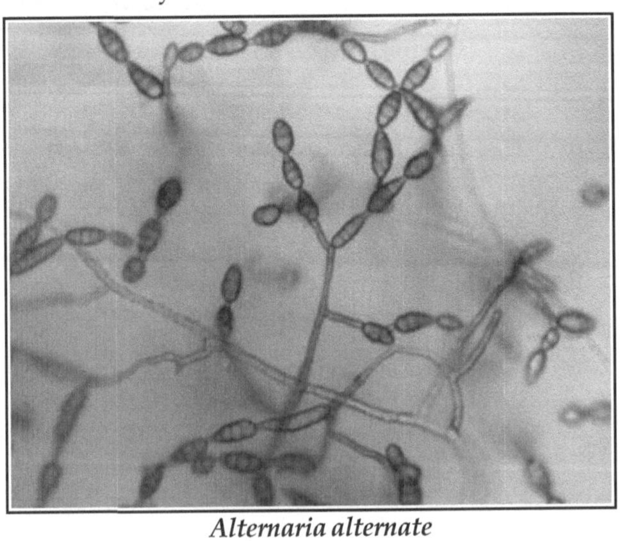

Alternaria alternate

Isolate Number-4

The fungus *Macrophomina* sp. produced black colonies on PDA and covers the entire petriplate (90mm) in eight days (24 ± 20) of incubation. The hyphae were septate. Pycnidia beared simple and rod-shaped conidiophores and were black, globose and ostiolate. Conidiophores appeared hyaline and narrow apically bearing hyaline and cylindrical conidia. The cultural and morphological characters of vegetative and rep roductive structures of the fungal isolate indicated its close identity with *Macrophomina phaseolina*

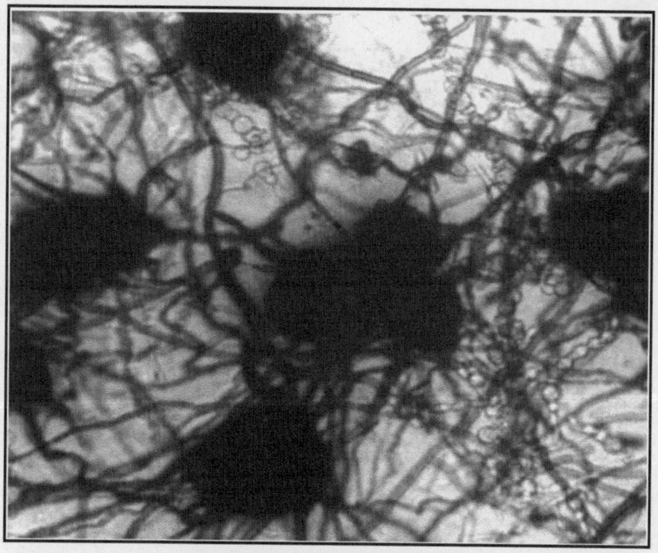

Mcrophomina phaseolina

Isolate Number-5

The fungus *Aspergillus* sp. produced hyaline, white to light yellow mycelium, grew rapidly and turned into dirty white to black colony, covering the entire petriplate (90 mm) within five days of incubation (24 ± 20). Mycelial growth appeared pale yellow in reverse side of petriplates. Stipes was long and smooth-walled and terminated into spherical vesicles. The hyphae were hyaline and septate. The conidiophores were thick walled, erect, unbranched, straight, hyaline to light brown, long aseptate and darker near the vesicle. The vesicle was globose and biseriate, thick walled and brown to black. The conidia produced in chain were globose showing rough surface texture, single celled, pale to dark brown on maturity. They measured 3-4.5 µm (Av.3.7 µm) in diameter. The cultural and morphological characters of vegetative and reproductive structures of the fungal isolate indicated its close identity with *Aspergillus niger*.

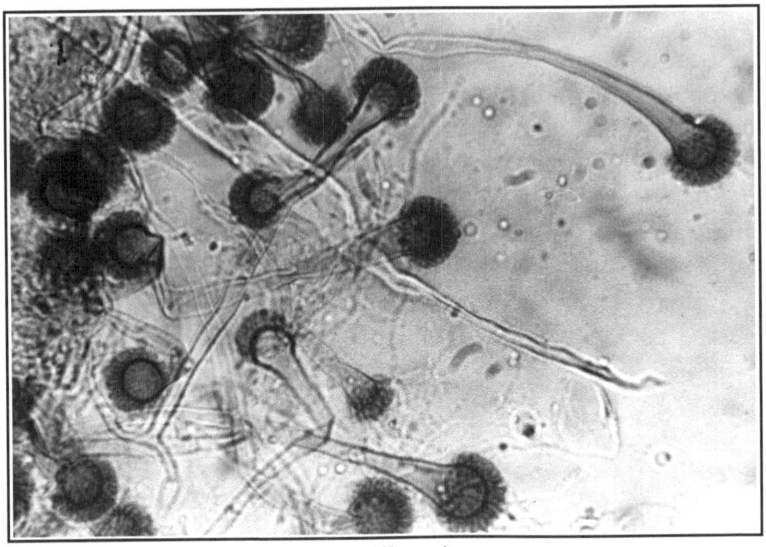

Aspergillus niger

Isolate Number-6

The fungus *Phoma* sp. produced mycelium was profuse, fluffy to dense, different colored and cover the entire petriplate (90 mm) in 8 days (24 ± 20) of incubation. The hyphae were hyaline and septate. Pycnidia were immersed or erumpent, dark brown to black, shiny or dull and produced on aerial mycelium. They were single or multiostiolate, variable in size and shape, globose .The morphological characters of vegetative and reproductive structures of the fungal isolate indicated its close identity with *Phoma sorghina*.

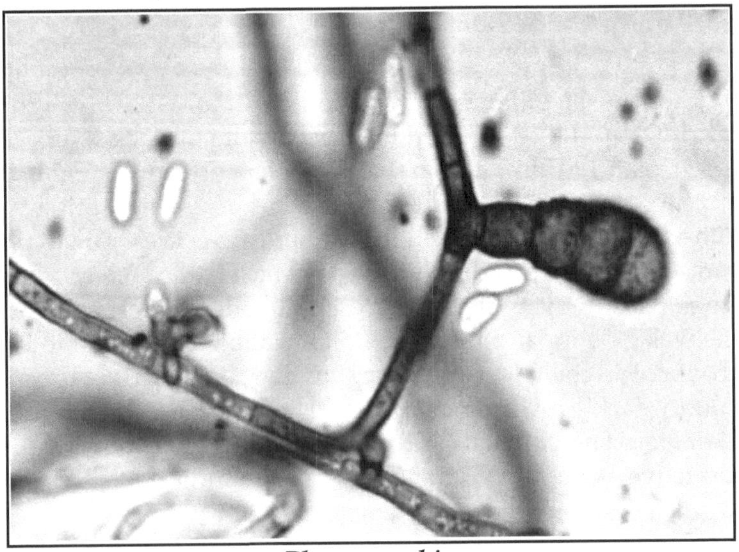

Phoma sorghina

Isolate Number-7

The fungus *Curvularia*sp. produced dark greenish mycelial growth with irregular margin which later on became grayish black in color and cover the entire petriplate (90 mm) within seven days (24 ± 20) of incubation. Conidiophores were solitary, straight or little curved and dark brown. Conidia were produced apically and laterally on conidiophores. The end cells of conidia were paler than two central cells. Conidia were mostly curved, curvature at the bigger cells with three transverse septa and cells were often hyaline, central cell was bigger and dark brown whereas apical cell was rounded, smooth walled and measured 17.43-23.97 × 10.03-14.87 μm (Av. 20.7 × 12.45 μm). The morphological characters of vegetative and reproductive structures of the fungal isolate indicated its close identity with *Curvularialunata.*

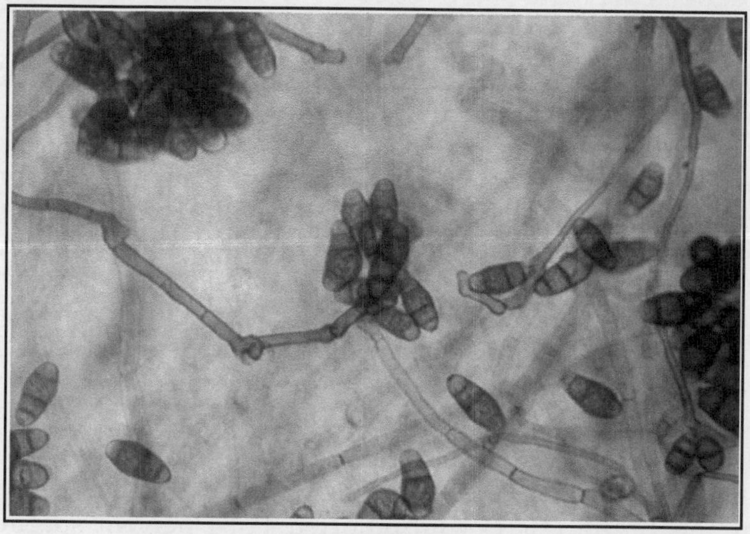

Curvularialunata

Pathogenicity Test *in vitro*

The pathogenic nature of *Fusarium moniliforme, Alternaria alternata, Macrophomina phaseolina* and *Colletotrichum graminicola* were tested on Kanpuri jowar in vitro condition. The data presented in Table 2.2 revealed that inoculation of all the pathogens isolated from sorghum grains had reduced seed germination and increased seedling mortality compared to uninoculated control. In control, seed germination was cent per cent and normal healthy seedling growth was observed. The minimum seed germination was found in *Fusarium moniliforme*(32.0%) inoculated seed and *Colletotrichum graminicola* (59.0%) inoculated seed. While maximum seedling mortality occurred in *Fusarium moniliforme* (68.00%) followed by *Colletotrichum graminicola* (41.00%), and *Alternaria alternata* (35.00%) inoculated seed tested in vitro. The rest of inoculated pathogen also reduce the seed germination and increase seedling mortality as compared to control. This clearly indicate that *Fusarium moniliforme,* and *Colletotrichum graminicola* are more responsible for reduction of seed germination, causing grain rot and seedling mortality.

Table 2.2: Effect of Seed Inoculation with Different Fungi on Seed Germination and Seedling Mortality *in vitro*

Name of Isolate	Present Seed Germination (%)	Present Seedling Mortality (%)	Seed not Germinated
Macrophomina Phaseolina	74.00	26.00	Seed rot
Alternaria alternate	65.00	35.00	Seed rot
Fusarium Moniliforme	32.00	68.00	Seed rot
Colletotrichum Graminicola	59.00	41.00	Seed rot
Control	100.0	0.00	Normal seed germination

Results on seed germination of sorghum as influenced by cultural filtrates of various fungi are presented in table 2.2 which revealed significant adverse effect on seed germination. It is possible that metabolites produced during growth and development of fungi in cultural medium might have adversely affected the metabolic activity of seeds during seed germination. The production of secondary metabolites by *F.moniliforme* is known to degrade seed quality and reduces seed viability (castor and frederikson, 1980). Tripathi (1974) observed that the inhibition of seed germination in sorghum by *C.graminicola* and *F.moniliforme* was due to extracellular thermostable toxins and that by a. flavus by the production of aflatoxins.

Detrimental effects of toxins produced by fusarium spp. The results for minimum adverse effect of *C. lunata*seed inoculation tallied with those of Somani and Indira (2001) who reported 11.84 percent sorghum seed germination reduction. Similar results were obtained by Kotgire (2009), Sajjan *et al.* (2014) and Jidda and Anaso (2014).

CONCLUSION

Sorghum is the emerging fourth most important crop after rice, wheat and maize and cultivated widely throughout the tropical, subtropical and temperate regions. It is an important cereal crop grown when conditions are congenial for the seed infection by large number of fungi, some of them are seed transmitted, resulting into poor seed germination and plant stand in the field affecting the quality and yield.

Therefore, the investigations on the grain molds of sorghum seeds collected from from farmers field were undertaken on various aspects, *viz.*, detection of external and internal fungi, their effect on seed germination, seedling mortality and management of sorghum grain molds.

The pathological investigations of the discolored diseased seed were undertaken by recording the natural symptoms and signs. The microscopic examination and repeated isolation from discolored seed sample revealed the presence of *Fusarium* sp., *Colletotrichum* sp., *Curvularia* sp., *Alternaria* sp., *Macrophomina* sp., *Phoma* sp. And *Aspergillus* sp. Among, the fungi isolated from sorghum grains, *Fusarium* sp., *Alternaria* sp., and *Colletotrichum* sp. were found associated both externally and internally while, the rest were found to be associated externally only. After purification of each isolate, the cultural and morphological characters of vegetative and reproductive structures of each isolate were studied. The following fungi were identified as *Fusarium moniliforme, Colletotrichum graminicola, Macrophomina phaseolina, Curvularialunata, Alternaria alternata, Phoma sorghina*, and *Aspergillus niger.*

The pathogenicity test conducted for four fungi *viz., Fusarium moniliforme, Alternaria alternata, Colletotrichum graminicola*and *Macrophomina phaseolina*proved to be positive. These pathogensadversely affect seed germination and cause seedling mortality in *in vitro*. Incase of *Fusarium moniliforme* seedling mortality *in vitro* was 68.00 per cent, in case of *Colletotrichum graminicola* it was 41.00 in case of *Macrophomina phaseolina*it was 26.00 and in case of *Alternaria alternata* it was 35.00 per cent. The reisolation from diseased seeds and blighted seedlingsyielded the same respective pathogen, used for inoculation.

The germination was drastically reduced by seed inoculation with fungi. *Fusarium moniliforme* (32.00%), *Colletorichum graminicola* (59.00%), *Alternaria alternate* (66.20%) and *Macrophomina phaseolina*(74.00%) inoculated seed.

REFERENCES

Adegbola Adetayo Jacob, Awagu Emenike Fidelis, Kamaldeen Oladimeji Salaudeen, and Kashetu Rukayat Queen (2013) Nigerian Stored Products Research Institute, P. M. B 3032, Kano, Nigeria. 2Department of Applied Zoology, Bayero University, Kano, Nigeria.

Anonymous, (1980). Diseases and Their Control: in Jowar. Indian Council of Delhi Agricultural Research, New, India, pp. 22-29.

Bhagwat, V.Y. and Pedgaonkar, S.M. (1973). Pink Mold on Grain Sorghum. *Sorghum Newsletter*, 17: 60-61.

Balota, M (2012). Sorghum (sorghum vulgare L.) Marketability. Grain Colour and Relationship to Feed Values.Virginia Cooperative Extension. www.ext.vt.edu.

Berenji, J and Dahlberg, J (2004). Perspectives of Sorghum in Europe. Journal Agrocon Crop Science, 1905: 332-338.

Banerjee UC (1990). Production of Beta-glucosidase (cellobiase) by *Curvularia* sp. Lett. Appl. Microbiol. 10(5): 197-199.

Banerjee UC, Chakrabarti S (1992). Production and Properties of Carboxymethylcellulase 3(endo-1,4-b-glucanase) from *Curvularialunata*. World J. Microbiol. Biotech. 8(4): 423-424.

Bonzi, S., 2007. Efficacy of Four Aqueous Plant Extracts Against Seed-borne Fungi of Sorghum (Sorghum bicolor (L.) Moench): Particular Case of *Colletotrichum graminicola*

(Ces.) Wilson and *Phoma sorghina* (Sacc.) Boerema, Dorenbosch and Van Kesteren. Memory of Master 2 (DEA), Rural Development Institute, Polytechnic University of Bobo-Dioulasso, Burkina Faso, pp: 39.

Bora, L.C. and Gogoi, R. (1992). Seed Borne Microflora of Deep Water Rice. Oryza, 29: 355-357.

Castor, L.L. and Frederikson, R.A. (1980). *Fusarium* and *Curvularia* Grain Mold in Texas. *Sorghum Dis.*, pp. 93-192.

Chandrashekar A, Bandyopadhyay R and Hall AJ. (eds.) 2000. Technical and Institutional Options for Sorghum Grain Mold Management: Proceedings of an International Consultation, 18-19 May 2000, ICRISAT, Patancheru, India. Patancheru 502 324, Andhra Pradesh, India: International Crops Research Institute for the Semi-Arid Tropics. 229 pp.

Esele, J.P., Frederiksen, R.A., and Miller, F.R. 1993. The Association of Genes Controlling Caryopsis Traits with Grain Mold Resistance in Sorghum. Phytopathology 83: 490-495.

Eva HH, Line A, Thomas S, Schafer J, Charlotte J (2003). *Curvularia* Haloperoxidase: Antimicrobial Activity and Potential Application as a Surface Disinfectant. Applied Envir. Microbiol. 69(8): 4611-4617.

Evans HC, Reeder RH (2001). Fungi Associated with Eichhornia Crassipes (Water Hyacinth) in the Upper Amazon Basin and Prospects for Their Use in Biological Control. pp. 62-70. In: M.H. Julien, M.P. Hill, T.D. (ed.). Center and Ding Jianqing ACIAR Proceedings 102.

FAO (1995). Sorghum and Millet in Human Nutrition. FAO Food and Nutrition Series, NO. 27, Food and Agriculture Organisation of the United Nations, Rome.

Freire SVP (1995). Atividade Celulolítica e aspectos citológicos de *Curvularia pallescens*. Recife, (Dissertação Mestrado. Departamento de Biologia, Universidade Federal Rural de Pernambuco) p. 95.

Gallegos, H.M. and Castro, M.A. (1977). The Occurrence in Mexico of *Curvularialunata* on Sorghum Kernels. *Plant Dis. Reptr.*, 61(12): 1082-1083.

Girish AG, Rao VP and Thakur RP. 2004. Diversity of Grain Mold Fungi on Selected Sorghum Genotypes. Indian Phytopathology 57(1): 84-87.

Green, C (2012). Sorghum Grain Nutrition. www.ehow.com.

Gwary, D.M., T.D. Rabo and A.B. Anaso, 2003. The Development of Anthracnose Symptoms on Sorghum Geneotypes in the Nigerian Savanna. J. Pl. Dis. Protection, 111: 96-103.

Gwary, D.M., T.D. Rabo and A.B. Anaso, 2002. Assessment of Leaf Anthracnose Caused by Colletotrichum Sublineolum on Sorghum Geneotypes in the Sudan Savanna. Agricultura Tropica et Subtropica, 35: 53-9.

Hallgreen, L, Rexen, F, Petersen, PB, and Munck, L (1992). Industrial Utilization of whole Crop Sorghum for Food and Industry. pp. 121-130. In: Utilization of Sorghum and Millets (Gomez, MI, House, LR, Rooney, LW, and Dendy, DAV, eds.) Patancheru, A.P. 502 324, India: International Crops Research Institute for Semi – Arid Tropics

Halt, M. 1994 Aspergillus Flavus and Aflatoxin B1 in Flour Production. Eur. J. Epidermiol. 10: 555-558.

Hiremath, R.V.; Palaxappa, M.G. and Lakhman, M. (1993). Evaluation of Sorghum Genotypes for Resistence to Grain Molds. *Karnatka J. Agril. Sci.*, 6(2): 155-159.

ISTA, (1976). International Rules for Seed Testing. Seed Sci. and Tech., 4: 3-49.

Jambunathan, R and Subramanian, V (1988). Grain Quality and Utilization of Sorghum and Pearl Millet. In Biotechnology in Tropical Crop Improvement. Proceedings of the International Biotechnology Workshop, Patancheru, India, 12-15 Janvier 1987, pp. 133-139.

Joi, M.B. and Ahmed, L. (1976). Seed Borne Mycoflora of Rice (Oryza sativa L.). J. Mah.Agril. Univ., 1 (1): 37-39.

Jidda, M.B. and anaso A.B. (2014). Mycoflora Associated with Masakwa Sorghum (sorghum bicolor l. moench) in the North Eastern Part of Nigeria. J. Stored pro. Posth. Res. 5(4): 20-25

Jyoti S, Sing RP (1985). Temperature Relation and Cellulolytic Activity of Weed Fungi Occurring in the Beds of Pleurotus Sajor Caju. Indian J. Plant Pathol. 3: 7-10.

Kim-Jisoo L (1998). Seed Transmission of Bipolaris Coicis, B. cynodontis, B. Maydis and *Curvularialunata* Causing Leaf Blight of Job's Tears. Korean J. Plant Path. 14(4): 287-293.

Kotgire , G. (2009). Studies on Ear-infecting Fungi of Sorghum (*Sorghum bicolor* (L.) Moench). M.Sc. (Agri.) Thesis Submitted to B.A. College of Agriculture, AAU, Anand.

Knudsen, E., Kirleis, A., Eggum, B. and Munck, L. (1988). Carbohydrate Composition and Nutritional Quality for Rats of Sorghum Prepared from.

Martin, JH, and MacMasters (1950). Industrial Uses for Sorghum. The Yearbook of Agriculture, Year book of Agriculture Series.United States Department of Agriculture. US Government Printing Office: Washington 1950.

Marley, P.S., 1996. Sorghum Pathology: In: Cropping Scheme Meeting Report, Cereal Research Programme, pp: 24-7. Institute of Agricultural Research, Ahmadu Bello University Zaria.

Narnaware, S.W.; Wadibhasme, S.S. and Wavre S.H. (2006). Effect of Weather Conditions on Grain Mold Diseases Incidence in Sorghum. *J.Pl.Dis.Sci.*, 1(2): 245-246.

Navi, S.S.; Bandyopadhya, R.; Reddy, R.K.; Thakur, R.P. and Yang, X.B. (2005). Effect of Wetness Duration and Grain Development Stages on Sorghum Grain Mold Infection. *Plant Dis*., 89: 872-878.

Navi, S.S.; Banyopadhyay, R.; Hall, A.J. and Bramel, P. (1999). A Pictorial Guide for the Identification of Mold Fungi on Sorghum Grain. Inf. Bull. 59 (in Eng, Fr). International Crops Research Institute for the Semi-Arid Tropics, Andhra Pradesh, India.

Nitharwal PD, Gour HN, Agarwal S (1991). Effects of Different Factors on the Production of Cellulase by *Curvularialunata*. Folia Microbiol. 36: 357-361.

Ou, S.H. (1985). Rice Diseases. CMI, Kew Survey, U.K. pp. 294.

Padwick, G.W. (1950). Mannual of Rice Diseases, 198 pp. Kew., Common Wealth Mycological Institute.

Pande, S., L.K. Naghogho, R Bandgopadhygay and R.I. Karunakar, 1991. Variation in Pathogenicity and Cultural Characteristics of Sorghum Isolates of *Colletotrichum graminicola* in India. Pl. Dis., 75: 778-83.

Parimelazhagan T, Francis K (1999). Antifungal Activity of Clerodendrum Viscosum Against Cuvularia *lunata* in Rice Seeds. Ind. J. Myc. Plant Pathol. 29(1): 139-141.

Rao, K.N. and Williams, R.J. (1978). The ICRISAT Sorghum Pathology Programme. International Sorghum Workshop 6-13, ICRISAT, Hyderabad, India.

Rashid, M.M. (2001). Detection of *Curvularia* sp. on Boro Rice Seeds of Dinajpur. Online *J.Bio. Sci*., 1(7): 591-592.

Richardson, M.J. 1990. An Annotated List of Seed Borne Diseases. Int. Seed Test. Assoc. Zurich, Switzerland.

Sajjan, A.S.; Gaudar, R.B.; Basavarajappa, M.P. and birader, B.D. (2014). Study of Seed Borne Pathogens Associated with Rabi Sorghum (Sorghum Bicolor l. moench) Genotypes. adv. Crop sci. tech. 2(3):1-3.

Sahu, R.K. and Agarwal, V.K. (2003). Effect of Fungicidal Seed Treatment on Seed Born Fungi Germination and Seedling Vigour of Rusty Shield Bearer. (Peltophoram Terruineum) J. Mycol. Pl. Pathol., 33(1) 84-88.

Sisterna MN, Bello GMD (1998). *Curvularia* Protuberate: A New Seedborne Pathogen of Rice. Acta-Phytopathologica-et-Entomologica – Hungarica 33(1-2): 111-114.

Somani R.B. and Indira , S. (2001). Effect of Grain Molds Culture Filtrates on Germination and Seedling Vigour in Sorghum. *Annals of Pl. Physiology*, 14 (2): 166-168.

Somwanshi, S.D. (2005). Studies on Sorghum Grain Mold. M.Sc. (Agri.) Thesis Submitted to MAU, Parbhani, M.S.

Tailor, H.C. (1998). Management of Sorghum Grain Molds. M.Sc. (Agri.) Thesis Submitted to G.A.U., S.K. Nagar.

Tarkegn, G.; Mclearn, N.W. and Swart, W.J. (2004). Relationship Between Grain Development Stage and Sorghum Cultivar Susceptibility to Grain Mold. *African Plant Prot.*, 10 (1) 53-62.

Tarr, S.A. (1962). Diseases of Sorghum, Sudan Grass and Broom Corn. Kew (Surrey), UK; Commenwealth Mycological Institute, pp. 380.

Thakur, R.P.; Rao, V.P.; Agarkar, G.D.; Solunke, R.B.; Bhat, B. and Navi, S.S. (2006). Variation in Occurrence and Severity of Major Sorghum Grain Mold Pathogens in India. *Indian Phytopath.*, 59: 410-416.

Thompson, L (2010). Sorghum Grain Nutrition. www.livestrong.com USDA and NRCS (2006) "Sorghum". www.grains .org.

Tripathi, R.K. (1974). Head Fungi of Sorghum, Phytotoxins and Their Effect on Seed Germination. *Indian Phytopath.*, 27: 499-501.

USDA., 1960. Index of Plant Disease in the United States. Agricultural Hand Book. 165: 187-211.

Zida, P.E., P. Sérémé, L. Vibeke, P. Sankara, I. Somda and N. Adama, 2008. Importance of Seed-borne Fungi of Sorghum and Pearl Millet in Burkina Faso and Their Control Using Plant Extracts. Pak. J. Biol. Sci., 11: 321-331.

Pages: 33-52

SEED TREATMENT, PLANT HEALTH AND AGRO-TECHNOLOGY

Edited by: Dr. Avnish Chauhan and Dr. Pawan Kumar 'Bharti'

ISBN: 978-93-5056-810-1

Edition: **2016**

Published by: **Discovery Publishing House Pvt. Ltd., New Delhi (India)**

3

Relative Abundances and Advances in Seed Production of Seed Spices Crop

Chandan Singh Ahirwar[1] and D.K. Singh[2]

ABSTRACT

India is known as the 'Land of Spices' and is the largest producer, consumer and exporter of spices and spice products. Out of the 109 spices listed by the International Organisation for Standardization (ISO), India produces as many as 63 owing to its varied agro-climatic regions. Spices not only add flavor, aroma and taste to our food but also enhance keeping quality and medicinal values of food. The prevailing worldwide demand for seed spices is more than 200000 tones, out of which India alone contributes 188,550 tonnes annually (2012-13) valued Rs. 170600 lakhs. India is exporting only 15.28% of its production (Indian Horticulture Database, 20113-14).

Spices are the source of livelihood and employment for large number of people in the country, both for rural population, who grow them, and the urban population, who process and trade them. Out of total 63 spices grown in India, 20 spices are classified as seed spices with 36% share in area and 17% share in production of total spices. Main seed spices of India are Coriander, Cumin, Fennel, Fenugreek, Dill, Ajwain, Celery, Anise, Nigella and Caraway. Seed spice crops are extensively cultivated during rabi season in the arid and semi

1 Ph.D. Scholar, Department of Vegetable Science, College of Agriculture, Govind Ballabh Pant University of Agriculture and Technology, Pantnagar, Uttarakhand - 263 145, (India).

2 Professor, Department of Vegetable Science, College of Agriculture, Govind Ballabh Pant University of Agriculture and Technology, Pantnagar, Uttarakhand - 263 145, (India).

arid region of India, covering an area of 13.95 lakh ha with production of 12.34 lakh tones) (Annual report, NRCSS, 2013-14)

Standardization of NPK levels for coriander and cumin under protected environment in the scenario of climate change was studied by NRCSS, Ajmer (Annual report, 2013-14). In coriander, number of seeds per umbellate and highest yield (1841.11 kg/ha) was obtained under plastic walk in tunnel with 100% recommended dose of fertilizer. In case of cumin insect proof net tunnel with 80% recommended dose of fertilizer treatment, exhibited better plant growth and development in number of seeds per umbellate and highest seed yield (736.25 kg/ha). The minimum incidence of aphids (7.89/umbel) was recorded under the same treatment as compared to open field condition (28.26/umbel).

Key words: Recent Advances, Spices, Seed production, Seed spices.

Introduction

India is known as the 'Land of Spices' and is the largest producer, consumer and exporter of spices and spice products. Spices are nature's gift to humankind. Spices not only add flavour and taste to our food but also enhance keeping quality and medicinal values of food. Spices have a profound influence on the course of human civilization. They permeate our everyday life, provide succor, cure and relax us. Ancient civilization from Egypt, Arab and Rome made extensive use of spices, not only to add flavour to foods and beverages, but as medicines, disinfectants, incenses, stimulants and even as aphrodisiac agents. Non leafy parts (e.g. bud, fruit, seed, bark, rhizome, and bulb) of spices plants were used flavouring or seasoning agents to foods and beverages, and as herbal medicines. Out of the 109 spices listed by the International Organisation for Standardization (ISO), India produces as many as 63 owing to its varied agro-climatic regions. Almost all the states and Union territories (UTs) of the country grow one or the other spices.

It is a source livelihood and employment for large number of people in the country, both for rural population, who grow them, and the urban population, who process and trade in them. Out of the total 63 spices grown in India, 20 are classified as seed spices with 36 per cent share in area and 17 per cent share in production of total spice in India. Main seed spices of India are coriander, cumin, fennel, fenugreek, dill, ajwain, celery, anise, nigella and caraway. Seed spice crops are extensively cultivated in the arid and semi arid region of India during rabi season covering an area of 13.95 lakh ha with production of 12.34 lakh tones annually.

The prevailing world wide demand for seed spices is more than 200000 tones, of which India alone contributes 188550 tonnes annually (2012-13) valued at Rs. 170600 lakhs. India is exporting only 15.28 per cent of its production. If our consumption level remains same then to meet global demand and to retain our prime position as seed spices export we have to double our production within five year period. This is a great challenge for us as other countries like Bulgaria for coriander, Syria for cumin, Egypt for fennel, Morocco for fenugreek are competing with higher yield per unit area.

National Research Centre on Seed Spices, Tabiji, Ajmer came into existence on 22 April 2000 as per the recommendation of the working group of Department of Agricultural Research and Education which approved establishment of National Research Centre on Seed Spices, Ajmer during IX five year plan. Thus, this institute was set up with a broad-based framework to address diverse agricultural issues related to water and land resources management, crop improvement, crop protection, agroprocessing and socio-economic aspects in a holistic manner for enhancing research capacity and for providing a backstopping for improvement in productivity, sustainability and quality with reference to export value of seed spices which play an important role in national economy.

The Centre has now completed a decade and has achieved many major achievements which have left a strong impression among all the stakeholders involved with seed spices and has been successful in ensuring an increase in the income of seed spices growing farmers, provide good produce to the consumers as well as raise the profit of all the stakeholder which in turn has fulfilled the dream of earning more foreign exchange in the country.

The experiment was conducted at Ajmer (Rajasthan) to study the influence of seed yield by treatment of sheep manure, vermicompost and bio-fertilizer on growth and yield of ajowan (Trachyspermum ammi).The recorded was highest seed (16.35 q ha-1) and biological yield (49.49 q ha-1) of ajowan was obtained with application of sheep manure @ t 10 ha-1 with Azotobacter sp. (Meena *et al.*, 2009).

Application of different sources of organic as well as inorganic sources significantly influenced the yield and yield attributes of coriander over absolute control (Mehta *et al.*, 2011). The results revealed that application of sheep manure, vermicompost at all levels and recommended doses of fertilizers with or without bio fertilizer resulted significantly higher yield attributing characters viz. umbels plant^{-1}, umbellates umbel^{-1}, and seeds umbellate-^{1} and yield over absolute control. The application of sheep manure @ 7.5 t ha^{-1} with bio-fertilizer exhibited the highest yield of coriander being at par with 4.0 t vermicompost and 10.0 t ha^{-1} sheep manure with bio-fertilizer.

In order to study the effect of salicylic acid (SA) and Methyl jasmonate (MeJa) on growth, yield and essential oil (EO) quantity and quality of cumin (*Cuminum cyminum* L.) the resulted in significant promotion of plant height and number of branches and umbels per plant. seed yield and EO yield significantly increased by the application of 0.1 mM SA (Rahimi *et al.*, 2013).

The experiment conducted by Malik *et al.*, (2009) at CCSHAU, Hisar on fennel recorded more plant height, umbellate per umbel, secondary branches per plant, umbel per plant, 1000-seed weight, and primary branches per plant and seeds per umbel in variety HF-33. The highest seed yield was obtained in HF-125 (2149.7 kg/ha) followed by UF-207 (2024.0 kg/ha) and HF-118 (2003.3 kg/ha).

Presently following ten seed spice crops are the mandate crops:

1. Coriander (*Coriandrum sativum* L.)
2. Cumin (*Cuminum cyminum* L.)
3. Fennel (*Foeniculum vulgare* Mill.)
4. Fenugreek (*Trigonella foenum-graecum, Trigonella corniculata* L.)
5. Ajwain (*Trachyspermum ammi* Sprague)
6. Dill (*Anethum graveolens* L., *Anethum sowa* Kurz.)
7. Nigella (*Nigella sativa* L.)
8. Anise (*Pimpenella anisum* L.)
9. Celery (*Apium graveolens* L.)
10. Caraway (*Carum carvi* L.)

Objectives

1. Efficient agro-techniques for achieving the high production and productivity.
2. Evolving better and efficient management system for control of pests and diseases.
3. Study of nutritional and water management aspects.
4. Development of package on organic farming of the seed spices for export, based on environment friendly production and potential technology.
5. Research on seed technology for production of quality seeds of improved varieties.
6. Study of economics of production and marketing.
7. Development of pre and post harvest technology for better processing, storage and utilization.
8. Development of export oriented technology for export of raw and value-added products.
9. Transfer of technology for farmers and extension agencies.

Crop-wise area, production and productivity of major spice crops in India:

Seed Spices Crops	Area in '000 HA	Production in '000 MT	Productivity in MT/HA
Coriander	543	524	1.0
Cumin	594	394	0.7
Fennel	100	143	1.4
Fenugreek	93	113	1.2
Ajwan	35	27	0.8
Clove	2	1	0.5

(NHB, 2013-14)

Leading all Spices Producing States during 2012-13 (in '000 MT)

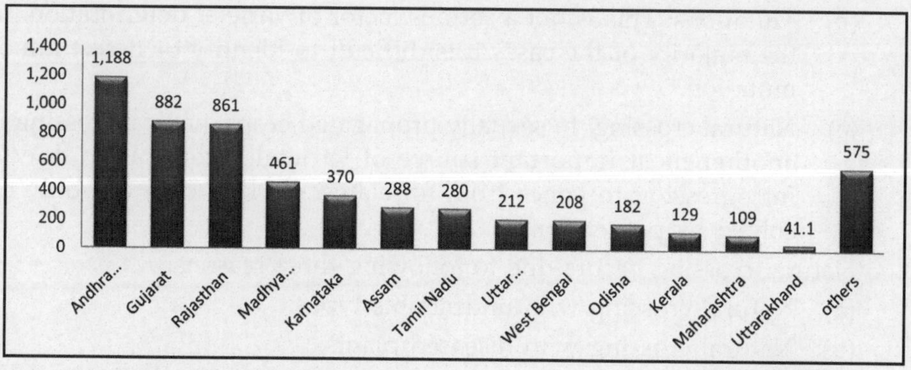

(NHB, 2013-14)

Principle of Seed Production

Production of genetically pure and otherwise good quality pedigree seed is an exacting task requiring high technical skills and comparatively heavy financial investment. During seed production strict attention must be given to the maintenance of genetic purity and other qualities of seeds in order to exploit the full dividends sought to be obtained by introduction of new superior crop plant varieties. In other words, seed production must be carried out under standardized and well-organized condition.

A. Genetic Principle

1. Deterioration of varieties: Genetic purity (Truness to type) of a variety can deteriorate due to several factor during production cycles. The important factors of apparent and real deterioration of varieties).
2. Developmental variation: When the seed crops are grown in difficult environment, under different soil and fertility conditions, or different climate conditions, or under different photoperiods, or at different

elevation for several consecutive generations, the developmental variation may arise some times as differential growth response. To minimize the opportunity for such shifts to occur in varieties it is advisable to grow them in their areas of adaptation and growing seasons.

(a) Mechanical mixtures: This is the most important source of variety deterioration during seed production. Mechanical mixtures may often take place at the time of sowing, if more than one variety is sown with same seed drill; through volunteer plants of the same crop in the seed field; or through different varieties grown in adjacent fields. Often the seed produce of all the varieties are kept on same threshing floor, resulting in considerable varietal mixture. To avoid this sort mechanical contamination it would be necessary to rogue the seed fields, and practice the utmost care during the seed production, harvesting, threshing and further handling

(b) Mutations: This is not a serious factor of varietal deterioration. In the majority of the cases it is difficult to identify or detect minor mutation.

(c) Natural crossing: In sexually propagated crops, natural crossing is another most important source of varietal deterioration due to introgression to genes from unrelated stocks which can only be solved by prevention.

3. Natural crossing occurs due to following three reasons:

(a) Natural crossing with undesirable types.

(b) Natural crossing with diseased plants.

(c) Natural crossing with off- type plants.

Natural crossing occurs due to following factors:

(a) The breeding system of species

(b) Isolation systems

(c) Varietal mass

(d) Pollinating agent

(a) **Minor genetic variations:** Minor genetic variations may exist even in the Varieties appearing phenotypically uniform and homogeneous at the time of their release. During later production cycle some of this variation may be lost because of selective elimination by the environment. To overcome these yields trials are suggested

(b) **Selective influence of diseases:** The selective influence of diseases in varietal deterioration is also of considerable importance. New crop varieties often become susceptible to new races of diseases often caused by obligate parasites and are out of seed programmes. Similarly the vegetatively propagated stocks deteriorate fast if infected by viral, fungal and bacterial diseases. During seed production it is, therefore, very important to produce disease free seeds/stocks.

(c) **Techniques of plant breeders:** In certain instances, serious instabilities may occur in varieties due to cytogenetically irregularities not properly assessed in the new varieties prior to their release. Other factors, such as break down in male sterility, certain environmental conditions, and other heritable variations may considerably lower the genetic purity.

(d) **Maintenance of Genetic Purity During seed Production**: The various steps suggested), to maintain varietal purity, are as follows.

(*i*) Use of approved seed only in seed multiplication.

(*ii*) Inspection and approval of fields prior to planting.

(*iii*) Field inspection and approval of growing crops at critical stages for verification of genetic purity, detection of mixtures, weeds, and for freedom from noxious weeds and seed borne diseases etc.

(*iv*) Sampling and sealing of cleaned lots

(*v*) Growing of samples of potentially approved stocks for comparison with authentic stocks.

The various steps suggested for maintaining genetic purity are as follows:

(a) Providing adequate isolation to prevent contamination by natural crossing or mechanical mixtures

(b) Rouging of seed fields prior to the stage at which they could contaminate the seed crop.

(c) Periodic testing of varieties for genetic purity.

(d) Avoiding genetic shifts by growing crops in areas in their adaptation only.

(e) Certification of seed crops to maintain genetic purity and quality of seed.

(f) Adopting the generation system.

(g) Grow out tests.

Agronomic principles:

1. **Selection of a Agro-climatic Region:**

(a) A crop variety to be grown for seed production in an area must be adapted to the photoperiod and temperature conditions prevailing in that area.

2. **Selection of seed plot:**

(a) The plot selected for seed crop must be free from volunteer plants, weed plants and have good soil texture and fertility The soil of the seed plot should be comparatively free from soil borne diseases and insects pests.

3. **Isolation of Seed crops:**
   (a) The seed crop must be isolated from other nearby fields of the same crops and the other contaminating crops as per requirement of the certification standards.
4. **Preparation of Land:**
   (a) Good land preparation helps in improved germination, good stand establishment and destruction of potential weeds. It also aids in water management and good uniform irrigation.
5. **Selection of variety:**
   (a) The variety of seed production must be carefully selected, should possess disease resistance, earliness, grain quality, a higher yielder, and adapted to the agro-climatic conditions of the region.
6. **Seed treatment:**
   (a) Depending upon the requirement the following seed treatment may be given.
7. **Chemical seed treatment.**
8. **Bacterial inoculation for the legumes.**
9. **Seed treatment for breaking dormancy.**
10. **Time of planting:**
    (a) The seed crops should invariably be sown at their normal planting time. Depending upon the incidence of diseases and pests, some adjustments, could be made, if necessary.
11. **Seed Rate:**
    (a) Lower seed rates than usual for raising commercial crop are desirable because they facilitate rouging operations and inspection of seed crops.
12. **Method of sowing:**
    (a) The most efficient and ideal method of sowing is by mechanical drilling.
13. **Depth of sowing:**
    (a) Depth of sowing is extremely important in ensuring good plant stand. Small seeds should usually be planted shallow, but large seeds could be planted a little deeper.
14. **Rouging:** Adequate and timely rouging is extremely important in seed production. Rouging in most of the field crops may be done at many of the following stages as per needs of the seed crop.
    (a) Vegetative/pre-flowering stage
    (b) Flowering stage
    (c) Maturity stage

Supplementary pollination: Provision of honey bees in hives in close proximity to the seed fields of crops largely cross pollinated by the insects, ensure good seed set thereby greatly increase seed yields.

15. **Weed control:** Good weed control is the basic requirement in producing good quality seed. Weeds may cause contamination of the seed crop , in addition to reduction in yield.
16. **Disease and insect control:** Successful disease and insect control is another important factor in raising healthy seed crops. Apart from reduction of yield, the quality of seeds from diseased and insect damaged plants is invariably poor.
17. **Nutrition:** In the nutrition of seed crops, nitrogen, phosphorus, potassium, and several other elements play an important role for proper development of plants and seed. It is, therefore, advisable to know and identify the nutritional requirements of seed crops and apply adequate fertilizers.
18. **Irrigation:** Irrigation can be important at planting for seed crops on dry soils to ensure good uniform germination and adequate crop stands. Excess moisture or prolonged drought adversely affects germination and frequently results in poor crop stands.
19. **Harvesting of Seed crops:** It is of great importance to harvest a seed crop at the time that will allow both the maximum yield and the best quality seed.
20. **Drying of seeds:** In order to preserve seed viability and vigour it is necessary to dry seeds to safe moisture content levels.
21. **Storage of raw seeds:** The best method of sowing seed for short periods is in sacks or bags in ordinary buildings or godowns.

Requirement of Field Standard for Seed Production of Spices:

	General Requirements			Specific Requirements		
Crape	Contaminants	Isolation Distance (mtr.)		Factor	Maximum permitted %	
		Foundation	Certified		Foundation	Certified
Coriander	Fields of other variety	200	100	Off type plants	0.10	0.50
	Fields of same variety not conforming to varietal purity	200	100	Objectionable weed plants	None	None
Cumin	Fields of other variety	800	400	Off type plants	0.10	0.50
	Fields of same variety not conforming to varietal purity	800	400	Objectionable weed plants	0.05	0.10

(Contd...)

Crape	General Requirements			Specific Requirements		
	Contaminants	Isolation Distance (mtr.)		Factor	Maximum permitted %	
		Foundation	Certified		Foundation	Certified
Dill	Fields of other variety	200	100	Off type plants	0.10	0.50
	Fields of same variety not conforming to varietal purity	200	100	Objectionable weed plants	None	None
Ajowain	Fields of other variety			Off type plants	0.10	0.50
	Fields of same variety not conforming to varietal purity	200	100	Objectionable weed plants	None	None
Fennel	Fields of other variety	200	100	Off type plants	0.10	0.50
	Fields of same variety not conforming to varietal purity	200	100	Objectionable weed plants	None	0.05

Requirement of Seed standards for seed production of spices

	Factor	Standards for Each Class	
		Foundation	Certified
Coriander	Pure seed (minimum)	97.0%	97.0%
	Inert matter (maximum)	3.0%	3.0%
	Other crop seeds (maximum)	10/kg	20/kg
	Objectionable weed seeds (maximum)	None	None
	Germination (minimum)	65%	65%
	Moisture (maximum)	10%	10%
	For vapour-proof containers (maximum)	8%	8%
	Factor	Standards for Each Class	
		Foundation	Certified
Ajawain	Pure seed (minimum)	97.0%	97.0%
	Inert matter (maximum)	3.0%	3.0%
	Other crop seeds (maximum)	10/kg	20/kg
	Weed seeds (maximum)	10/kg	20/kg
	Germination (minimum)	65%	65%
	Moisture (maximum)	10%	10%
	For vapour-proof containers (maximum)	8%	8%

(Contd...)

	Factor	Standards for Each Class	
		Foundation	Certified
Cumin	Pure seed (minimum)	97.0%	97.0%
	Inert matter (maximum)	3.0%	3.0%
	Other crop seeds (maximum)	10/kg	20/kg
	Weed seeds (maximum)	10/kg	20/kg
	Objectionable weed seed (maximum)	5/kg	10/kg
	Germination (minimum)	65%	65%
	Moisture (maximum)	10%	10%
	For vapour-proof containers (maximum)	8%	8%
	Factor	Standards for Each Class	
		Foundation	Certified
Fennel	Pure seed (minimum)	97.0%	97.0%
	Inert matter (maximum)	3.0%	3.0%
	Other crop seeds (maximum)	10/kg	20/kg
	Weed seeds (maximum)	10/kg	20/kg
	*Objectionable weed seeds (maximum)	5/kg	10/kg
	Germination (minimum)	65%	65%
	Moisture (maximum)	10%	10%
	For vapour-proof containers (maximum)	8%	8%
	Factor	Standards for Each Class	
		Foundation	Certified
Dill seed	Pure seed (minimum)	97.0%	97.0%
	Inert matter (maximum)	3.0%	3.0%
	Other crop seeds (maximum)	10/kg	20/kg
	Weed seeds (maximum)	10/kg	20/kg
	Germination (minimum)	65%	65%
	Moisture (maximum)	10%	10%
	For vapour-proof containers (maximum)	8%	8%

Source: Indian minimum seed certification standards(2013). The central seed certification board department of agriculture & Co-operation ministry of agriculture government of India New Delhi.

Research Achievements in seed Spice crops:

1. **Management of plant genetic resources of seed spice crops:** Total germplasm available at National Research Centre on Seed Spices, Ajmer. The total collection of 842 active germplasm accessions comprising of four major seed spices crops viz coriander, cumin, fennel and fenugreek are maintained in the National Conservatory.

Sl.No.	Crop	Indigenous	Exotic	Total
01	Cumin	100	7	107
02	Coriander	169	3	172
03	Fenugreek	82	59	171
04	Fennel	118	3	121
05	Ajwain	99	1	100
06	Dill	106	5	111
07	Nigella	21	3	24
08	Celery	36	–	36
09	Anise	18	–	18
10	Caraway	8	2	10
11	Total	759	83	842

(*NRCSS, 2013-14*)

2. **Crop Improvement in seed spice crops:** On the selections basis of better yield traits, quality and resistance to biotic and abiotic stresses, the selections were made from the base population of the respective germplasm. The following elite selections of coriander, cumin, fennel, and fenugreek have been developed.

Crop	Respective Germplasm	Specific Features
Coriander:	ACr-01-209, ACr-01-255	Dual purpose use: Leaves and seed as spices
Cumi	AC-01-3, AC-01-167	Resistance to Fusarium wilt
	AC-01-167	High essential oil content ranging between 3.5 to 4%.
Fennel	AF-01-87,	Dwarf character and earliness
	AF-01-119	Khariv and Ravi season
Fenugreek	NRCSS-AM-1, NRCSS-AM-2	Dual purpose use: Leaves and seed as spices

(*NRCSS, 2013-14*)

Influence of sheep manure, vermicompost and biofertilizer on growth and yield of ajowan (pooled data of two years) of ajowan

Treatment	Umbels plant-1	Umbellets umbel-1	No.of seed sumbellet-1	Seed yield (q ha-1)	Biologicalyield (q ha-1)
Absolute control	165.00	9.50	11.80	10.45	31.60
RDF	176.00	11.25	12.75	14.16	41.56
B (Azotobacter sp.)	170.00	10.50	12.30	12.25	35.85
RDF with B	179.00	12.48	13.10	14.85	43.85
S M @ 5 t ha-1	173.00	10.75	12.15	12.60	37.75
S M @ 7.5 t ha-1	176.00	11.00	12.20	13.40	40.55
S M @ 10 t ha-1	180.00	12.50	13.40	15.25	46.43
S M @ 5 t ha-1 + B	174.00	11.80	12.50	13.40	40.40
S M @ 7.5 t ha-1 + B	182.00	12.25	12.65	14.25	43.40
S M @ 10 t ha-1 + B	195.00	13.50	14.15	16.35	49.49
VC @ 2 t ha-1	172.00	10.55	12.10	11.90	35.15
VC @ 3 t ha-1	175.00	11.25	12.25	13.15	39.55
VC @ 4 t ha-1	177.00	12.45	13.30	14.95	44.35
VC @ 2 t ha-1 + B	180.00	11.70	12.40	12.80	39.70
VC @ 3 t ha-1 + B	183.00	12.00	12.60	14.25	42.20
VC@ 4 t ha-1 + B	193.00	13.25	14.00	15.20	45.60
CD (P= 0.05)	2.41	0.42	0.46	0.45	3.13

Effect of cuttings on vegetative growth and seed yield of coriander cv. Narnaul Selection

Treatment	Height 01 plant (cm)	Number 01 Branches per Plant	Number 01 Umbels per Plant	Yield of Leaves (q!hll)	Yield 01 Seed (q!hll)
C0	89.7	6.7	47.2	0.00	18.74
C1	70.9	9.0	54.6	36.63	22.33
C2	39.1	4.7	20.0	57.02	4.60
C3	28.2	3.4	9.9	65.29	0.89
CD at 5 %	2.21	0.59	2.39	0.39	0.17

C-0= no cutting, C-1= one cutting at 30 DAS, C-2=Second cuttings at 45 DAS, C-3=third cuttings at 60 DAS

Ahmad *et al.*, 2011 as reported that locally adapted plants can be considered as an alternative to commercial crops for cultivation in harsh environments within semi-arid regions. Nowadays, exploring these plants industrial benefits has motivated many farmers around the world to extend their cultivation. However, agronomic characters of these forgotten plants are still unknown. The main aim of this study was to evaluate the influence of fall sowing dates on yield and yield components of different Cumin (*Cuminum cyminum* L., *Apiaceae*) ecotypes in the semi-arid region of Khorasan Iran. An experiment of two years duration was performed using a split-plot randomized complete block design, employing sowing dates as main-plot factor, and cumin ecotypes as sub-plot factor in three replicates. Three levels of sowing dates included the following: mid October, mid November and mid December. Additonally, sub-plot treatments consisted of four local ecotypes of cumin from different regions of the Khorasan province (Gayen, Torbat, Sabzevar and Khaf). The plants' survival percentage in field conditions, number of umbels m-2, number of seeds per umbel, thousand seed weight, biological, and seed yield were measured in this experiment. The results showed that all study parameters were influenced by different sowing dates except thousand seed weight. The third sowing date resulted in the highest biological (110 g m-2 and 94 g m-2 in 2006 and 2007) and seed yield (50 g m-2 and 55 g m-2 in 2006 and 2007). There was a significant positive correlation between average minimum temperature and biological yield of cumin across all ecotypes and years. The results showed significant difference in productivity of different ecotypes of cumin from various parts of northeast of Iran. The Gayen and Khaf ecotypes showed the highest plant survival percentage, biological and seed yield across study ecotypes under the third sowing date. In conclusion, delayed fall sowing date and appropriate cumin ecotypes are able to increase yield of this plant in northeast of Iran.

Effects of different sowing dates on plant survival, number of umbels, seed number, thousand seed weight, biological and seed yield of cumin (*Cuminum cyminum* L.)

Sowing Dates	Plantsurvival (%)	Umbels (m-2)	Seed Number (m-2)	Thousand Seed Weight (g)	Biological Yield (g m-2)	Seed Yield (g m-2)
S1	64	1790	18	4.6	84	48
S2	68	1518	17	4.4	87	51
S3	100	1260	16	4.2	94	55

Letters indicated different sowing dates include mid October (S1), mid November (S2) and mid December (S3)

Breeding for high yield, quality and resistant to biotic and abiotic stress in fennel.

Initial Evaluation Trial of Fennel at NRCSS, Ajmer, and Annual report 2013-14

Nineteen selected populations were evaluated in initial trial at NRCSS. The analysis of variance revealed significant difference among the genotypes for all the traits including seed yield. The eed yield was ranging from 16 to 31 q/ha whereas the yield of check varieties were 25.09 q/ha (AF-1), 18.76 q/ha (GF-2), 22.89 q/ha (RF-143), 18.57 q/ha (RF-101) and 27.88 q/ha (RF-125). Among the tested entries three populations namely AF-05-12-1 (31.31 q/hac), AJ-FNL-2 (30.23 q/ha) and AF-05-7-1 (29.17 q/ha) were found superior over check varieties. Essential oil content in the populations was ranging from 0.29 to 2.86%. Maximum essential oil was observed in genotype AF-05-12-1 (2.86 %) whereas, as the best check RF-125 contained 2.54 % essential oil.

Essential oil and seed yield in elite populations of fennel

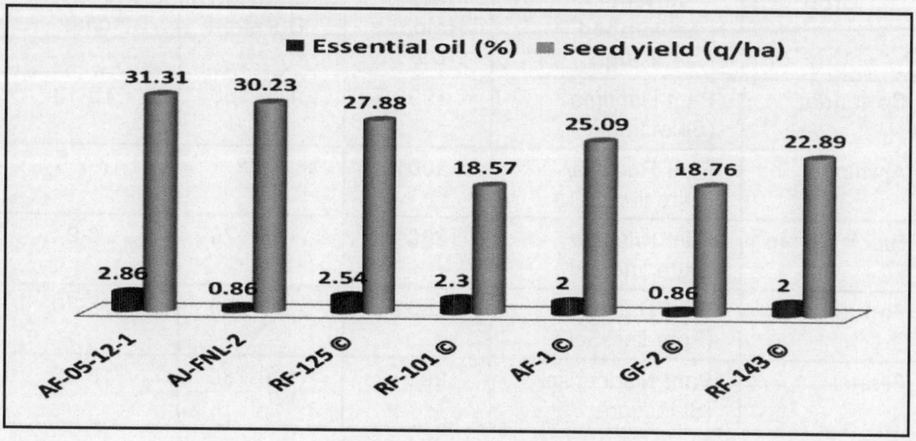

Breeder seed produced during 2012-13 at NRCSS, Ajmer:

Crop	Variety	Production (kg)
Coriander	Ajmer Coriander-1	458
Fennel	Ajmer Fennel-1	386
Fenugreek	Ajmer Fenugreek-1	756
Fenugreek	Ajmer Fenugreek-2	103
Fenugreek	Ajmer Fenugreek-3	709
Ajwain	Ajmer Ajwain-1	142
Ajwain	Ajmer Ajwain-2	27
Dill	Ajmer Dill-1	87
Dill	Ajmer Dill-2	110
Nigella	Ajmer Nigella-1	10
Anise	Ajmer Anise-1	23

Breeder Seed production of seed spices at VRC, GBPUA&T, Pantnagar

Crop	Variety	Production (kg)	
		2012-13	**2013-14**
Coriander	Pant Haritima	665	1400
Fennel	Pant Madhurika	16	30
Fenugreek	Pant Ragini	13	34
Fenugreek	Pusa early Bunching	100	325
Black Cumin	Pant Krishna	18	3

Varieties of Seed Spices released from GBPUA & T, Pantnagar

Crop	Varieties/ Developed Through	Year of Release (Days)	Maturity/ Duration	Seed Yield q/ha.
Coriander	Pant Haritima/ (Selection)	1993	150-160	15-18
Ajwain	Pant Ruchika/ (Pure line Sel.)	2001	172	7-7.5
Black Cumin	Pant Krishna/ (Pure line Sel.)	2001	165-170	8-9
Fenugreek	Pant Ragini/ (Pure line Sel.)	2001	170-175	15-20
Fennel	Pant Madhurika/ (Selection)	2001	180-185	18-20

Some other important varieties of seed spices in India

Crop	Varieties	Released Year	Sources	Seed Yield Kg/ha.	Special feature
Coriander	Guj. Coriander-1	1974	Jagudan, Gujarat	1100-1900	Suitable for early sowing, bild seeded for Rainfed area of Raj. and Guj.
	Guj. Coriander-2	1985	Jagudan, Gujarat	1450-2000	Semi spreading, dark green leaves,
	Hisar Sugandh UD-446	2001	Hisar	1400-1500	Dual purpose, Highly resist. To stem gall
	Lam CS-3	–	Guntur	1400	Dual purpose,
Cumin	Guj.Cumin-1	1983	Jagudan Guj.	700-1000	Bold, brown grains with tolerant to wilt
	RZ-19	1988	Jobner	500-1000	Tolerant to wilt & blight.
	Guj. Cumin-1	1991	Jobner	700-1000	Moderately tolerant to powdery mildew, wilt & blight
	MC-43	1970	Jobner	580-860	Moderately tolerant to powdery mildew, wilt & blight
Black Cumin	Pant Krishna	2001	Pantnagar	10q/ha	Bold black seed
	NS-44		Jabalpur	405-605	Bold black seed
	Azad Kalaunji		Kanpur	10-12	–
	NS-32		Jabalpur	405-6.5	Bold black seed
Fennel	Co-1	1985	Coimbatore	567-825	Diffuse branching, for drought, saline. Hilly area
	Guj.fennel-1	1985	Jagudan Guj.	1695-3000	Moderately tolerant to leaf blight, leaf spot
	Azad Saunf-1	1996	Kanpur	1800	Rest. To blight & root rot
	Pant Madhurkia	2001	Pantnagar	1800-2000	Tolerant to leaf blight & leaf spot
	Guj.fennel-1	1997	Jagudan Guj.	1940	Suitable for rainfed & Irrig.
Fenugreek	Co-1	1982	Coimbatore	680-750	Dual purpose, rest. To root rot
	Hisar Madhvi	–	Hisar	1900-2000	Dual purpose, rest. To DM

(Contd...)

Crop	Varieties	Released Year	Sources	Seed Yield Kg/ha.	Special feature
	Pant Ragini	2001	Pantnagar	1500-2000	Dual purpose, rest. To PM
Ajwain	Guj. Ajowain-1	–	Gujarat	8.0q/ha	High yielding
	Pant Ruchika	–	Pantnagar	7-75 q/ha	Brown seed
	Lam selection-1		Guntur	8.0q/ha	Erect, 80 cm tall
	Lam selection-2	–	Guntur	10q/ha	Bushy with 40-45 cm

Export of spices from india (qty. In tonnes & value in rs. Lakhs)

Item	2009-10		2013-14 (Est.)	
	Qty.	Value	Qty.	Value
Coriander	47,250	22585.50	45,750	37,185.65
Cumin	49,750	54824.50	121,500	160,006.00
Celery	5,000	2662.50	5,600	3,661.48
Fennel	6,800	5623.60	17,300	16,001.42
Fenugreek	21,000	6972.00	35,575	13,378.37
Other seeds spices	15,500	5890.00	27,800	15,425.65

Seed supply chain in India:

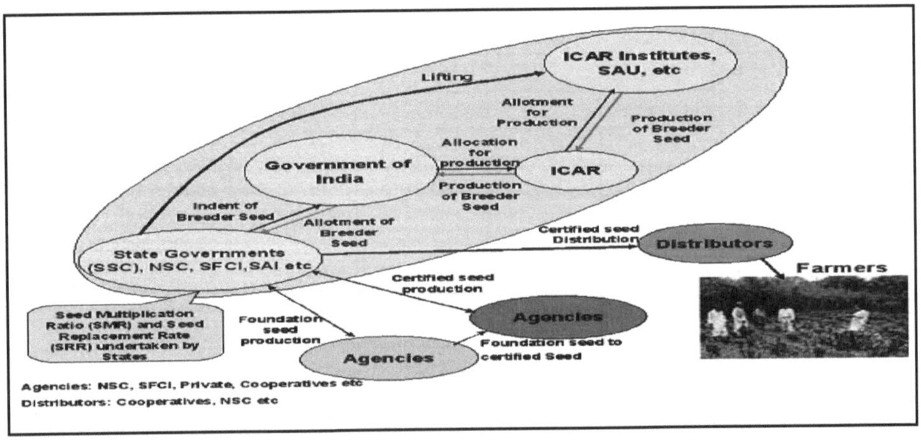

Source: http://seednet.gov.in/Material/Channels of seed Supply.htm

Conclusion

India is considered having the richest germplasm of seed spices crops and also varied agro climatic conditions present here provide good opportunity for cultivation of different seed spices. So there is vast scope for earning foreign exchange by export of seeds as well as spice products from various seed spices. But the region demands some unusual horticulture practices to flourish. For this the linkages among different national and international activities engaged with the seed spices research should be strengthened and improved varieties should be cultivated by farmers with scientifically recommended package of practices.

REFERENCES

Ahmad, Nezami.; Ehsan, EyshiRezaei; Zeinab, Khorasani and Khorramdel and M. Bannayan (2011): Evaluation of the Impacts of Fall Sowing Dates on Different Ecotypes of Cumin (*Cuminum cyminum, Apiaceae* L.) Productivity in Northeast of Iran. *Notulae Scientia Biologicae,* 3.4: 123-128.

Annual Report (2013-14): (NRCSS) National Research Center on Seed Spices, Tabiji, Ajmer - 305206 (Rajasthan) (India).

Antuno, D. Moretti, L.F., F., Lovato, F.S., (2002): Seed Yield, Yield Components, Oil Content and Essential Oil Content and Composition of *Nigella sativa* L. and *Nigella damascena* L. Ind.C rops Prod. 15, 59-69.

Choudhary, O.P. (2006): Diversity, Foraging Behaviour of Floral Visitors and Pollination Ecology of Fennel (*Foeniculum vulgare* Mill.). *J. Spice Aeromatic Crops*.15 (1): 34-41.

Choudhary, O.P. and Singh, J. (2007): Diversity, Temporal Abundance, Foraging Behaviour of Floral Visitors and Effect of Different Modes of Pollination on Coriander (*Coriandrum sativum* L.). *J. Spice Aeromatic crops*. 16(1): 8-14.

Davidson, M.H., Dugan, L.D., Burns, J.H., (1996): Apsyllium Enriched Cereal for Treatment of Hypercholesterolemia in Children: A Controlled Double Blind Crossover Study. Am. J. Clin. Nutr. 63, 96-102.

Day, A.D., Intalp, S., (1970): Some Effects of Soil Moisture Stress on Growth of Wheat (*Triticum aestivum* L.). Agron. J. 62, 27-29.

Dash, S.R., Kole, P.C. (2001): Studies on Variability, Heritability and Genetic Advance in Fenugreek. *Journal of Interacademicia*; 5 (1): 7-10.

Dashora A, Maloo, S.R. and Dashora, L.K. (2011): Variability, Correlation and Path Coefficient Analysis in Fenugreek (*Trigonella foenum-graecum* L.) Under Water Limited Conditions. *Journal of Spices and Aromatic Crops*; 20 (1): 38-42.

Datta, S., Chatterjee, R. and Mukherjee, S. (2005): Variability, Heritability and Path Analysis Studies in Fenugreek. *Indian Journal of Horticulture*; 62 (1): 96-98.

Deore, B. P. and Bharud, R.W. (1990): Growth, Yield and Storability of Fenugreek as Influenced by Foliar Spray of Growth Substances. *J. Maharashtra Agricult. Univ.* 15: 208-210.

Doorenbos, J., Kassam, A.K., (1979): Yield Response to Water. Irrigation and Drainage Paper 33. FAO, United Nations, Rome, pp. 176.

Frayer, J.K. (1930): Chromosome Atlas of Flowering Plant.*Georg Allen and Urwin London; pp*. 519.

Farooqi, A.H.A. and Sharma, S. (1988): Effect of Growth Retardants on Growth and Essential Oil Content in Japanese Mint, *Plant Growth Regul*. 7: 39-45.

Gul, H., Khattak, A.M., Amin, N. (2006): Accelerating the Growth of (*Araucaria heterophylla*) Seedlings Through Different Gibberellic Acid Concentrations and Nitrogen Levels. *J. Agric. Biol. Sci.*, 1: 25-29.

Herrera, C.M. (1987): Components of Pollinator "Quality": Comparative Analysis of a Diverse Insect Assemblage. *Oikos* 50: 79-90.

Herrera, C.M. (2005): Plant Generalization on Pollinators: Species Property or Local Phenomenon? *American Journal of Botany* 92:13-20.

Idrees, M., Khan, M.M.A., Aftab, T. and Naeem, M. (2010): Synergistic Effects of Gibberellic Acid and Triacontanol on Growth, Physiology, Enzyme Activities and Essential Oil Content of *Coriandrum sativum* L. *The Asian Australasian J. Plant Sci. Biotechnol.* 4: 24-29.

Indian Minimum Seed Certification Standards (2013): The Central Seed Certification Board Department of Agriculture & Co-operation Ministry of Agriculture Government of India New Delhi. 396 P.

Indian Horticulture Database (2013-14): National Horticulture Board, Ministry of Agriculture, Government of India 85, Institutional Area, Sector-18, Gurgaon, India. pp. 17.

Malik, T.P.; Tehlan, S.K. and Thakral, K.K. (2009): Performance of Fennel (*Foeniculum vulgare*) Genotypes for Seed Yield. *Annals of Horticulture* 2. 2: 243-245.

Mehta, R.S.; Anwer, M.M.; Malhotra, S.K.; Lal, G.; Aishwath, O.P.; Meena, S.S.; Kant, K. and Khan, M.A. (2011): Growth and Yield of Coriander (*Coriandrum sativum* L.) as Affected by Sheep Manure, Vermi-compost and Bio-fertilizer. *International J. Seed Spices.* 1.1: 22-28.

Meena, S.S.; Mehta R.S. and Vashishtha B.B. (2009): Influence of Sheep Manure, Vermicompost and Azotobacter sp. on Growth and Yield of Ajowan (Trachyspermum Ammi Sprague) *Journal of Spices and Aromatic Crops.*, 18.2: 100-103.

Rahimi, Abdol Rahman.; Rokhzadi, Asad Sheno and Karami Amini. Ezzat (2013): Effect of Salicylic Acid and Methyl Jasmonate on Growth and Secondary Metabolites in *Cuminum cyminum L.* Journal of Biodiversity and Environmental Sciences (JBES) 3. 12:140-149.

Singh, Dhirendra K. (2010): Spices and Condiments. *Practical Manual*, GBPUA&T, Pantnagar. 75-83 P.

Pages: 53-78

SEED TREATMENT, PLANT HEALTH AND AGRO-TECHNOLOGY

Edited by: Dr. Avnish Chauhan and Dr. Pawan Kumar 'Bharti'

ISBN: 978-93-5056-810-1

Edition: 2016

Published by: Discovery Publishing House Pvt. Ltd., New Delhi (India)

4

Health Benefit and Medicinal Uses of Jatropha Plant

Farouk K El-Baz[1]*, Hanan F Aly[2], Safaa A Saad[1]

ABSTRACT

Jatropha curcas is a species of flowering plants belongs to Euphorbiaceae family. *It is* a multipurpose plant that gains a lot of economic importance because of its several potentials in industrial application and medicinal values. *J. curcas* has been used as traditional medicine to cure various infections. Medically it is used for diseases like cancer, piles, snakebite, paralysis, dropsy etc. Jatropha contains many medicinal values for human and veterinary purposes and has a vast potential for deriving therapeutically values for usage in various segments. Preparations of all parts of the plant, including seeds, leaves and bark, fresh or as a decoction, are used in traditional medicine.

Introduction

Plants gained an increasing interest due to their containing of bioactive compounds that lead to several medicinal virtues and a great importance for health. Many searches joined between the major pharmacological proprieties of medicinal plants and their biological activities (*Kadri et al., 2013*). Recently, the use of plants as herbal therapy has been considered popularity among clinicians and represents a good source of therapeutic compounds because of their beneficial effects with minimum toxicity, natural origins, lower side effects and relatively lower costs as compared to synthetic drugs.

1 Plant Biochemistry Department, National Research Centre, Dokki, Cairo, Egypt.

2 Therapeutic Chemistry Department, National Research Centre, Dokki, Cairo, Egypt.

J. curcas is plant belonging to the Euphorbiaceae family that is used to be planted as living fence or for medicinal use (*Heller, 1996*). The genus *Jatropha* is one of 300 genera belonging to the family Euphorbiaceae (*Bailey, 1953*). The plant is believed to be a native of South America and Africa but later the Portuguese settlers helped in its spreading to other continents of the world (*Gubitz et al., 1999*). The common use of *J. curcas* is the production of bio-fuel. However, *Prasad et al.* (*2012*) pointed to taking the medicinal role of *J. curcas* into consideration because of its promising potentials in the pharmaceutical field beside to commercializing on the medicinal product derived from *J. curcas* may turn out to be more profitable than using *J. curcas* as fuel substitution and promotion is needed to increase awareness to the public on this plant various potentials in medicinal uses.

The plant possesses anti-inflammatory, anti-metastatic, anti-tumor, coagulant and anti-coagulant, disinfectant, antiparasitic, wound healing, insecticidal, pregnancy terminating activity and anti-diarrhoea effect (*Laxane et al., 2013*). *J. curcas* was reported to be abortifacient, anodyne, antiseptic, diuretic, emetic, hemostat, lactagogue, narcotic, purgative, rubefacient, stypt and vulnerary; physic nut is a folk remedy for alopecia, ascites, burns, convulsions, cough, dermatitis, diarrhea, dropsy, dysentery, dyspepsia, eczema, fever, gonorrhea, hernia, incontinence, inflammation, jaundice, neuralgia, paralysis, parturition, pneumonia, rash, rheumatism, scabies, sciatica, sores, stomachache, syphilis, tetanus, thrush, tumors, ulcers, uterosis, and yellow fever (*Laxane et al., 2013*).

Therefore, the current chapter sheds light on the health benefit of *J. curcas* to display its medicinal uses and provide brief biological significance of this plant along with its up-to-date therapeutic applications.

Materials and Methods

Materials

Authentic reference material and chemicals

Folin-Ciocalteu reagent, 2, 2-diphenyl-1-picrylhydrazyl (DPPH), sodium carbonate, potassium ferricyanide ($K_3Fe\ (CN)_6$), ammonium molybdate and aluminum chloride were purchased from Sigma Chemical Co., Ltd (St. Louis, MO, USA). Butylated hydroxyltoluene (BHT) and gallic acid were purchased from Sigma-Aldrich. L-(tosyl-amido-2-phenyl) ethyl chloromethyl ketone and agarose were obtained from Merck, Sigma and Himedia (Mumbai, India). All other reagents and solvents were of analytical grade. All kits were the products of Biosystems (Alcobendas, Madrid, Spain), Sigma Chemical Company (St. Louis, MO, USA), Biodiagnostic Company (Cairo, Egypt).

Collection and Identification of Plant Material

The fresh plant organs of *J. curcas* were collected from the farm. The plant was authenticated by Agricultural Engineer Terese Labib, El Orman Botanical Garden, Cairo, Egypt.

Botanical Classification

Kingdom: Plantae
Order: Malpighiales
Family: Euphorbiaceae
Subfamily: Crotonoideae
Tribe: Jatropheae
Genus: Jatropha L.

Botanical Description

- **The whole tree**

The plant is regarded as a small tree or shrub with height generally ranging from 3-5 meter. *J. curcas* tree has a straight trunk and grey or reddish bark masked by large white patches *Kamal et al.* (2011).

- **Roots**

There are five roots formed from seedlings, one central and four peripheral (*Solsoloy and solsoloy*, 1997). A tap root is not usually formed by vegetative propagated plants

- **Leaves**

Morphology of leaves is variable. In general, leaves color is green to pale green. They are alternate and three to five-lobed (*Nahar* and *Ozores-Hampton*, 2011).

- **Flowers**

They are yellowish green and unisexual; occasionally hermaphrodite flowers occur. Flowers blossom in June. Additionally, *Kamal et al.* (*2011*) showed that flowering occurs during the wet season but it occurs within the year in permanently humid regions.

The inflorescence contains both of male and female flowers in ratio 29:1 (*Solomon* and *Ezradaman*, 2002) and can be formed in the leaf axil. Plants are monoecious and can also present hermaphroditic flowers occasionally. The rare hermaphrodite flowers can be self-pollinating (*Staubmann et al.*, 1999a).

- **Fruits**

They are small capsule-like, round fruit; about 2.5 - 4 cm in diameter. They are green and fleshy when immature, becoming dark brown when rip and splitting to release 2 or 3 black seeds each about 2 cm long. Fruits get ripen in Agust.

- **Seeds**

The seed resembles castor seed in shape but are smaller in size and dark brown in color. They become mature when the capsule color changes from green to yellow. They contain around 20% saturated fatty acids and 80% unsaturated fatty acids, and they yield 25-40% oil by weight. Also, they contain other chemical compounds such as raffinose, fructose, stachyose, glucose, saccharose, galactose, protein (*Nahar* and *Ozores-Hampton*, 2011) and phorbol ester.

Preparation of Samples

The plant samples of *J. curcas* were washed with tap water followed with distilled water to remove any dust and dirt. The plant samples were air dried under shade condition then grinded and homogenized to coarse powder finally stored in opaque screw tight jars until use.

Methods

Phytochemical Screening

The powdered samples of *J. curcas* were screened for qualitative detection of flavonoids, tannins, phenolics, saponins, coumarines and sterols and/or triterpenes applying chemical tests of *Harborne* (1988); *Harborne* (1998) and *Dahiru et al.* (2006).

Successive and Crude Extracts Preparation

Powdered samples of *J. curcas* were extracted by soaking using successive three solvents with different polarities (*Niranjana et al.,* 2013).

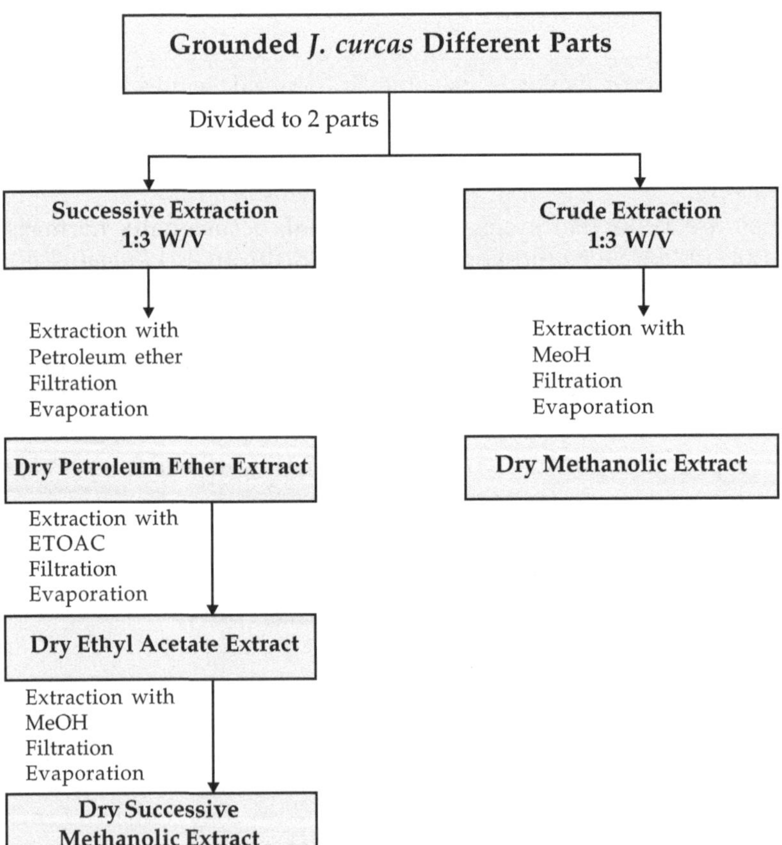

Fig. 4.1: **Scheme of the Extraction Procedure Followed**

Solvents used were: petroleum ether, ethyl acetate and methanol with percentage of extraction 1:3 w/v. While crude extracts were prepared by soaking powdered samples in methanol on shaker at 150 rpm for 48 hrs. The extracts were filtered using a Buchner funnel and Whatman No. 4 filter paper. The filtrate was concentrated using Rotary evaporator at 40°C under vacuum. The resulting dry extracts were re-dissolved in fresh methanol to make (10 µg/µl) stock solution and kept at 4°C for further analysis.

Determination of Polyphenolic (Total and Total Flavonoid Content)

Total phenolic content of each extract was determined using the Folin-Ciocalteu reagent (*Javanmardi et al.*, 2003). While total flavonoid content was determined according to the method of *Woisky and Salatino* (*1998*).

Antioxidant Activity

Antioxidant activity was determined by three methods; DPPH free radical scavenging, total antioxidant and reducing power activity. Quantitative measurement of radical scavenging properties of different *J. curcas* samples extract was carried out according to the method of *Blois* (1958). Total antioxidant activity of *J. curcas* extracts was determined according the method of *Prieto et al.* (1999). Also, determination of reducing power activity was carried out according to method of (*Zhao et al.*, 2008).

Antimicrobial Activity

Antimicrobial activity of *J. curcas* extracts was determined by using agar-well diffusion method described by (*Albayrak et al.*, 2010).

Antiviral Bioassay

(a) Cytotoxicity by MTT assay

Cell toxicity activity was carried out to identify the cell culture safe doses of the tested extracts by using MTT method (*Mossman*, 1983).

(b) Antiviral activity by plaque reduction assay

Antiviral activity of *J. curcas* extracts was investigated by plaque reduction assay according to the method of (*Hayden et al.*, 1980).

Anticancer Activity

Anticancer test was carried out by MTT assay according to the method of (*Plumb*, 2004).

Antidiabetic Activity

Glucose was determined in serum by colorimetric assay method according to *Trinder* (1959).

Results and Discussion

Health Benefit

The chemical compounds founded in herbal products are a part of the physiological functions of living organisms and hence they are believed to have better compatibility with the human body. In addition, bioactive compounds present in the medicinal plants provide the bountiful resource of active compounds for the pharmaceutical, cosmetics and food industries, and more recently in agriculture for pest control (*Rice*, 1995).

Accordingly, *J. curcas* contains a lot of secondary metabolites. The secondary metabolites in *J. curcas* leaves were represented in alkaloids, flavonoids and triterpenes (*Staubmann et al.* 1999b and *Morton* 1981). Screening of *J. curcas* roots showed the existence of many isolated secondary metabolites such as diterpenoids jatropholol, jatropholone A and B (*Chen et al.*, 1988). Therefore, *J. curcas* has many of biological compounds with many biological activities. *J. curcas* different parts or their different extracts possessed several of biological activities such as antioxidant, anticancer, antiulcer, antimicrobial, antidiabetic ...... etc.

1. **Antioxidant activity**

Numerous studies have shown that medicinal plants are sources of diverse phytochemicals (*Saxena et al.*, 2013). Many of which display antioxidant properties that can protect the human body against cellular oxidation reactions, free radicals and reactive oxygen species (ROS) effects (*Rahman*, 2007). Recently, the most commonly used synthetic antioxidants are butylated hydroxyanisole (BHA), butylated hydroxytoluene (BHT) and propylgallate. However, BHA and BHT have been restricted by legislative rules due to doubts over their toxic and carcinogenic effects (*Soubra et al.*, 2007). Hence, finding new source for natural antioxidants has increased greatly in the present years.

The study of *El Diwani et al.* (2009) indicated that some organs of *J. curcas* (root, leaf, stem and nodes) have different activities. The authors added that roots ethanolic extract was the most effective organ in terms of phenolic antioxidant properties followed by leaf and stem. The phytochemical contents and biological activities of the methanolic extract from different parts of *J. curcas* (leaves, stem bark, root and latex) were conducted by *Oskoueian et al.* (2011), where the latex and leaf extracts showed the highest antioxidant activity and the root exhibited anticancer therapeutic property against human colon adenocarcinoma (HT-29) cell line but its effect on human hepatocyte (Chang cell) was high.

Besides, *Oskoueian et al.* (2011a) studied the bioactive compounds and the biological activities of *J. curcas* kernel meal such as antimicrobial and antioxidant activities in methanolic and hot water extracts. The authors detected the occurrence of phenolics, flavonoids and saponins compounds in methanolic extract. HPLC analysis showed the presence of the phenolic compounds and flavonoids in hot water extract. Both of methanolic and hot water extracts showed antioxidant activities and antimicrobial effects against Gram negative and Gram positive bacteria. *Igbinosa et al.* (2011) evaluated the total phenol, flavonoids, flavonols and proanthocyanidin contents of the aqueous, ethanol and methanol stem bark extracts of *J. curcas.* They proved that *J. curcas* is a potential source of natural antioxidants and may be a good candidate for pharmaceutical plant based products.

2. **Antimicrobial activity**

Infectious diseases or transmissible diseases rising from microorganisms or infectious agents pose a health problem throughout the world (*Adenisa et al.*, 2000). Microbial pathogens are developing resistance against existing antibiotics therefore; the discovery of new pharmaceutical compounds is considered a great stress (*Sreedevi et al.*, 2013). Medicinal plants are the greatest asset to human health and represent a viable treasure for discovering new potential compounds with various therapeutic effects. Ethanol extract of sun-dried leaves of *J. curcas* inhibited the growth of *S. aureus* (*Le Grand et al.*, 1988). Additionally, *Haslam et al.* (1989) reported that *J. curcas* plant extracts and their products are used in many parts of the world as active herb remedies. Besides, *Fagbenro-Beyioku et al.* (1998) stated that *J. curcas* sap could be used as germicidal agent (any substance that kills germs or other microorganisms) against micrococcus species, Staphylococcus and Bacillus. Also, the authors mentioned the inhibitory effect of *J. curcas* sap on larval growth of mosquito that supports the cheap and readily available use of *J. curcas* as a disinfectant and malaria vector control agent. *J. curcas* latex has also been reported to have strong antimicrobial activities (*Oyi et al.*, 2002).

Ethanolic and aqueous extracts of *J. curcas* leaf and bark were studied for antibacterial activity against *Bacillus subtilis, Escherichia coli, Pseudomonas aeruginosa, Enterobacter aerogenes* and *Proteus vulgaris* where, ethanol extracts of bark was active against all bacteria and ethanol extract of leaf was active against all the microbes except *E. aerogenes* (*Sangeetha et al.*, 2009). In this concern, *Gupta et al.* (2010) evaluated the antibacterial, antifungal and cytotoxic effect of the crude extracts (petroleum ether, ethyl acetate and methanol extracts) and two purified compounds JC-1 and JC-2 isolated from the stem bark of *J. curcas*. The authors found that the isolated compounds produced the promising cytotoxic antibacterial activity against all the gram positive and negative bacteria, besides the antifungal activity of ethyl acetate extract against *Candida albicans, Aspergilus niger, Candida oryzae and Saccharromyces.*

Stem bark, root bark and kernel meal of *J. curcas* contained compounds with antibacterial activities and represent a potential source of antibacterial effect (*Namuli et al.*, 2011). Additionaly, the same authors determined the phytochemical compounds by spectrophotometry, high performance chromatography and gas chromatography-mass spectrometry analysis in *J. curcas* different extracts (hexane, water and methanol) of leaves, stem bark, root bark, root wood and kernel seeds and antibacterial activity. The authors found that phytochemicals detected by RP-HPLC were pyrogallol, gallic acid, naringin, rutin and vanillic acid and the main compounds detected by GC-MS were oxalic acid (root bark), acetic acid and oleic acid (stem bark). Also, they revealed that stem bark, root bark and kernel meal of *J. curcas* contained compounds with antibacterial activities. A cationic antimicrobial peptide (KVFLGLK, JCpep7) which isolated from *J. curcas* meal protein had antimicrobial activity against *Salmonella typhimurium, Shigella dysenteriae, P. aeruginosa, S. aureus, B. subtilis* and *Streptococcus pneumonia* with MIC values ranging from 24 to 64 µg/ml (*Xiao et al.*, 2011).

Gaikwad et al. (2012) studied the antimicrobial activity of *J. curcas* leaf, stem, root, latex and oil extracts against plant pathogenic fungi such as *A. flavus, Aspergillus niger, Alternaria alternate, Fusarium oxysporum and Rhizoctonia solani* and plant pathogenic bacteria *Erwini carotovora pv. Carotovora, P.aeruginosa, Xanthomonas campestris pv. Citri* and *Xanthomonas campestris pv. mangiferaeindicae* which gave various degree of inhibition towards pathogenes. *Nuchsuk et al* (2013) isolated and purified the Jc-SCRIP; a type 1 ribosome-inactivating protein from *J. curcas* seed coat also, studied its antimicrobial and anticancer effect that indicated its strong activity against Staphylococcus epidermidis human pathogenic bacteria and the cytotoxicity against human breast cancer adenocarcinoma, liver carcinoma cell and colon adenocarcinoma. Methanolic extract of *J. curcas* leaves revealed the presence of relevant antimicrobial compounds that have the potential as a cut flower solution to minimize microbial populations and extend flower vase life (*Rahman et al.*, 2014).

3. Antiviral activity

Virus is a small infectious agent that replicates only inside the living cells of other organisms and can infect all types of life forms. Medicinal plants have been traditionally used for different kinds of ailments including infectious diseases. There is an increasing need for substances with antiviral activity since the treatment of viral infections with the available antiviral drugs often leads to the problem of viral resistance.

Aqueous extract of *J. curcas* branches strongly inhibited the human immunodeficiency virus (HIV)-induced cytopathic effects with very low cytotoxicity (*Bbeassor et al.*, 1989). Various parts of *J. curcas* were reported for their antiviral activity against different strains of viruses. Hexane and chloroform fractions of *J. curcas* leaves produced a moderate protection of cells against the cytopathic effects of HIV in cultured human CCRF-CEM-SS lymphoblastoid cells (*Muanza et al.*, 1995). In addition, *Matasuse et al.* (1998) studied the antiviral effect of the water extract of *J. curcas* stem bark and concluded that the extract showed good suppressive effect on HIV growth and the antiviral activity had a high selective index. The water extract of the branches inhibits HIV induces cytopathic effects with low cytotoxicity (*Matsuse et al.*, 1999).

Previous studies using *J. curcas* stem bark extracts have shown inhibition of HIV-induced cytopathic effects (*Matsuse et al.*, 1999 and *Oskoueian et al.*, 2011). Also, *Huang et al.* (2008) introduced a new kind of ribosome-inactivating protein (curcin 2) induced by several different kinds of stress from *J. curcas* leaves, under the control of the CaMV (cauliflower mosaic virus) 35S promoter into the tobacco genome by Agrobacterium tumefaciens-mediated transformation method. The obtained results showed an increased tolerance to tobacco mosaic virus (TMV) and a fungal pathogen *Rhizoctonia solani* by delaying the development of systemic symptoms of TMV and reducing the damage caused by the fungal disease. A study, that scanned traditional medicines in the management of HIV/AIDS (Acquired Immune Deficiency Syndrome) in Tanzania, found that *J. curcas* leaves were being used for treatment in HIV related conditions such as skin rash and oral candidiasis (*Kisangau et al.*, 2007). The anti-HIV effect of 12-deoxyphorbol-13-phenylacetate, a compound synthesized from *J. curcas* phorbol esters, has been demonstrated; it inhibits HIV entry into target cells (*Wender et al.*, 2008 and *Makkar* and *Becker*, 2009). Immunomodulatory effect of *J. curcas* leaves aqueous methanolic extract had been reported by *Abd-Alla et al.* (2009). The results showed that, chicks treated with the aqueous methanolic extract exhibited protection against Newcastle disease challenge virus after being vaccinated. Besides, *Igbinosa et al.* (2009) mentioned that the water extract of *J. curcas* branches strongly inhibited HIV *in vitro* by depressing of reverse transcriptase (RT) enzyme activity and that also induced cytopathic effects with low cytotoxicity.

Devappa et al. (2010) determined the medicinal importance of the bioactive protein curcin as a successful immune-conjugate in chemotherapy and several cyclic peptides presented in *J. curcas* seeds as they have clinical significance and showed their potential in pharmacy and the immediate benefits of research on *J. curcas* proteins and peptides would be in the area of nutrition and clinical diagnosis. The branches latex of *J. curcas* has been found to be strong inhibitors to watermelon mosaic virus (*Esimone et al.*, 2008). Methanolic and aqueous extracts of mosaic virus (*Esimone et al.*, 2008). Methanolic and aqueous extracts of *J. curcas* leaf showed effective anti-viral and probable entry inhibition activity against potentially drug-resistant HIV so; *J. curcas* represents a good candidate for anti-HIV therapy with further research (*Dahake et al.*, 2012).

4. **Anticancer activity**

Herbal medicine is one of the most commonly used complementary and alternative therapies (CAM) by people with cancer. Some studies have shown that as many as 6 out of every 10 people with cancer (60%) use herbal remedies alongside conventional cancer treatments. There are many different types of herbal medicines and some of them overlap with foods.

Previous searches indicated the anticancer effect of *J. curcas* plant. Defatted seeds ethanol extract of *J. curcas* was active on leukemia cell line LEUK-P388 in cell culture (*Reddy et al.*, 1988). Twig and ethanolic extract of defatted leaves has showed activity against Lymphocytic leukemia (*Thomas*, 1989). Stem bark of *J. curcas* has anticancer effect due to its containing of alkaloids (*Nobori et al.*, 1994). Some compounds with antitumor activities were reportedly found in this plant (*Van den Berg et al.*, 1995). The latex of *J. curcas* contains an alkaloid called jatrophine that is believed to have anticancer activity (*Lin et al.*, 2003 and *Thomas et al.*, 2008). The most of research programmes are directed towards the investigation of constitutive diterpenes and lignans in *J. curcas* due to they have antitumor effect. Accordingly, curcin from *J. curcas* had a powerful antitumor activity on human gastric cancer cells (SGC-7901), Sp2/0 (mouse myeloma cell line), and human hepatoma *via* inhibitory action upon protein synthesis in reticulocyte lysate (*Lin et al.*, 2003).

Muangman et al. (2005) referred to the antimetastatic potential of curcusone-B, a diterpene isolated from *J. curcas.* The authors added that the treatment with curcusone-B resulted in a strong reduction of *in vitro* invasion, motility and secretion of matrix-metalloproteinases (MMP) of the cancer cells, whereas the ability to adhere to a Matrigel-coated surface was variably sensitive to curcusone B treatment. Therefore, curcusone-B, had a potential suppression towards the metastatic processes, which may be of therapeutic benefit for the treatment of metastatic cancers. In addition, *Balaji et al.* (2009) reported the inhibition effect for metastatic colony formation of lung melanoma cells B16F10 in C57BL/6 mice.

Moreover, Curcusone C, curcusone D, multidione, 15-epi-4Z-jatrogrossidentadion, 4E-jatrossidentadion, 4Z-jatrossidentadion, 2 hydroxyjatrogrossidion and 2-epi-hydroxyisojatrogrossidion (Pure diterpenoids isolated from *J. curcas*) showed strong cytotoxicity against L5178y mouse lymphoma cells (*Aiyelaagbe et al.*, 2011). *Nazeema* and *Girija* (2013) assessed the cytotoxicity of crude methanolic and ethanolic fractions of *J. curcas* stem on Hela cell lines as antiproliferative agents in addition to, identifying the compounds responsible for the cytotoxicity effect. The results revealed the cytotoxicity of the extract and the presence of alkaloids, phenolic and flavonoids. Also, *Nuchsuk et al.* (2013) studied the antimicrobial and anticancer effect of *J. curcas* that indicated its strong activity against *Staphylococcus epidermidis* human pathogenic bacteria and the cytotoxicity against human breast cancer adenocarcinoma, liver carcinoma cell and colon adenocarcinoma. Moreover, *Van den Berg et al.* (1995) referred to some compounds like (curcacycline A) with antitumor activities reportedly found in *J. curcas.*

5. Antidiabetic activity

Diabetes mellitus (DM), is a metabolic syndrome of etiologies characterized by chronic hyperglycemia with abnormalities in carbohydrate, fat and protein metabolism due to defect insulin secretions. DM is a serious health problem being the third greatest cause of death all over the world (*Gomathi et al.*, 2013) and if not treated, it is responsible for many complications affecting various organs in the body. Complications of diabetes can lead to death (*Weiss* and *Sumpio*, 2006). Referring to the WHO estimations, if the disease is not given urgent attention, death cases related with diabetes will increase by more than 50% in the next 10 years. A report from American Diabetes Association referred to the direct medical cost of diabetes and diseases linked with diabetes are enormous, e.g., it was over $132 billion in 2002.

Although the direct use of plant extracts in developed countries continued to decrease in the late nineteenth and early twentieth century, medicinal plants still play a key role in health care system of many parts of the world (*Tapsell et al.*, 2006).[1] Hypoglycemic herbs increase insulin secretion, enhance glucose uptake by adipose or muscle tissues and inhibit glucose absorption from intestine and glucose production from liver (*Hongxiang et al.*, 2009). *J. curcas* produced hepatoprotective effect where, *Imtiyaz et al.* (2010) investigated the hepatoprotective effect of *J. curcas* petroleum ether, alcoholic and aqueous leaf extracts against carbon tetrachloride ($CC1_4$)-induced acute hepatotoxicity in rats. The obtained results showed the protective effect by lowering serum levels of various biochemical parameters such as serum glutamyl oxalacetic acid transaminase (SGOT), serum glutamyl pyruvate transaminase (SGPT), alkaline phosphatase (ALP) and total bilirubin level (TBL).

Chloroform extract of leaves of *J. curcas* at different doses showed antidiabetic activity in albino rats. It decreased the elevated level of serum glucose, normalized pancreatic á-amylase activity and also reversed the cholesterol, triglyceride levels as compared to untreated diabetic rats (*Patil et al.*, 2011). The antidiabetic effect of *J. curcas* root aqueous extract was studied by *Aladodo et al.* (2013). The authors declared that, the aqueous root extract of *J. curcas* at 250 and 450 mg/kg body weight possessed hypoglycemic activity and also ameliorate anemic condition of alloxan-induced diabetic rats. In addition to, *Farag et al.* (2014) reported the hypoglycemic and antidiabetic activities of *J. curcas* aerial parts ethanolic extract in mice at a dose of 400 mg/kg body weight in alloxan-induced diabetic mice. However, the researches on the antidiabetic activity of *J. curcas* still little.

Medicinal Application

Traditional medicine using the plant extracts continues to provide over 80% of health coverage of the world's population, especially in the developing world (*WHO*, 2002). Secondary metabolites in medicinal plants are organic compounds that are not directly implicated in the normal growth, or development, of an organism. They often play an important role in plant defense against herbivores and other interspecies defenses. Humans use secondary metabolites as medicines, flavorings and drugs.

Jatropha species belongs to the family Euphorbiaceae and are used in traditional folklore medicine to cure various ailments in Africa, Asia and Latin America. The nomenclature of *J. curcas* is related to its medicinal applications where, it is derived from the Greek word *jatr´os* (doctor) and *troph´e* (food), which implies medicinal uses (*Kumar* and *Sharma*, 2008). The common use of *J. curcas* is the production of bio-fuel. However, *J. curcas* possesses various medicinal uses. A part of this, effort has been made to compile all the information reported on its pharmacological, phytochemical, toxicological studies and commercial applications. This information will be helpful to create interest towards the plant and may be useful in developing new formulations, as they more effective and having more therapeutic value. All parts of *J. curcas* (seeds, leaves, bark, stem....etc.) have been used in traditional medicine and for veterinary purposes for a long time (*Duke*, 1988).

- **The plant**

J. curcas is a folk remedy for alopecia, anasorca, ascites, burns, carbuncles, convulsions, cough, dermatitis, diarrhea, dropsy, dysentery, dyspepsia, eczema, erysipelas, fever, gonorrhea, hernia, incontinence, inflammation, jaundice, neuralgia, paralysis, parturition, pleurisy, pneumonia, rash, rheumatism, scabies, sciatica, sores, stomach, syphilis, tetanus, thrush, tumor, ulcer, uterosi, whitlow, yaw and yellow fever (*List* and *Horhammer*, 1979; *Duke* and *Wain*, 1981). Other ethnomedicinal uses of *J. curcas* include stryptic, vermifuge, vulnerary, alopecia, anasorea, ascites, burns, carbuncles, convulsions, cough, dermatitis, diarrhea, dropsy, dysentery, dyspepsia, eczema, fever, erysipelas, jaundice, paralysis, rashes, rheumatism, yellow fever, tetanus, ulcer, stomach ache, sores, heart burns, thrush, uterosis, whitlows and yaws (*Agbogidi et al.*, 2013). The plant is rich in many photochemicals including xylose (seeds), vitex (bark), sovitexin (leaf), and curcusones (whole plant) (*Hasfort*, 2000; *Osemene et al.*, 2013).

Moreover, shrub is used in hepatotoxicity and anti-obesity. *J. curcas* various solvent extracts has an abortive effect (*Goonasekera et al.*, 1995). Pohlianin A has antifungal and anti-malarial activity (*Auvin-Guette et al.*, 1999). It was reported that *J. curcas* for curing malaria (*Ankrah et al.*, 2003). The plant was traditionally used to cure diseases like piles, cancer, snakes bites, dropsy and paralysis (*Okujagu et al.*, 2006). Several biological effects were reported for the plant like wound healing (*Shetty et al.*, 2006), inhibition of cell protein synthesis (*Shimada*, 2006), anti-inflammation and anti-ulcer activities (*Parekh* and *Chanda*, 2007). *Feitosa et al.* (2011) screened eighteen medicinal plants including *J. curcas* for their inhibitory activity on acetyl cholinesterase (the responsible for Alzheimer's disease) and found that the most active and interesting plants were *Ipomoea asarifolia, J. curcas, Jatropha gossypiifolia, Kalanchoe brasiliensis* and *Senna alata. Sharma et al.* (2012) referred to using of the plant in curing allergies, burns, cuts, wound inflammation, smallpox, leprosy and leucoderma.

- **Roots**

Venezuelans take the root decoction for cure dysentery (*Morton*, 1981). Ethanol (70%) extract of *J. curcas* fresh root of, administered intraperitoneally to mice was active in metrazole induced convulsions (*Adesina*, 1982). Root was used for ringworm, eczema and scabies (*Perry*, 1980 and *Duke* and *Ayensu*, 1985). Root decoction used as a mouth wash for bleeding gums and toothache. In past the crushed root of *J. curcas* was applied to cure the inflammation by Bhil tribes from Rajasthan area in India on empirical basis (*Joshi*, 1995). *Mujmdar et al.* (2000) attributed the anti-diarrhea activity of root extract in albino mice to inhibition combination of elevated prostaglandin biosynthesis and reduction in propulsive movements of small intestine.

The decoction of roots bark is used to rinse the mouth to relieve toothache and sour throat among the tribal's inhabitants of southern Andhra Pradesh (*Parotta*, 2001). However, *Okujagu et al.* (2006) reported that the using of *J.curcas* roots in treating chest disease or using the cooked roots with gruel to cure kidney diseases. Yellow oil from the roots showed anti-helmintic properties (*Sirisomboon et al.*, 2007). The plant contains an antidote against snake venom and root extract also helps to check bleeding from gums (*Thomas et al.*, 2008).

Anti-inflammatory activity of topical application of *J. curcas* root powder in paste form in TPA-induced ear inflammation was confirmed in albino mice and successive solvent extraction of these roots was carried out by ether and methanol. The methanol extract exhibited systemic and significant antiinflammatory activity in acute carrageenan induced rat paw edema (*Mujumdar and Misar*, 2004). The authors added that the methanol extract also showed activity against formalin-induced rat paw edema, turpentine-induced exudative changes and cotton pellet-induced granular tissue formation after oral treatment for 7 days in albino rats. Moreover, *Mujmdar et al.* (2004) mentioned that the anti-inflammatory activity might be due to effects on several mediators and arachidonic acid metabolism involving cyclo-oxygenase pathway resulting in prostaglandin formation; anti-proliferative activity leading to reduction in granular tissue formation and leukocyte migration from the vessels. *Mujmdar et al.* (2005) found that, the methanol fraction had effect against castor oil induced diarrhoea and intraluminal accumulation of fluid. In addition, authors declared that methanol fraction reduced gastrointestinal motility after charcoal meal administration in albino mice.

- **Stem**

The cytotoxic effect of the ethyl acetate extract of *J. curcas* stem bark towards brine shrimp nauplii gave LC_{50} value of 19.95μg/ml. Flavonoid, a secondary metabolic compound from stem bark, exhibited a lot of biological activities like analgesic, anti-allergic, antimicrobial, anti-inflammatory, anti-angionic, cytostatic and antioxidant properties (*Hodek et al.*, 2002). Tannins, another bioactive component in *J.curcas* stem bark that has many biological activities which are presented in anti-diarrhea activity (*Dharmananda*, 2003). *J. curcas* crude bark extract accelerates the healing process by increasing the skin breaking strength, granulation tissue breaking strength, wound contraction, dry granulation tissue weight and hydroxyproline levels (*Shetty et al.*, 2006).

Besides, the authors observed a significant decrease in epithelization period in addition to, the histopathological examination of granulation tissue showed much advanced phase of healing, with more collagen, which has organized to form bundles. On the other hand, tender/twig/stem can be used in toothache, gum inflammation, gum bleeding and pyorrhoea. Amyrin from bark is considered analgesic, antiedemic, anti-inflammatory, antinoceceptive, antiulcer, gastroprotective and hepatoprotective (*Duke et al.*, 2002). *J. curcas* is able to protect skeletal muscle cells *in vitro* against the deleterious effects of ethanol (*Paulillo et al.*, 2012). Stems of young leaves have been used to successfully treat urinary infections (*Agbogidi et al.*, 2013).

- **Leaves**

Cameroon natives used the decoction of leaf in arthritis (*Watt* and *Breyer-Brandwijk*, 1962). Leaves are utilized as anti-parasitic, applied to scabies, rubefacient for paralysis, rheumatism; also applied to hard tumors (*Hartwell*, 1971). Colombians drink the leaf decoction for venereal disease (*Morton*, 1981). The infusion from the leaves is prepared to cure vaginal bleeding (*Singh et al.*, 1984). The IC50 of dichloromethane, methanol and methanol/water (1:1) extracts of *J. curcas* leaves against chloroquine resistant strain W2 of Plasmodium falciparum was found to be > 50 μg/ml (*Bbeassor et al.*, 1989). *Staubmann et al.* (1999) stated that the leaves of *J. curcas* are applied to wounds to get it cured, decoction of leaves was used externally and internally to treat fever and direct application of leaves was followed to treat jaundice. The IC_{50} of petroleum ether/ethyl acetate (1:1) and methanol extracts of *J. curcas* leaves against *Plasmodium falciparum* was found to be > 50 μg/ml (*Kohler et al.*, 2002). The leaves are regarded as antiparasitic, applied to scabies, rubefacient for paralysis, rheumatism and also applied to hard tumor (*Duke et al.*, 2002; *Aliyu*, 2006).

Aqueous extracts of *J. curcas* leaves were evaluated for anti-helmintic activity on adult Indian earthworms *Pheretima poshtuma* and indicated significant activity (*Ahirrao et al.*, 2008). The biological activities of α-amyrin from leaves as analgesic, antiedemic anti-inflammatory, antinociceptive, antitumor, antiulcer, cytotoxic, gastroprotective, hepatoprotective and insectifuge. Crushed leaves applied to the breast encourage lactation, besides using their juice to treat colic and dysentery (*Parveen et al.*, 2007). Aqueous extract of leaves of *J. curcas* showed anti-helmintic activity against *Pheritim aposhtuma* (*Ahirrao et al.*, 2008). Methanolic extract of *J. curcas* leaves showed anti-ulcer activity by using aspirin induced gastric lesions in whister rats (*Kannappan et al.*, 2008). *Uche* and *Aprioku* (2008) investigated the analgesic and anti-inflammatory effect of methanolic extract of *J. curcas* leaves and reported the significant reduction in the acetic acid-induced writhing mice, also recommended using *Jatropha curcas* for cute inflammatory disorders and diseases associated with pains.

Akinpelu et al. (2009) assessed the phytochemical compounds and antibacterial activities of the methanolic extracts of the leaves of *J. curcas* as medicinal plant used for the treatment of illness such as jaundice, diarrhoea, dysentery, sexually transmitted diseases and several other diseases caused by micro-organisms. They added that the methanolic extracts gained antibacterial activity against eight of the thirteen tested bacterial while, the phytochemical results indicated the presence of alkaloids, saponins, steroids and tannins in *J.curcas* extracts.

Jaikumar et al. (2010) investigated the antiulcer effect of methanolic extract of *J. curcas* leaves on pylorus ligation and Aspirin-induced gastric ulcers in Wister rats where, the treatment of *J. curcas* extract exhibited antiulcer effect represented in reduction of the acid parameters like gastric volume, pH, total acidity, total proteins, ulcer index and total acid output. The leaves have acrid taste, which is considered as an excretory product or secondary metabolites, may be of therapeutic use and have action on metabolism (*Mishra et al.*, 2010). Ethanol and water extracts of *J. curcas* leaves exhibited anti-inflammatory activity comparable to ibuprofen (*Sangeetha et al.*, 2009). The leaves contain apigenin, vitexin and ansovitexin which when combined with other factors enable them to be used against muscular pains (*Agbogidi and Ekeke*, 2011).

James et al. (2011) showed that formulating *J. curcas* extract into ointment is effective for wound repairing and enhance the harnessing of the extract in the formulation of commercial dermatological ointments, which highly supports the verbal claim and the use of *J. curcas* to cure wound healings. *Laxane et al.* (2013) found that the different uses of leaves by different people for curing such as Colombians drink the leaf decoction for venereal disease, Bahamans drink the decoction for heartburn, Costa Ricans poultice leaves onto erysipelas and splenosis, Guatemalans place heated leaves on the breast as a lactagogue and Barbadians use the leaf tea for marasmus. *Azikiwe et al.* (2014) studied the possible coagulant activity of *J. curcas* leaves *via* some *in vivo* and *in vitro* haemostatic studies on rats to scientifically demonstrate its coagulant effect and declared that both of *J. curcas* extracts (aqueous and ethanolic extracts) had shortened the time of blood clotting and the prothrombin, activated partial thromboplastin time and platelets count were normal and same with control.

- **Seeds**

Seeds are used as a cure for dropsy, gout, paralysi and skin ailments (*Watt* and *Breyer-Brandwijk*, 1962). In south Sudan, the seed and the fruit are used as a contraceptive (*List and Horhammer*, 1979). Seed is viewed as aperients (*Duke*, 1983). *Goonasekera et al.* (1995) showed abortifacient properties in female rats which gave 100% anti-fertility of the methanol, petroleum ether and dichloromethane extract of fruit. The plant seeds are not only a source of biofuel but they also contain many pharmaceutical metabolites with a big importance that supports the commercial exploitation of seeds in biopharmaceutical field and bio-energy production (*Debnath et al.*, 2008).

The aqueous and hydro-alcoholic extracts of *J. curcas* seeds were investigated to know their anthelmintic activity where, they produced a good egg-hatching-inhibition of parasites *Haemonchus contortus* (*Eguale* and *Giday*, 2009). The nut of the plant has also been used traditionally for the treatment of many ailments including burns, convulsions, fever and inflammation (*Mishra et al.*, 2010). *J. curcas* press cake (residue after oil extraction) strongly supports its use as a potential coagulant agent (*Abidin et al.*, 2011). The hexane, ethyl acetate and ethanol extracts of *J.curcas* seeds inhibited egg hatching in Haemonchus contortus (*Monteiro et al.*, 2011). Seeds are used as contraceptives.

- **Oil**

J. curcas kernel oil has 36% linoleic acid content that has possible interest for skin care industry. Oil is used traditionally for the treatment of sciatica, dropsy, paralysis, rheumatism, dysentery, diarrhea and certain skin diseases (*Desai*, 1975; *Dymock et al.*, 1976; *Nadkarni*, 1976; *Agarwal*, 1986; *Ambasta*, 1986; *Anonymous*, 2001). The seed oil is emetic, laxative, purgative and for skin ailments (*Duke*, 1983). Oil has been found useful for medicinal and veterinary purposes (*Gubitz et al.*, 1999).

When the oil is mixed with benzyl benzoate, it becomes effective against scabies and dermatitis (*Priminick*, 2002). The oil from *J. curcas* seeds is used in helping with rashes and parasitic skin diseases (*Okolie et al.*, 2007). *Laxane et al.* (2013) reported the using oil massage by Mauritians for ascitic limbs. The oil from *J. curcas* seeds is used in helping with rashes and parasitic skin diseases (*Kemberling*, 2014).

- **Sap**

The sap is used for treatment of piles, snakebite, skin diseases, paralysis, dropsy, malarial fever, arthritis, gout, jaundice and resistance to various stresses (*Heller*, 1996; *Openshaw*, 2000). The sap from twigs is considered as a styptic and can treat ulcer and dress wounds (*Mishra et al.*, 2010). Sap form *J. curcas* bark is used to dress wounds and ulcers and can also be used to stop bleeding (*Kemberling*, 2014).

- **Latex**

The latex combined with the powdered leaves is applied to sluggish wounds when formulated as enema, it used for the treatment of gonorrhea (*Irvine*, 1961). Latex used to dress sores, ulcers and inflamed tongues (*Perry*, 1980). *Nath* and *Dutta* (1991 and 1997) studied the ability of curcain (a proteolytic enzyme extracted from the latex of *J. curcas* shoots) ointments to cure healings in mice which gave healing of wounds better compared to the control ointments nitrofurazone (furcin ointment, SK&F) and propamidine isoethionate (antiseptic cream, M&B). The healing effect of curcain a proteolytic enzyme from the latex on wound has been demonstrated (*Nath* and *Dutta,* 1992). The latex is externally applied to cure rheumatism and skin ailments (*Thomas et al.*, 2008; *Salas et al.*, 1994).

Van den Berg et al. (1995) reported the inhibition effect of Curcacycline A (a cyclic octapeptide isolated from the ethanolic extract of *J.curcas* latex) on each of the classical pathway activity of human complement and the proliferation of human T-cells. Curcacycline A isolated from latex inhibits classical pathway of human complement and proliferation of human T-cells (*Van den Berg et al.*, 1995) while Curcacycline B has the ability to encourage rotamase activity of cyclophilin B (*Catherine et al.*, 1997). The latex of *J. curcas* has anticoagulant activities (*Osoniyi* and *Onajobi*, 2003). The authors mentioned that ethyl acetate and butanol extracts of *J. curcas* latex resulted in a partial separation of the two opposing activities: at low concentrations, the ethyl acetate fraction exhibited a procoagulant activity, while the butanol fraction had the highest anticoagulant activity. The residual aqueous fraction had no significant effect on the clotting time of blood and the PT but slightly prolonged the APTT. It is also used as an antiseptic against cuts and wounds (*Oyi et al.*, 2007). Laxane et al (*2013*) referred to applying the latex of *J.curcas* to bee and wasp stings.

- **Twig**

Twig was used as a toothbrush to Gumboils and strengthens the gums (*Parveen et al.*, 2007).

REFERENCES

Abd-Alla, H.I. Moharram, F.A. Gaara, A.H. and El-Safty, M.M. (2009): Phytoconstituents and Immunomodulatory Activity of *Jatropha curcas* L. Leaves on Humoral and Cell-mediated Immune Response in Chicks. Zeitschrift für Naturforschung, 64: 495-501.

Abidin, Z.Z. Ismail, N. Yunus, R. Ahamad, I.S. and Idris, A. (2011): Preliminary Study on Jatropha Curcas as Coagulant in Wastewater Treatment. Environ Technol, 32: 971-7.

Adesina, S.K. (1982): Studies on Some Plants Used as Anticonvulsants in Amerindian and African Traditional Medicine. Fitoterapia, 53: 147.

Adenisa, S.K. Idowu, Q. Ogundaini, A.O. Oladimeji, H. Olugbade, T.A. Onawunmi, G.O. Pais, M. (2000): Antimicrobial Constituents of the Leaves of *Acalypha wilkesiana* and *Acalypha hispida*. Phytotherapy Research, 14: 371-374.

Agbogidi, O.M. Ekeke, E.A. (2011): *Jatropha curcas* Linn an Important but Neglected Plant Species in Nigeria. Journal of Biological and Chemical Research, 281: 52-62.

Agbogidi, O.M. Akparobi, S.O. and Eruotor, P.G. (2013): Health and Environmental Benefits of *Jatropha curcas* Linn. Unique Research Journal of Agricultural Sciences, 1: 076-079.

Agarwal, V.S. (1986): Economic Plants of India. Kailash Prakashan, Calcutta, p. 196.

Albayrak, S. Aksoy, A. Sagdic, O. and Hamzaoglu, E. (2010): Compositions, Antioxidant and Antimicrobial Activities of Helichrysum (Asteraceae) Species Collected from Turkey. Food Chemistry, 119: 114-122.

Aladodo, R.A. Muhammad, N.O. and Balogun, E.A. (2013): Effects of Aqueous Root Extract of *Jatropha curcas* on Hyperglycemic and Haematological Indices in Alloxan-induced Diabetic Rats. Fountain Journal of Natural and Applied Sciences, 2: 52-58.

Ahirrao, R.A. Pawar, S.P. Borse, LB. Borse, S.L. Desai, S.G. and Muth, A.K. (2008): Anthelmintic Activity of Leaves of *Jatropha curcas* linn and *Vitex negundo* linn. Pharmacology online News Letters.1, 279-293. *Pharmacology online*, 1: 276-279.

Aiyelaagbe, O.O. Hamid, A.A. Fattorusso, E. Taglialatela-Scafati, O. Schroder, H.C. and Muller, W.E.G. (2011): Cytotoxic Activity of Crude Extracts as well as of Pure Components from Jatropha Species, Plants Used Extensively in African Traditional Medicine. Hindawi Publishing Corporation, 2011, Article ID 134954, 1-7.

Akinpelu, D.A. Aiyegoro, O.A. and Okoh, A.I. (2009): The Bioactive Potentials of Two Medicinal Plants Commonly Used as Folklore Remedies Among some Tribes in West Africa. Afr.J.Biotechnol, 8: 1660-1664.

Aliyu, B.S. (2006): Some Ethnomdicinal Plants of the Savannah Regions of West Africa: Description and Phytochemicals. Triumph Publishing Company Ltd., Kano.

Ambasta S.P. (1986): The Useful Plants of India. Publication and Information Directorate, CSIR, New Delhi, p. 302.

Ankrah, N.A. Nyarko, A.K. Addo, P.G. Ofosuhene, M. Dzokoto, C. Marley, E. Addae, M.M. and Ekuban, F.A. (2003): Evaluation of Efficacy and Safety of a Herbal Medicine Used for the Treatment of Malaria. Phytother. Res, 17: 697-701.

Anonymous, (2001): The Wealth of India, Raw Materials, Vol. V, (Council of Scientific and Industrial research, New Delhi, 293-297.

Auvin-Guette, C. Baraguey, C. Blond, A. Lezenven, F. Pousset, J.L. and Bodo, B. (1997): Curcacycline B, a Cyclic Nonapeptide from Jatropha Curcas Enhancing Rotamase Activity of Cyclophilin, 38, 2845.

Azikiwe, C.C.A. Ifezulike, C.C. Amazu, L.U. and Nwabali, M.O. (2014): Haemostatic Activities of *Jatropha curcas* (Linn) in rats, Drug discovery, 8: 16-20.

Bailey, L.H. (1953): The Standard Cyclopedia of Horticulture. Vol. III, The Mcmillan Co., New York, Toronto.

Balaji, R. Rekha, N. Deecaraman, M. and Manikandan, L. (2009): Antimetastatic and Antiproliferative Activity of Methanolic Fraction of *Jatropha curcas* Against B16F10 Melanoma Induced Lung Metastasis in C57BL/6 mice. Afr J Pharm Pharmacol, 3: 547-555.

Bbeassor, M. Kossou, Y. Amegbo, K. De Souza, C. Koumaglo, K. and Denke, A. (1989): Antimalarial Effects of Eight African Medicinal Plants. J Ethnopharmacol, 25: 115-118.

Blois, M.S. (1958): Antioxidant Determinations by the Use of Stable Free Radical, Nature, 26: 1199-1200.

Catherine, A. Carine, B. Alain, B, Francoise, L. Jean-Louis, P. and Bernard, B. (1997). Curcacycline B, a Cyclic Nonapeptide from *Jatropha curcas* Enhancing Rotamase Activity of Cyclophilin. Tetrahedron Lett, 38: 2845-2848.

Chen, M. Hou, L. and Zhang, G. (1988): The Diterpenoids from *Jatropha curcas*. Zhiwu Xueboa, 30: 308-311.

Dahake, R. Roy, S. Patil, D. Chowdhary, A. and Deshmukh, R.A. (2012): Evaluation of Anti-viral Activity of *Jatropha curcas* Leaf Extracts Against Potentially Drug-resistant HIV Isolates. BMC Infectious Diseases, 12, 14.

Dahiru, D. Sini, J.M. John-Africa L (2006): Antidiarrhoeal Activity of *Ziziphus mauritiana* Root Extract in Rodents, Afr. J. Biotechnol, 5: 941-945.

Dharmananda, S. (2003): Gallnuts and the Uses of Tannins in Chinese Medicine. In: Proceedings of Institute for Tradit. Med, Portland, Oregon.

Debnath, P.K. Gode, K.D. Das, G. Sanyal, A.K. (1974): Br J Pharmacol, 51: 231-6.

Debnath, M., and Bisen, P.S. (2008). Jatropha Curcas L., a Multipurpose Stress Resistant Plant with a Potential for Ethnomedicine and Renewable Energy. Curr Pharm Biotechnol, 9: 288-306.

Desai, V.G. (1975): Aushadhi Sangraha. Shri Gajanan Book Depot, Dadar, Mumbai, p. 914 (in Marathi).

Devappa, R.K. Makkar, H.P. and Becker, K. (2010): Nutritional, Biochemical, and Pharmaceutical Potential of Proteins and Peptides from Jatropha: Review. J. Agric. Food Chem, 58: 6543-6555.

Dharmananda, S. (2003): Gallnuts and the Uses of Tannins in Chinese Medicine. In: Proceedings of Institute for Tradit. Med, Portland, Oregon.

Duke, J.A. and Wain, K.K. (1981): Medicinal Plants of the World. Computer Index with more than 85,000 Entries. 3 vols.

Duke, J.A. (1983): Handbook of Energy Crops. Purdue University. Centre for New Crops and Plant Products.Unpublished.

Duke, J.A. and Ayensu, E.S. (1985): Medicinal Plants of China. Reference Publications, Inc. Algonac, MI.

Duke, J.A. (1988): CRC Handbook of Medicinal Herbs. CRC Press, Boca Raton, Florida, 253-254.

Duke, J.A. Bogenschutz-Godwin, M.J. DuCellier, J. and Duke, P.A.K. (2002): Handbook of Medicinal Herbs. 2nd Edition, Boca Raton, CRC Press.

Dymock, C. Warden, C.J.H. and Hooper, D. (1976): Pharmacographica Indica – A History of the Principal Drugs of Vegetable Origin. Bishen Singh Mahindra Pal Singh, Dehra Dun, p. 274 (reprint).

Eguale, T. and Giday, M. (2009): In vitroanthelmintic Activity of Three Medicinal Plants Against Haemonchus contortus. Int J Green Pharm, 3: 29-34.

El Diwani, G. El Rafie, S. and Hawash, S. (2009): Antioxidant Activity of Extracts Obtained from Residues of Nodes Leaves Stem and Root of Egyptian *Jatropha curcas*. African Journal of Pharmacy and Pharmacology, 3: 521-530.

Esimone, C.O. Nworu, C.S. and Jackson, C.L. (2008): Cutaneous Wound Healing Activity of a Herbal Ointment Containing the Leaf Extract of *Jatropha curcas* L. (Euphorbiaceae). Int J Appl Res Nat Prod, 1: 1-4.

Fagbenro-Beyioku, A.F. Oyibo, W.A. and Anuforom, B.C. (1998): Disinfectant/Antiparaistic Activities of *Jatropha curcas*. East Afr. Med. J, 75: 508-511.

Farag, M. Al-Rehaily, A. Ahmad, M. and Mothana, R. (2014): Detection of Hypoglycemic and Antidiabetic Fraction in Ethanol Extract of *Jatropha curcas* Aerial Parts. Pharmacology & Pharmacy, 5: 663-669.

Feitosa, C.M. Freitas, R.M. Luz, N.N.N. Bezerra, M.Z.B. and Trevisan, M.T.S. (2011): Acetylcholinesterase Inhibition by Somes Promising Brazilian Medicinal Plants. Braz. J. Biol, 71: 783-789.

Gaikwad, R.S. Kakde, R.B. Kulkarni, A.U. Gaikwad, D.R. and Panchal, V.H. (2012): *In vitro* Antimicrobial Activity of Crude Extracts of Jatropha Species. Current Botany, 3: 09-15.

Gomathi, D. Ravikumar, G. Kalaiselvi, M. Devaki, K. and Uma, C. (2013): Efficacy of *Evolvulus alsinoides* (L.) L. on Insulin and Antioxidants Activity in Pancreas of Streptozotocin Induced Diabetic Rats. Journal of Diabetes & Metabolic Disorders, 12: 39.

Goonasekera, M.M. Gunawardana, V.K. Jayasena K. Mohammed S.G. and Balasubramania S. (1995): Pregnancy Terminating Effects of Jatrophacurcasin Rats. J. ethnopharmacol, 47: 117-123.

Gosh, L. and Singh, L (2010): Study of Factors Influencing Vegetative Propagation of *Jatropha curcas*. Indian Forester, 136: 1637-1648.

Gubitz, G.M. Mittelbach M.and Trabi, M. (1999): Exploitation of the Tropical Oil Seed Plant *Jatropha curcas* L. Bioresour. Technol, 67: 73-82.

Gupta, D.D. Haque, E. Islam, N.; Mondal, S. and Shibib, B.A. (2010): Antimicrobial and Cytotoxic Activities of *Jatropha curcas* (Euphorbiaceae). Dhaka Univ. J. Pharm. Sci, 9:139-142.

Harborne, J.B. (1988): The Flavonoids: Advances in Research Since 1980. (New York: Chapman and Hall).

Harborne, J.B. (1998): Phytochemical Methods: A Guide to Modern Technique of Plant Analysis, Champman and Hall, London.

Hartwell, J.L. (1971): Plants Used Against Cancer. A Survey Lloydia, 30-34.

Hasfort, E.E. (2000): The Cultural Life of Early Domestic Plant Use. Antiquity, 72: 773-7783.

Haslam, E. Lilley, T.H. Martin, Y. and Magnolotto, R. (1989): Traditional Herbal Medicine; The Roles of Polyphenols, Plants Medica, 4: 1-8.

Hayden, F.G. Cote, K.M. and Douglas, R.G. (1980): Plaque Inhibition Assay for Drug Susceptibility Testing of Influenza Viruses. Antimicrobial Agents and Chemotherapy, 17: 865-870.

Heller, J. (1996): Physic Nut. Jatropha Curcas - Promoting the Conservation and Use of Underutilized and Neglected Crops. Gatersleben, Inst Plant Genet Crop; 1996. Plant Research/Rome, International Plant Genetic Resources Institute.

Hodek, P. Trefil, P. and Stiborova, M. (2002): Flavonoids -Potent and Versatile Biologically Active Compounds Interacting with Cytochrome P450. Chemico-Biol. Int, 139: 1-21.

Hongxiang, H. George, T. and Vay Liang, W. (2009): Hypoglycemic Herbs and Their Action Mechanisms. Chin. Med, 4: 11-14.

Huang, M. Hou, P. Wei, Q. Xu, Y. and Chen, F. (2008): A Ribosome-inactivating Protein (curcin 2) Induced from *Jatropha curcas* can Reduce Viral and Fungal Infection in Transgenic Tobacco. Plant Growth Regul, 54: 115-123.

Igbinosa, O.O. Igbinosa, E.O. and Aiyegoro, O.A. (2009): Antimicrobial Activity and Phytochemical Screening of Stem Bark Extracts from *Jatropha curcas* (Linn). African Journal of Pharmacy and Pharmacology, 3: 058-062.

Igbinosa, O.O. Igbinosa, I.H. Chigor, V.N. Uzunuigbe, O.E. Oyedemi, S.O. Odjadjare, E.E. Okoh, A.I. and Igbinosa, E.O. (2011): Polyphenolic Contents and Antioxidant Potential of Stem Bark Extracts from *Jatropha curcas* (Linn). Int J Mol Sci, 12: 2958-2971.

Imtiyaz, S. Patil, K.S. Singh, A. Kute, S.H. and Mahajan, S.M. (2010): Hepatoprotective Activity of *Jatropha curcas* Leaf Extract Against Carbon Tetrachloride-induced Hepatotoxicity. Journal of Tropical Medicinal Plants, 11: 53-59.

Irvine, F.R. (1961): Woody Plants of Ghana (With Special Reference to Their Uses). 2nd Ed. OUP, London, 233-237.

Jaikumar, S. Ramaswamy, S. Asokan, B.R. Mohan, T. and Gnanavel, M. (2010): Anti Ulcer Activity of Methanolic Extract of *Jatropha curcas* (Linn.) on Aspirin-induced Gastric Lesions inWistar Strain Rats. Research Journal of Pharmaceutical, Biological and Chemical Sciences, 1: 886.

James, O. Unekwojo, E.G. and Ojochenemi,, A.A. (2011): Assessment of Biological Activities: A Comparison of Pergularia Daemia and Jatropha curcas Leaf Extracts. British Biotechnology Journal, 1: 85-100.

Javanmardi, J. Stushnoff, C. Locke, E. and Vivanco, J.M. (2003): Antioxidant Activity and Total Phenolic Content of Iranian Ocimum Accessions, Food Chemistry, 83: 547-550.

Joshi, P. (1995): Ethnobotany of the Primitive Tribesin Rajasthan. Printwell, Jaipur, India, 89.

Kadri, H. Djilani, S.E. and Djilani, A. (2013): Phtochemical Constituents, Antioxidant Activity, Total Phenolic and Flavonoid Contents of *Arisarum vulgare* Seeds. Acta Sci. Pol., Technol. Aliment, 12: 169-173.

Kamal, S. Manmohan, S. and Birendra, S. (2011): A Review on Chemical and Medicobiological Applications of *Jatropha curcas*. International Research Journal of Pharmacy, 2: 61-66.

Kannappan, N. Jaikumar, S. Manavalan, R. and Muthu A.K. (2008): Antiulcer Activity of Methanolic Extract of *Jatropha Curcas* (Linn.) on Aspirin-Induced Gastric Lesions in Wistar Rats. Pharmacologyonline, 1: 279-293.

Kemberling, J. (2014): Medicinal Uses for *Jatropha Curcas*. *e*How Contributor.

Kisangau, D.P. Lyaruu, H.V. Hosea, K.M. and Joseph, C.C. (2007): Use of Traditional Medicines in the Management of HIV/AIDS Opportunistic Infections in Tanzania: A Case in the Bukoba Rural District. J Ethnobiol Ethnomed, 3: 29.

Hodek, P.P. Trefil,, and Stiborova, A. (2002): Flavonoids-potent and Versatile Biologically Active Compounds Interacting with Cytochrome P450.Chemico-Biological Interactions, 139: 1-21.

Kohler, I.K. Jenett-Siems, K. Siems, M.A. Hernandez, R.A. Ibarra, W.G. Berendsohn, Bienzle, U. and Eich, E. (2002): In Vitroantiplasmodial Investigation of Medicinal Plants from El Salvador. Z Naturforsch C, 57: 277-281.

Kumar, A. and Sharma, S. (2008): An Evaluation of Multipurpose Oil Seed Crop for Industrial Uses *(Jatropha curcas L.)*: A Review. Industrial Crops and Products, 28: 1-10.

Laxane, S.N. Swarnkar, S. Mruthunjaya, K. Sachin, B.Z. and Manjunath, S.M. (2013): *Jatropha curcas*: A Systemic Review on Pharmacological, Phytochemical, Toxicological Profiles and Commercial Applications. Research Journal of Pharmaceutical, Biological and Chemical Sciences, 4: 989-1010.

Le Grand, A. Wondergem, P.A. Verpoorte, R. and Pousset, J.L. (1988): Anti-infectious Phytotherapies of the Tree-savannah of Senegal (West-Africa) II. Antimicrobial Activity of 33 Species. J Ethnopharmacol, 22: 25-31.

Lin, Y.F. Yan, L. Tang and Chen, F. (2003): Antitumor Effects of Curcin from Seeds of *Jatropha curcas*. Acta Pharmacol., Sin, b24: 241-246.

List, P.H. and Horhammer, L. (1979): Hager's Handbuch der pharmazeutischen praxis. vols 2-6. Springer-Verlag, Berlin.

Makkar, H. and Becker, K. (2009): *Jatropha curcas*, a Promising Crop for the Generation of Biodiesel and Value-added Coproducts. Eur J Lipid Sci Technol, 111: 773-787.

Matsuse, T. Lim, Y.A. Hatton, M. Correa, M. and Gupta, M.P. (1998): A Search for Antiviral Properties in Panamanian Medicinal Plants. The Effects on HIV and its Essential Enzymes. J. Ethnopharm, 64: 15-22.

Matsuse, T.I. Lim, Y.A. Hattori, M. Correa, M. and Gupta, M.P. (1999): A Search for Anti-viral Properties in Panamanian Medicinal Plants. The Effect on HIV and Essential Enzymes. J. Ethnopharmacol, 64: 15-22.

Mishra S.B. (2010): Antidiabetic Effect of *Jatropha curcas* L. Leaves Extract in Normal and Alloxan-induced Diabetic Rats. International Journal of Pharmaceutical Sciences, 2: 482-87.

Monteiro, V.B. Bevilaqua, C.M.L. Morais, S.M. Machado, L.K. Lourdes F.A. Camurc, a-Vasconcelosc, Claudio C. Campello, Wesley, L.C. Ribeiro, Mayara de, A. Mesquita, A. (2011): Anthelmintic Activity of *Jatropha curcas* L. Seeds on Haemonchus Contortus Maria. Veterinary Parasitology, 182: 259-263.

Morton, J.F. (1981): Atlas of Medicinal Plants of Middle America-Bahamas to Yucatan. C.C. Thomas, Spring Field, IL.

Mossman, T. (1983): Rapid Colorimetric Assay for Cellular Growth and Survival: Application to Proliferation and Cytotoxicity Assays. Journal of Immunological *Methods*, 65: 55-63.

Muangman, S. Thippornwong, M. and Tohtong, R. (2005): Anti-metastatic Effects of Curcusone B, a Diterpene from *Jatropha curcas*. In vivo, 19: 265-268.

Muanza, D.N. Euler, K.L. Wiliams, L. and Newman, D.J. (1995): Screening of Antitumour and Anti-HIV Activities of Nine Medicinal Plants from Zaire. Int J Pharmacogn, 33: 98-106.

Mujumdar, A.M. Upadhye, A.S. and Misar, A.V. (2000): Studies on Antidiarroheal Activity of *Jatropha curcus* Root Extract in Albino mice. Journal of Ethynopharmacology, 70: 183-187.

Mujumdar, A.M. and Misar A.V. (2004). Anti-inflammatory Activity of *Jatropha curcas* Roots in Mice and Rats. Journal of Ethnopharmacology, 90: 11-15.

Mujumdar, A.M. Misar, A.V. and Upadhye, A.S. (2005): Antidiarrhoeal Activity of Ethanol Extract of the Bark of *Dalgergia lanceolaria*. J. Ethnopharmacol, 102: 213-216.

Nadkarni, A.K. (1976): Dr. K.M. Nadkarni's Indian Material Medica, Vol. I (Originally K.M. Nadkarni (Ed.)). Popular Prakashan, Bombay, p. 705 (revised).

Nahar, K. and Ozores-Hampton, M. (2011): *Jatropha:* An Alternative Substitute to Fossil Fuel. Gainesville: University of Florida, Institute of Food and Agricultral Sciences, Retrieved, 1-9.

Namuli, A. Abdullah, N. Sieo, C.C. Zuhainis, S.W. and Oskoueian, E. (2011): Phytochemical Compounds and Antibacterial Activity of *Jatropha curcas* Extracts. Journal of Medicinal Plants Research, 5: 3982-3990.

Nath, L.K. and Dutta, S.K. (1991): Extraction and Purification of Curcain, a Protease from the Latex of Jatropha Curcas Linn. Ind. J. Pharmacol, 43: 111-114.

Nath, L.K. and Dutta, S.K. (1992): Wound Healing Response of the Proteolytic Enzyme Curcain. Indian Journal of Pharmacology, 24/2.

Nath, L.K.and Dutta, S.K. (1997): Acute Toxicity Studies and Wound Healing Response of Curcain, a Proteolytic Enzyme Extract from the Latex of *Jatropha curcas* L. In: Gubitz, G.M., Mittelbach, M., Trabi, M., (Eds.), Biofuel and Industrial Products from *Jatropha curcas*. DBV Graz, 82-86.

Nazeema, T.H. and Girija, S. (2013): Characterisation of the Active Antiproliferative Principles of *Jatropha curcas* and *Jatropha gossippifolia* on Hela Cell Lines. International Journal of Pharmacy and Pharmaceutical Sciences, 5: 346-355.

Niranjana, K. Sathiyaseelanb, V. and Jeyaseelana, E.C. (2013): Screening for Anti-microbial and Phyto Chemical Properties of Different Solvents Extracts of Leafs of *Pongamia pinnata,* International Journal of Scientific and Research Publications, 3: 1-3.

Nobori, T. Miurak, K. Wu, D.J. Lois, A. Takabayashik, K. and Carson, D.A. (1994): Deletion of the Cyclin-dependent kinase-4 inhibitor gene in Multiple Human Cancers. Nature, 368: 753-756.

Nuchsuk, C. Wetprasit, N. Roytrakul, S. Choowongkomon, K. T-Thienprasert, N. Yokthongwattana, C. Arpornsuwan, T. and Ratanapo, S. (2013): Bioactivities of Jc-SCRIP, a Type 1 ribosome-inactivating Protein from *Jatropha curcas* Seed Coat. Chemical Biology & Drug Design, 82: 453-462.

Okoli, R.I. Aigbe, O. Ohafu-Obode, J.O. and Mensah, J.K. (2007): Medicinal Herbs Used for Managing some Common Ailments Among Esan People Edo State, Nigeria.Pakistan Journal of Nutrition, 65: 470-490.

Okujagu, T.F. Etatuvie, S.O. Eze, I. Jimoh, B. Nweke, C. and Mbaoji, C. (2006): Medicinal Plants of Nigeria; South-west Nigeria. In Collaboration with Lagos State Traditional Medicine Board and Botany Department, University of Lagos. 1st ed 2006, 1: 20.

Openshaw, k. (2000): A Review of Jatropha Curcas: An Oil Plant of Unfulfilled Promise. Biom. Bioen, 19: 1-15.

Osemene, K.P. Ilori, M.O. and Elujoba, A.A. (2013): Examining the Nature of Herbal Research and Development in Nigeria International Journal of Biology, Pharmacy and Allied Sciences, 1: 133-142.

Oskoueian, E. Abdullah, N. Ahmed, S. Saad, W.Z. Omar, A. and Ho, Y.W. (2011): Bioactive Compounds and Biological Activities of *Jatropha curcas* L. kernel meal Extract. International Journal of Molecular Sciences, 12: 5955-5970.

Oskouelan, E.N. Abdullah, W.Z. Saad, A.R. Omar, S. Ahmad, W.B. Kuan, N.A. Zolkifil, R. Hendra and Ho, Y.W. (2011a): Antioxidant, Anti-inflammatory and Anticancer Activities of Methanolic Extracts from *Jatropha curcas* Linn. J. Med. Plants Res, 5: 49-57.

Osoniyi, O. and Onajobi, F. (2003). Coagulant and Anticoagulant Activities in *Jatropha Curcas*. J. Ethnopharmacol, 89: 101-105.

Oyi, A.R. Onaolapo, J.A. and Adigun, J.O. (2002): Phytochemical and Antimicrobial Screening of the Latex of *Jatropha curcas* Linn (Euphorbiaceae) Journal of Phytomedicine and Therapeuticsl, (1&2): 63-74.

Oyi, A.R. Onaolapo, J.A. Haruna, A.K. and Morah, C.O. (2007): Antimicrobial Screening and Stability Studies of Crude Extract of *Jatropha curcas* Linn Latex (Euphorbiaceae). Nigerian. J. Pharmace. Sci, 6: 14-20.

Parekh, J. and Chanda, S. (2007): *In vitro* Antibacterial Activity of Crudemethanol Extract of Woodfordia Fruticosa Kurz Flower (Lythacease).Braz. J. Microbiol, 38: 2.

Parotta, J.A. (2001): Healing Plants of Peninsular India. CAB International, Wallingford U.K, 299-300.

Parveen, B.U. Shikha, R. and Ashawani, K. (2007): Traditional Uses of Medicinal Plants Among the Rural Communities of Churu District in the Thar Desert, India. J. Ethnopharmacol, 113: 387-399.

Patil, R.N. Patil, R.Y. Ahirwar, B. and Ahirwar, D. (2011): Evaluation of Antidiabetic and Related Actions of Some Indian Medicinal Plants in Diabetic Rats. Asian Pacific Journal of Tropical Medicine. 1: 20-23.

Paulillo, L.C. Mo, C.L. Isaacson, J. Lessa, L. Lopes, E. Romero-Suarez, S. Brotto, L. Abreu, E. Gutheil, W. and Brotto, M. (2012): *Jatropha curcas:* From Biodiesel Generation to Medicinal Applications, 192-199.

Perry, L.M. (1980): Medicinal Plants of East and Southeast Asia. MIT Press, Cambridge.

Plumb, J.A (2004): Cell Sensitivity Assays: The MTT Assay. Methods Mol Med. 88: 165-9.

Prasad, C. Krishna, M. Reddy, C. and Mohan, K. (2012): Performance Evaluation of Non-edible Vegetable Oils as Substitute Fuels in Low Heat Rejection Diesel Engines, J. of Automobile Eng, 214: 181-187.

Prieto, P. Pineda, M. and Agular, M. (1999): Spectrophotometric Quantitation Antioxidant Capacity Through the Formation of a Phosphomolybdenum Complex, Analytical Biochemistry, 269: 337-341.

Prminik, K. (2002): Properties and Use of *Jatropha curcas* Oil and Diesel Fuel Blends Compression Ignition Engines. Renewable Energy, 28: 239-248.

Rahman, K. (2007): Studies on Free Radicals, Antioxidants, and Co-factors," Clinical Interventions in Aging, 2,: 219-236.

Rahman, M.M. Ahmad, S.H. Mohamed, M.T.M. and M. Rahman, Z.A. (2014): Antimicrobial Compounds from Leaf Extracts of *Jatropha curcas*, *Psidium guajava*, and *Andrographis paniculata*. Hindawi Publishing Corporation, 1-8.

Reddy, M.B. Reddy, K.R. and Reddy, M.N. (1988): A Survey of Medicinal Plants of Chenchu Tribes of Andhra Pradesh, India. Int J Crude Drug Res, 26: 198-196.

Rice, E.L. (1995): Biological Control of Weeds and Plant Diseases. Adv. Applied Allelopathy, Univ. Oklahoma Press.

Salas, J. Tello, V. Zavaleta, A. Villegas, L. and Salas, M. (1994): Effect of *Jatropha curcas* Latex. Rev-Biol-Trop, 4: 323-326.

Sangeetha, J.K. Divya, M.V. Prashanth, A. Vamsikrishna, G. and Rani L. (2009): Anti-inflammatory and Antibacterial Activity of *Jatropha curcas* Linn. JPRHC, 2: 258-262.

Saxena, M. Saxena, J. Nema, R., Singhand, D. and Gupta, A. (2013): Phytochemistry of Medicinal Plants. Journal of Pharmacognosy and Phytochemistry, 1:168-182.

Sharma, A.K. Gangwar, M. Tilak, R. Nath, G. and Sinha, A.S.K. (2012): Comparative *in vitro* antimicrobial and Phytochemical Evaluation of Methanolic Extract of Root, Stem and Leaf of *Jatropha curcas* Linn, Pharmacognosy Journal, 4: 34-40.

Shetty, S. Udupa, S.L. Udupa, A.L. and Vollala, V.R. (2006): Wound Healing Activities of Bark Extract of *Jatropha curcas* Linn in Albino Rats. Saudi Med. J, 27: 1473-1476.

Shimada, T. (2006): Salivary Proteins as a Defense Against Dietarytannins. J. Chem. Ecol, 32: 1149-1163.

Singh, Y.N. Ikahihifo, T. Panuve, M. and Slatter, C. (1984): Folk Medicine in Tongga. A Study on the Use of Herbal Medicines for Obstetric and Gynecological Conditions and Disorders. J. Ethnopharmacol, 12: 305-329.

Sirisomboon, P. Kitchaiya, P. Pholpho, T. and Mahuttanyavanitch, W. (2007): Physical and Mechanical Properties of Jatropha Curcas L. Fruits, Nuts and Kernels. Biol. Eng, 97: 201-207.

Solomon, R. and Ezradanam, V. (2002): Pollination Ecology and Fruiting Behaviour in a Monoecious Species, *Jatropha curcas* L. (Euphorbiaceae), Current Science, 83: 1395-1398.

Solsoloy, A.D. and Solsoloy, T.S. (1997): Pesticidal Efficacy of Formulated *J. curcas* Oil on Pests of Selected Field Crops. Pages 216-226 *in* Biofuel and Industrial Products from *Jatropha curcas* (Gübitz GM, Mittelbach M and Trabi M, eds.). Graz: Dbv-Verlag University.

Soubra, L. Sarkis, D. Hilan, C. and Verger, P. (2007): Dietary Exposure of Children and Teenagers to Benzoates, Sulphites, butylhydroxyanisol (BHA) and butylhydroxytoluen (BHT) in Beirut (Lebanon), Regul. Toxicol. Pharm, 47: 68-77.

Sreedevi, S. Remani, K.N. and Sailas (2013): Biotic Stress Induced Biochemical and Isozyme Variations in Ginger and Tomato by *Ralstonia solanacearum*. American Journal of Plant Sciences. 4. 1601-1610.

Staubmann, R. Ncube, I. Gubitz, G.M. Steiner, W. and Read, J.S. (1999a): Esterase and Lipase Activity in Jatropha Curcas L. Seeds. Journal of Biotechnology, 75: 117-126.

Staubmann, R. Schubert-Zsilavecz, M. Hiermann, A. and Kartnig, T. (1999b). A Complex of 5-hydroxypyrrolidin-2-one and pyrimidine-2, 4-dione Isolated from *Jatropha curcas*. Phytochemistry, 50: 337-338.

Tapsell, L.C. Hemphill, I. Cobiac, L. Patch, C.S. Sullivan, D.R.; Fenech, M. Roodenrys, S. Keogh, J.B. Clifton, P.M. Williams, P.G, Fazio, V.A. and Inge, K.E. (2006): Health Benefits of Herbs and Spices: The Past, the Present, the Future. The Medical Journal of Australia, 185(supplement4): S4-24.

Thomas, O.O. (1989): Re-examination of the Antimicrobial Activities of *Xylopia aethiopica, Carica papaya, Ocimum gratissimum* and *Jatropha curcas.* Fitoterapia, 60: 147-155.

Thomas, R. Sah, N.K. and Sharma, P.B. (2008): Therapeutic Biology of *Jatropha curcas*: A Mini Review. *Current Pharmaceutical Biotechnology*, 9: 315-324.

Trinder, P. (1959): Determination of Blood Glucose Using 4-aminophenazone. J. Clin. Path, 22: 246-251.

Uche, F.I. and Aprioku, J.S. (2008): The Phytochemical Constituents, Analgesic and Anti-inflammatory Effects of Methanol Extract of Jatropha Curcasleaves in Mice and Wister albino rats J.Appl.Sci.Environ Manage,12: 99-102.

Van den Berg, A.J. Horsten, S.F. Kettenes, V. Bosch, J.J. Kroes, B.H. Beukelman, C.J. Loeflang, B.R. and Labadie, R.P. (1995): Curcacycline A: A Novel Cyclic Octapeptide Isolated from the Latex of *Jatropha curcas Linn*. FEBS Letters, 358: 215-218.

Watt, J.M. and Breyer-Brandwijk, M.G. (1962): The Medicinal and Poisonous Plants of Southern and Eastern Africa. 2nd ed. E.&S. Livingstone, Ltd., Edinburgh and London.

Wender, P.A. Galliher, W.C. Goun, E.A.; Jones, L.R. and Pillow T.H. (2008): The Design of Guanidinium-rich Transporters and Their Internalization Mechanisms. Adv. Drug Deliv. Rev, 60: 452-472.

Weiss, J.S. and Sumpio, B.E. (2006): Review of Prevalence and Outcome of Vascular Disease in Patients with Diabetes Mellitus. Eur J Vasc Endovasc Surg, 31: 143-50.

World Health Organisation (2002): Traditional Medicine: Growing Needs and Potential. WHO Policy Perspectives on Medicines. World Health Organisation, Geneva, 1-6.

Woisky, R. and Salatino, A. (1998): Analysis of Propolis: Some Parameters and Procedures for Chemical Quality Control, J. Apic. Res, 37: 99-105.

Xiao, J. Zhang, H. Niu, L. and Wang, X. (2011): Efficient Screening of a Novel Antimicrobial Peptide from *Jatropha curcas* by Cell Membrane Affinity Chromatography. J Agr Food Chem, 59: 1145-1151.

Zhao, H. Fan, W. Dong, J. Lu, J. Chen, J. Shan, L. Lin, Y. and Kong, W. (2008): Evaluation of Antioxidant Activities and Total Phenolic Contents of Typical Malting Barley Varieties, Food Chemistry, 107: 296-304.

Pages: 79-105

SEED TREATMENT, PLANT HEALTH AND AGRO-TECHNOLOGY

Edited by: **Dr. Avnish Chauhan** and **Dr. Pawan Kumar 'Bharti'**

ISBN: 978-93-5056-810-1

Edition: **2016**

Published by: **Discovery Publishing House Pvt. Ltd., New Delhi (India)**

5

Broccoli
Phyto-chemicals and Potential Health Benefits

Farouk K. El –Baz*, Zeinab A. Salama and **Alaa A. Gaafar**

ABSTRACT

Numerous epidemiological studies indicated that *Brassica* vegetables in general and broccoli in particular, protect humans against cancer since they are rich sources of phenolics, flavonoids, vitamins and glucosinolates as well as mineral nutrients. Some criteria have been proposed to evaluate the possibilities of developing new "functional foods" to reduce the risk of specific cancers; largely in broccoli, which is associated with cancer protection. Therefore, this review will be focuses on the content, composition, antioxidant capacity of both lipid - and water-soluble antioxidants in broccoli, health-promoting properties chemical and biological characterization of the pharmaceutical in broccoli. The present review aims to summarize the current knowledge regarding the biological activities of brassica-derived phytochemicals regarding chemo preventive, anti-inflammatory, and epigenetic pathways.

Key words: Broccoli; Phenolic compounds; glucosinolates; minerals; antioxidant, biological activity.

Importance of *Brassicaceae*

In recent years, increasing attention has been paid to the role of diet in human health and the pharmacologically active chemicals in the form of foods. Obtaining vegetables and fruits with enhanced nutritional and medicinal

Plant Biochemistry Department, National Research centre, ID: 60014618
33 El Bohouth st. (former El Tahrir st.), Dokki, Giza, Egypt.

qualities will become a much larger component of private and public breeding programmes (*Ambrosone* and *Tang* 2009 and *Angeloni et al.*, 2009). Several studies have indicated that a high intake of plant products is associated with a reduced risk of a number of chronic diseases, such as atherosclerosis and cancer (*Ambrosone* and *Tang* 2009).

Cruciferous or *Brassica* vegetables are so named because they come from plants in the family known to botanists as Cruciferae or Brassicaceae. Many commonly consumed cruciferous vegetables come from the *Brassica* genus, including broccoli, Brussels sprouts, cabbage, cauliflower, collard greens, kale, kohlrabi, mustard, rutabaga, turnips, bok choy, and Chinese cabbage . Arugula, horse radish, radish, wasabi, and are also cruciferous vegetables. These vegetables possess both antioxidant and anticarcinogenic properties (*Cohen, Kristal, & Stanford*, 2000; *Chu, Sun, Wu, & Liu*, 2002; *Verhoeven, Verhagen, Goldbohm, van den Brandt, & van Poppel*, 1997).

Broccoli (*Brassica olaracea*, var. *Italica*) is mainly consumed for its florets, has already been characterized in terms of glucosinolates (*Rosa et al.*, 1996) and phenolics (*Ferreres et al.*, 2005; *Sousa et al.*, 2005). Much attention has been focused on broccoli as a source of bioactive compounds such as phenolics, flavonoids and glucosinolates, which possess antioxidant and anticancer effects (*Gundgaard et al.*, 2003 and *Williamson et al.*, 1998; *Zhang et al.*, 2004 and *Yoldas et al.*, 2008).

Broccoli

It is a significant source of phenolics such as sinapic acid (*Vallejo et al.*, 2003a). Apart from other nutritional antioxidants, broccoli is also a significant source of calcium, folic acid, carotenoids, ascorbic acid and known to reduce risk of breast and prostate cancer (*Beecher*, 1994; *Williamson et al.*, 1998).

Fertilization and Quantity and Quality of Broccoli

The quality and quantity of phenolics in plant vary significantly due to different factors, such as (1) genetic determinants (*Vallejo et al.*, 2003 and *Vallejo et al.*, 2003a); (2) environmental condition (temperature, light, water availability, nutrient availability) (*Zhao et al.*, 1994; *Rosa et al.*, 1996); (3) agricultural practices (date of harvest, etc.); and (4) post-harvest conditions (*Rodriguez and Rosa*, 1999).

Fertilization is the most important and controllable factor affecting the nutritional value of vegetables. The type and value of fertilizer and the level of application directly influence the level of nutrients available in plants and indirectly influence plant physiology and the biosynthesis of secondary compounds in plants. Organic food production is characterized by the absence of isoflavones, has been demonstrated to inhibit synthetic compound (herbicides, pesticides) and readily soluble fertilizers and relies more on natural mechanisms of controlling the growth, yield and diseases. Application of compost to sandy soil increased organic matter, cation exchange capacity, available nutrients and biological properties (*Lombardi-Boccia et al.*, 2004).

Manach et al., (2004) reported that emphasis on multi-strain biofertilizer has already been studied. Biofertilizers are biological preparations essentially; sufficient densities of potent strains of microorganisms, having a tangible beneficial role in fitting a proper rhizosphere for plant growth .Some researchers suggest that, of all the measures of nutrient quality, concentrations of phytochemicals have the potential to differ the most between organic and conventional foods (*Woese et al.*, 1997). It has been claimed that due to their higher amounts of secondary phenolic metabolites, organically produced plant foods could be expected to be more health-promoting than conventional foods (*Lundega* and *Rtensson*, 2003). Organically grown cabbage, spinach, Welsh onion, and green pepper generally had higher levels of flavonoids and antioxidant activity (*Young et al.*, 2000).

Organic manure can serve as alternative practice to mineral fertilizers (*Gupta et al.*, 1988, *Wong et al.*, 1999 and *Naeem et al.*, 2006) for improving soil structure (*Bin, 1983* and *Dauda et al.*, 2008) and microbial biomass (*Suresh et al.*, 2004). Therefore, utilization of produced manures for vegetable production may increase crop yields with less use of chemical fertilizers. In recent times, consumers are demanding higher quality and safer food and highly interested in organic products. Organic fertilization has a stimulatory effect on accumulation of phenolics in broccoli florets. It is well known that, the higher concentrations of phenolics in florets can be explained by the role of organic fertilizers in the biosynthesis which induces the acetate shikimate pathway, resulting in higher production of flavonoids and phenolics (*Sousa et al.*, 2008). The results given in (Table 5.1) that the yield of TPC (total phenolic content) was highly significantly increased by organic fertilization application. It increased by more than 216% compared to control treatment. However, the response to biofertilizer treatment was less effective. A similar trend was obtained in case of TFC and TGsC (total flavonoids and total glucosinolates).

Table 5.1: Effect of Organic and Bioorganic Fertilizers on Yield Florets Fresh and Dry Weight of Two Cultivars of Broccoli

Cultivars	Treatments	Florets Dry Weight %	Yield of Florets FW (Ton/fed)	Yield Increases of Florets FW %
Calabrese	100% NPK (Control)	14.31 ± 0.37	4.113 ± 0.16	100%
	50% NPK + 50% Organic	18.82 ± 1.29	6.53 ± 0.11	159
	50% NPK + 50% Organic + Bio	19.77± 0.60	8.20± 0. 12	199
Southernstar	100% NPK (Control)	14.24± 0.55	6.07± 0.20	100 %
	50% NPK + 50% Organic	17.52 ± 1.22	7.40 ± 0.26	122
	50% NPK + 50% Organic + Bio	17.32 ± 0.25	9.96 ± 0.02	164
	L.S.D at 0.05	1.28	0.23	–

All values are means of three replicates and are significantly different at $p > 0.05$ ± standard deviation.

Source: Naguib *et al.*, 2012

The effect of organic production methods on the overall nutritive value has been recently studied.

Many studies have investigated the relative nutrient value of organically and bioorganic fertilization produced food. Fertilization is the most important and controllable factor affecting the nutritional value of vegetables. The type and value of fertilizer and the level of application directly influence the level of nutrients available in plants and indirectly influence plant physiology and the biosynthesis of secondary compounds in plants. Secondary compounds in plants are known as secondary metabolites or phyto nutrients. General categories of these compounds in broccoli are phenolics including flavonoids, terpenes and nitrogen compounds including alkaloids and sulfur compounds. These compounds are used in the treatment of human diseases. They can quench free radicals, act as antiproliferative agents, promote detoxifying enzymes, induce differentiation of cancer cells, stimulate the immune system and inhibit tumor blood vessel formation (*Heaton,* 2001).

Naguib et al., (2012) studied the Influence of organic and bio-organic fertilization on yield florets fresh and dry weights of two broccoli cultivars in Table 5.1, it is clear from the data presented (Table 5.2) that the yield of florets in both cultivars of broccoli was significantly increased as a result of organic and bioorganic treatments. The yield was increased by 59% and 99% in Calabrese cultivar and by 22% and 64% in Southern star cultivar by the application of organic and bio-organic fertilizers respectively. The highest florets' yield of both cultivars of broccoli plants was recorded by the combined effect of bio-organic fertilizer and 50% organic +50% mineral treatment. This superiority in florets' yield might be referred to the increase in vegetative growth due to the reflection of the high soil fertility resulting by bio- organic fertilization and organic manuring (Table 5.1). The beneficial effect of organic and bio-organic fertilization on increasing the yield may be due to the increase in the organic matter content as was reported by *Wilkinson* (1979).

Table 5.2: Effect of Organic and Bioorganic Fertilization on Total Phenolics (TPC), Total Flavonoids (TFC) and Total Glucosinolates (TGsC) Contents of Florets in Two Cultivars of Broccoli

Cultivars	Treatments	TPC (mg*/g as DW)	TPC Increases %	TFC (mg**/g as DW)	TFC increases %	TGsC (µmol/g as DW)	TGsC increases %
Calabrese	100% NPK (Control)	9.15 ± 0.36	100%	5.46 ± 0.21	100%	48.72 ± 0.19	100%
	50% NPK + 50% Organic	13.82 ± 0.42	151	9.27 ± 0.16	170	71.34 ± 0.14	146
	50% NPK + 50% Organic + Bio	11.56 ± 0.19	126	7.18 ± 0.15	132	57.35 ± 0.18	118
Southernstar	100% NPK (Control)	7.68 ± 0.34	100%	4.52 ± 0.17	100%	44.04 ± 0.18	100%
	50% NPK + 50% Organic	10.86 ± 0.50	141	6.76 ± 0.17	150	62.11 ± 0.14	141
	50% NPK + 50% Organic + Bio	8.45 ± 0.51	110	5.91 ± 0.27	131	53.01 ± 0.09	120
L.S.D at 0.05		0.34	–	0.26	–	1.62	–

* As gallic acid.

** As quercetin.

All values are means of three replicates and are significantly different at *p* e" 0.05 ± standard deviation.

Source: Naguib et al., (2012)

In addition, (*Arisha et al.*, 2003) reported that the release of organic acids decreases the pH value of the plant growth medium so leads to the improvement of the soil conditions and in turn improves root growth and enhances nutrients uptake. *Naguib et al.*, (2012) added that The application of organic and bio-organic fertilizers significantly increased TPC in Calabrese cultivar from 9.15 mg/g DW (control) to 13.83 mg/g DW (organic) and 11.56

mg/g DW (bio-organic) respectively. These increases reached to more than 51% and 26% increase respectively. However, in Southern star cultivar it was increased from 7.68 mg/g (control) to 10.86 (41%) and 8.45 mg/g DW (10%) when organic and bio-organic fertilizers were applied respectively compared with control as shown in Table 5.2. In addition, flavonoid content of Calabrese cultivar showed significantly increases from 5.46 mg/g (control) to 9.27 mg/g DW and 7.18 mg/g DW with organic and bio-organic fertilizer respectively, (70-32% increase) compared to those of control. While, Southern star cultivar with organic and bio-organic fertilizer exhibited similar increases (50-31% increases) compared to those of control. Similar results of broccoli florets were recorded by *Heimler et al.* (2006).

Phytochemicals

Secondary compounds in plants are known as secondary metabolites or phytonutrients. General categories of these compounds in broccoli are phenolics including flavonoids, terpenes and nitrogen compounds including alkaloids and sulfur compounds. These compounds are used in the treatment of human diseases. They can quench free radicals, act as antiproliferative agents, promote detoxifying enzymes, induce differentiation of cancer cells, stimulate the immune system and inhibit tumor blood vessel formation (*Heaton*, 2001).

Vitamin C

Vitamin C, which includes ascorbic acid and its oxidation product—dehydroascorbic acid, has many biological activities in human body. *Block et al.* (2004) have found that vitamin C can reduce levels of C-reactive protein (CRP), a marker of inflammation and possibly a predictor of heart disease. More than 85% of vitamin C in human diets is supplied by fruits and vegetables (*Davey et al.*, 2000; *Lee & Kader*, 2000). Biological function of L- ascorbic acid can be defined as an enzyme cofactor, a radical scavenger, and as a donor/acceptor in electron transport at the plasma membrane. Ascorbic acid is able to scavenge the superoxide and hydroxyl radicals, as well as regenerate a-tocopherol (*Davey et al.*, 2000). Results clearly point towards a positive correlation between cancer prevention of many target organs and consumption of cruciferous vegetable or their active constituents. Broccoli contains many bioactive components including flavonoids (e.g. quercetin), minerals (e.g. selenium) and vitamins (e.g. Vitamin C) (*Bryant, et al.*, 2010). Variations in vitamin C content might be related to the differences in genotype (Table 5.3) (*Kurilich et al.*, 1999; *Vallejo et al.*, 2002). Climatic conditions also might alter vitamin C level (*Howard, Wong, Perry, & Klein*, 1999).

Table 5.3: Ascorbic Acid (AA) Content of *Brassica* Vegetables (mg/100g Edible Portion)

Vegetable	AA Content	References
Broccoli	34-93	Favell (1998)
	41-64	Franke et al. (2004)
	74.8	Bahorun et al. (2004)
	75	Hussein et al. (2000)
	84	Hrncirik et al. (2001)
	93	Chu et al. (2002)
	103	Zhang & Hamauzu (2004)
	112	Murcial et al. (2000))
	113	Davey et al. (2000)
	54-120	Kurilich et al. (1999)
	43-146	Vallejo et al. (2002)

Source: Podsedek A., (2006)

Phenolic Compounds

Phenolic compounds are a large group of the secondary metabolites widespread in plant kingdom. They are categorized into classes depending on their structure and subcategorized within each class according to the number and position of hydroxyl group and the presence of other substituents. The most widespread and diverse group of the polyphenols are the flavonoids which are built upon C6–C3–C6 flavone skeleton (Figures 5.1 & 5.2).

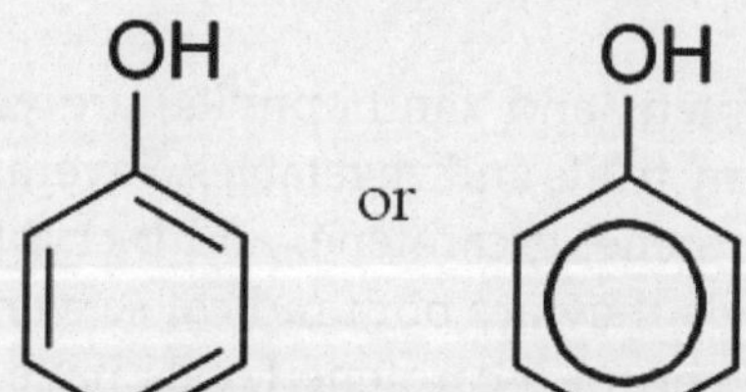

Fig. 5.1: **The Simplest Structure of Phenol**

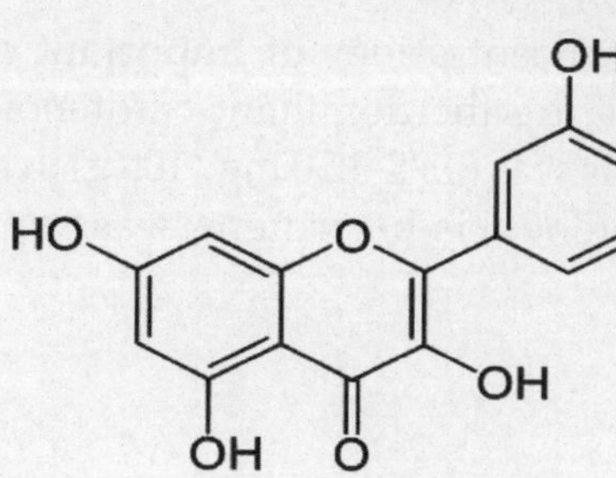

Fig. 5.2: **Qurstein**

In addition, other phenolic compounds such as benzoic acid or cinnamic acid derivatives have been identified in fruits and vegetables.

Phenolics are able to scavenge reactive oxygen spieces due to their electron donating properties. Their antioxidant effectiveness depends on the stability in different systems, as well as number and location of hydroxyl groups., phenolic compounds demonstrated higher antioxidant activity than antioxidant vitamins and carotenoids (*Vinson et al.*, 1995).

Broccoli is a significant source of phenolics such as sinapic acid (*Vallejo et al.*, 2003a). Apart from other nutritional antioxidants, broccoli is also a significant source of calcium, folic acid, carotenoids, ascorbic acid and known to reduce risk of breast and prostate cancer (*Beecher*, 1994, *Williamson et al.*, 1998).

Phenolic profiles of Brassica vegetables have been focused mainly on broccoli florets, which are popular in Western Europe countries and USA. Broccoli is a source of flavonol and hydroxycinnamoyl derivatives. *Price, et al.*, (1998) identified the main flavonol glycosides present in broccoli florets as quercetin and kaempferol 3-O-sophoroside. Three minor glucosides of these aglycones were also detected, namelyisoquercitrin, kaempferol 3-O-glucoside and kaempferol diglucoside. The predominant hydroxycinnamoyl acidswere identified as 1-sinapoyl-2-feruloylgentiobiose, 1,2- diferuloyl-gentiobiose, 1,2,20-trisinapoylgentiobiose, and neochlorogenic acid (*Vallejo et al.*, 2003a). In addition, 1,20-disinapoyl-2-feruloylgentiobiose and 1,2-disinapoylgentiobiose, 1-sinapoyl-2, 2-diferuloyl gentiobiose, isomeric form of 1,2,20-trisinapoylgentiobiose, and chlorogenic acidswere found in broccoli (*Price et al.*, 1979 & Vallejo *et al.*, 2003a).

Carotenoids

Carotenoids (carotens and xanthophylls) are yellow, orange, and red pigments present in many fruits and vegetables. Several of them are precursors of vitamin A (i.e. b-carotene, g-carotene, and b-cryptoxanthin), and due to conjugated double bonds they are both radical scavengers and quenchers of singlet oxygen. Lower serum b-carotene levels have been linked to higher rates of cancer and cardiovascular diseases, as well as to increased risk of myocardial infarction among smokers (*Rice-Evans et al.*, 1995).

Table 5.4 shows the concentrations of important dietary carotenoids from Lutein and b-carotene are the dominant carotenoids in broccoli. The amount of these xanthophylls was (0.78-3.50 mg/100 g) in broccoli. In addition to lutein and trans-b carotene, cis-b-carotene was reported by *Heinonen et al.*, (1989).

Table 5.4: Carotenoids Content of *Brassica* Vegetables (mg/100g Edible Portion)

Vegetable	α-carotene	β-carotene	Lutein+zeaxanthin	References
Broccoli	0.001	0.78	2.45	Holden et al. (1999)
	0	0.28	0.80	Muller (1997)
	Tr	1.00	1.80	Heinonen et al. 1989)
	0-0.07	0.37-2.42	NA	Kurilich et al. (1999)
	NA	1.24-1.92	2.42-3.50	de Sa et al. (2004)
	0	0.55	0.78	Mukovic.Gams. Draxl and Pfannhauser (2000)
	NA	0.63	1.05	Zhang and Hamauzu (2004)

Source: Podsedek A., (2006)

Vitamin E

Vitamin E shows protective effects against the coronary heart disease due to inhibition of LDL oxidation (*Stampfer* & *Rimm*, 1995).

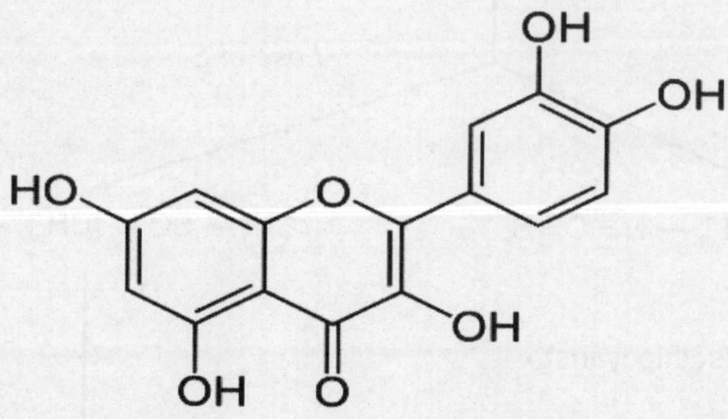

Fig. 5.3: **Gama-tocopherol**

There are only few data of tocopherol content in vegetables. The highest content of total tocopherols and tocotrienols in Brassica vegetables is as follows: broccoli (0.82 mg/100 g), Brussels sprouts (0.40 mg/100 g), cauliflower (0.35 mg/100 g), Chinese cabbage (0.24 mg/100 g) red cabbage (0.05 mg/100 g), white cabbage (0.04 mg/100 g). In contrast, Kurilich et al. (1999 reported that lower concentration of g-tocopherol than alpha -tocopherol in cauliflower.

In general, the best sources of lipid-soluble antioxidants are kale and broccoli. Brussels sprouts have moderate levels while cauliflower and cabbage are characterized by their relatively low amounts. These differences are probably caused by the differing varieties and growing conditions.

Glucosinolates

More than 140 structurally different glucosinolates (Figures 5.4 and 5.5) are known and about 10% are present in seeds of agriculturally common Brassica crops, although in varying quantities depending on the species.

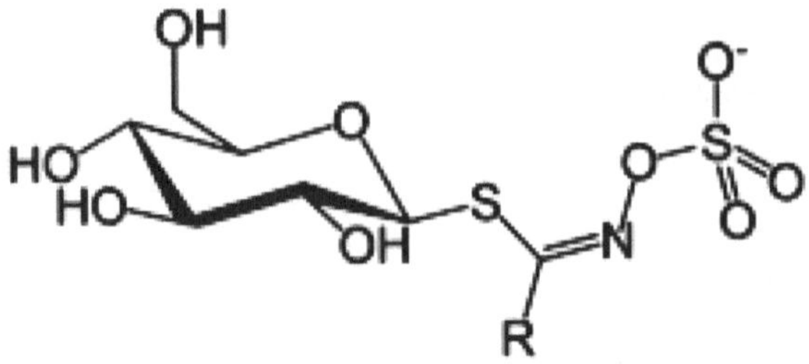

Fig. 5.4: **Chemical Structure of Glucosinolates**

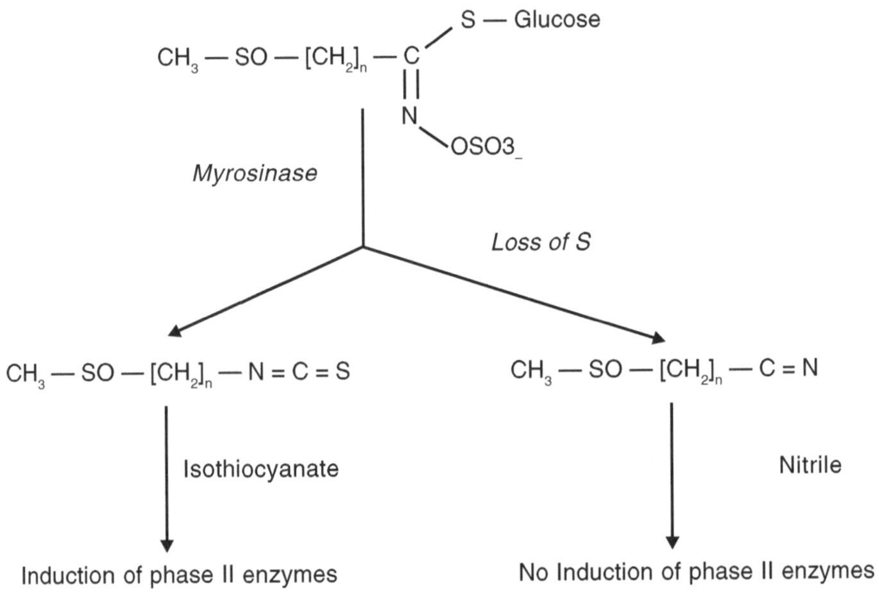

Fig. 5.5: **Hydrolysis of Glucosinolates**
Source: Moreno et al., 2006

The use of the remaining seed cake after oil extraction has traditionally been limited by the concentration of these compounds however, the extraction of glucosinolates from seed meal is nowadays possible and it further contributes to an increased quality of the seed meal for feed . Glucosinolates are hydrolysed by endogenous enzymes (myrosinases; EC 3.2.1.147) and a number of compounds are produced (Figure 5.4) depending on the parent glucosinolate and the environmental conditions (*Sørensen*, 1990). Among these compounds, 5-vinyl-oxazolidine-2-thione is known for their antinutritional effects on monogastric animals, whereas isothiocyanates are fungicidal, nematocidal and herbicidal (*Brown* and *Morra*, 1997). Isothiocyanates are very reactive compounds that can easily react with nucleophiles present in the environment, such as free amino groups or thiol groups.

Table 5.5: Glucosinolates Identified in Broccoli (*Brassica oleracea* L. var. italic cv. Youxiu)

Type	Trivial Name	Glucosinolate Side Chain
AG	Glucoraphanin	4- Methy lsulphiny lbuty l
	Glucoiberin	3- Methy lsulphiny lbuty l
	Progoitrin	2- (R)-2-hydroxy-3-buteny
IG	Glucoraphanin	3- Indolylmethy
	Neoglucobrassicin	1- Methoxy-3-indolylmethyl
	4- Methoxy glucobrassicin	4- Methoxy-3-indolylmethyl

AG: aliphatic glucosinolates; IG: indole glucosinolates

Source: Burow *et al.*, (2007).

One of the most important challenges for the agriculture is to enhance the food production and providing almost all the essential minerals and organic nutrients to humans in order to maintain health and organ functions. Humans need more than 22 mineral elements, some of them are required in large amounts, but others, such as Fe, Zn, Cu, I and Se, are required in trace amounts because higher concentrations can be harmful (*Welch & Graham*, 2004; *Grusak & Cakmak*, 2005).

Broccoli, contains high amounts of bioactive compounds and vitamins but also high content of minerals that can be an important supplement in nutrient-incomplete diets (*Agte et al.*, 2000). The main mineral elements (Na, K, Ca, Mg, Cl, S, N and P) present in broccoli are essential for human beings in amounts > 50 mg/day, while trace elements (Fe, Zn, Cu, Mn, I, F, Se, Cr, Mo, Co, Ni) are essential in concentrations of < 50 mg day-1 (*Martínez-Ballesta et al.*, 2010).These main and trace elements have very varied functions, e.g., as electrolytes, as enzymes constituents and as building materials, e.g. in bones and teeth.Most of the recent interest in Se nutrition, however, is not directed towards over-supplementation in amounts of 3-6-fold beyond the Recommended Dietary Allowance (RDA 55g/day); because there is evidence that such intakes are protective against cancer [*Aldrich et al.*, 2011]. Predominate forms of Se found in nature include salts such as sodium selenate and selenite and the amino acid selenocysteine; these forms are readily used by Se-deficient animals for production of selenoproteins. The amino acid selenomethionine (SeMet) may randomly substitute for methionine and thus may accumulate in general methionine-requiring proteins. Methylated amino acids such as Se-methyl selenocysteine (SeMSC) are metabolised primarily in the excre- tory pathway, and limited data suggests that methyl selenol generated in this pathway is the metabolite which is most respon- sible for preventing cancer (*Aldrich et al.*, 2011 and *Farooq et al.*, 2012). Broccoli hyperaccumulate Se in methylated forms and many other Brassicaceae species also accumulate Se (*Farooq et al.*, 2012). Data has demonstrated that Se in soil can be reliably transferred to plants and ultimately to humans, and the Se uptake from soil and accumulation in plants is affected by soil type, soil humidity and sulphur status, soil temperature, and soil and air temperature, light conditions and humidity, as found in broccoli. The main elements (Na, K, Ca, Mg, Cl and P) are essential for human beings in amounts >50 mg/day, while trace elements (Fe, Zn, Cu, Mn, I, F, Se, Cr, Mo, Co, Ni) are essential in concentrations of < 50 mg/day. These main and trace elements have very varied functions, e.g. as electrolytes, as enzymes constituents and as building materials, e.g. in bones and teeth.

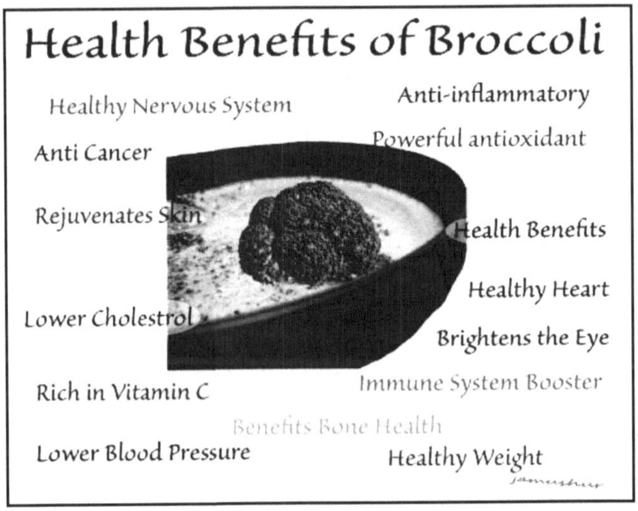

Fig. 5.6: **Health Benefits of Broccoli**

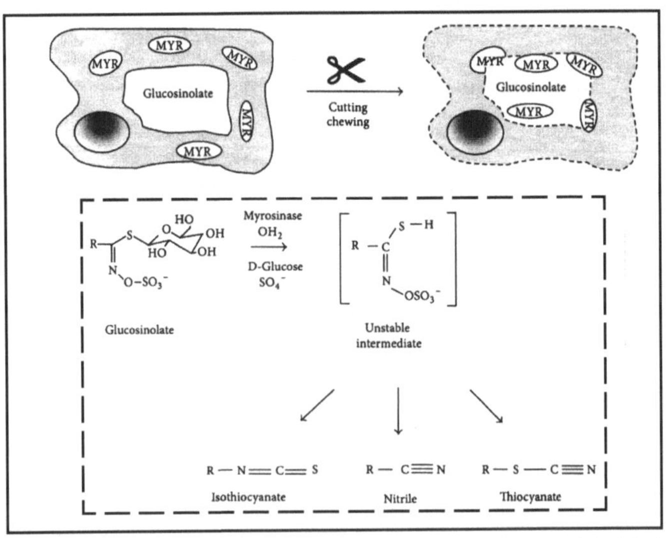

Fig. 5.7: **Myrosinase-mediated Hydrolysis of Glucosinolates with Main Break-down Products**

Table 5.6: Mineral Composition of Raw Broccoli Vegetables

Element	Content
N (g/100g)	1.71 ± 0.11
C (g/100g)	42.78± 0.61
Na (g/100g)	42.78 ± 0.61
K (g/100g)	0.05± 0.001
Ca(g/100g)	1.87± 0.01
Mg (g/100g)	0.13± 0.01
Fe (mg/Kg)	24.12± 1.51
Zn (mg/Kg)	12.01± 0.12
Cu (mg/Kg)	1.97±0.23
Mn(mg/Kg)	104.26±13.88

Source: Martínez-Ballesta et al., 2010

Health Benefits of Broccoli

Phytochemicals are strong antioxidants that can modify metabolic activity, aid in the detoxification of carcinogens, and even influence processes in a tumor cell. It is best to consume a variety of fruits and vegetables, rather than limiting oneself to those with highest anti-oxidant capacity (*Martínez-Ballesta et al.*, 2010).

This literature hows how eating fresh brocooli containing compounds such as phytochemicals can improve human health.

Broccoli has a high antioxidant capacity due to its high concentrations of vitamins A and B. Vitamin A has been known to have one of the greatest antioxidant activities (*Martínez-Ballesta et al.*, 2010)

The isothicyanate in broccoli is a potentially anticarcinogenic. A high intake of brassica vegetables may be associated with a decreased chronic disease risk. Health promoting effects of Brassicaceae have been partly attributed to glucosinolates and in particular to their hydrolyzation products including isothiocyanates. *In vitro* and *in vivo* studies suggest a chemopreventive activity of iso thiocyanates through the redox-sensitive transcription factor Nrf2. Furthermore, studies in cultured cells, in laboratory rodents, and also in humans support an anti-inflammatory effect of brassica-derived phytochemicals. However, the underlying mechanisms of how these compounds mediate their health promoting effects are yet not fully understood. Recent findings suggest that brassica-derived compounds are regulators of epigenetic mechanisms. It has been shown that isothiocyanates may inhibit histone deacetylase transferases and DNA methyl transferases in cultured cells. Only a few papers have dealt with the effect of brassica-derived compounds on epigenetic mechanisms in laboratory animals, whereas data in humans are currently lacking.

Broccoli's Anti-Inflammatory Benefits

Chronic inflammation can sometimes get triggered by overexposure to allergy-related substances. When threatened with dangerous levels of potential toxins, or dangerous numbers of overly-reactive, oxygen-containing molecules, signals are sent within our body to our inflammatory system, directing it to "kick in" and help protect our body from potential damage. In this context, broccoli has yet another anti-inflammatory trick up its sleeve, because it is a rich source of one particular phytonutrient (a flavonol) called kaempferol. Especially inside of our digestive tract, kaempferol has the ability to lessen the impact of allergy-related substances (by lowering the immune system's production of IgE-antibodies). The impact of allergy-related substances, the kaempferol in broccoli can help lower our risk of chronic inflammation and help protect our body from potential damage. One key signaling device is a molecule called NF-kappa B. When faced with the type of dangers described above, the NF-kappa B signaling system is used to "rev up" our inflammatory response and increase iNOS production of inflammatory components (for example, IL-6, IL-1beta, TNF-alpha, and COX-2). This process works beautifully in temporary, short-term circumstances when healing from injury is required. When it continues indefinitely at a constant pace, however, it can put us at risk for serious health problems, including the development of cancer.

Research studies have made it clear that the NF-kappa B signaling system that is used to "rev up" our inflammatory response can be significantly suppressed by isothiocyanates (ITCs). ITCs—the compounds made from glucosinolates found in broccoli and other cruciferous vegetables—actually help to shut down the genetic machinery used to produce NF-kappa B and other components of the inflammatory system. These anti-inflammatory benefits of ITCs have been demonstrated in the laboratory, and with consumption of the ITCs themselves. While they have yet to be demonstrated on consumption of broccoli in an everyday diet, future research is expected to show anti-inflammatory benefits from the routine consumption of broccoli (and its glucosinolates), not just from consumption of ITCs. *Prawan et al.*, (2010) extracted Broccoli (*Brassica oleracea* var. *italia*) florets with 80% methanol and the extract was sequentially fractionated with *n*-hexane, ethyl acetate, *n*-butanol, and distilled water. The extract and the fractions were evaluated for total phenolic content, sulforaphane content, antioxidant activity, and anti-inflammatory activity in lipopolysaccharide (LPS)-stimulated RAW 264.7 cells. The total phenolic content and sulforaphane content of the ethyl acetate fraction (EF) were 35.5 mg gallic acid equivalents/g and 620.2 µg/g, respectively. These values were higher than those of the 80% methanol extract and organic solvent fractions. The oxygen radical absorbance capacity of the EF [1,588.7 µM Trolox equivalents (TE)/mg] was 11-fold higher than that of the distilled water fraction (143.7 μM TE/mg). The EF inhibited nitric oxide release from LPS-stimulated RAW 264.7 cells in a dose-dependent manner and inhibited IκB-α degradation and nuclear factor-κB activation in LPS-stimulated RAW 264.7 cells. In conclusion, the EF of broccoli florets exerted potent antioxidant and anti-inflammatory effects (*Lakhan et al.*, 2009).

It has been found that Sulforaphane, a major component of broccoli, is known to possess anti-inflammatory and anti-cancer properties by suppressing LPS-induced COX-2 genes expression via modulation of multiple core promoter elements (i.e., NF-κB, C/EBP, and CREB) that regulate COX-2 transcription. However, the anti-inflammatory effects of organic solvent fractions from broccoli have not been reported yet. Furthermore, the effects of organic solvent fractions from broccoli on pro-inflammatory mediators have not been investigated in LPS-induced RAW 264.7 cells. Among, all of the commonly consumed cruciferous vegetables, broccoli stands out as the most concentrated source of a premiere antioxidant nutrient—vitamin C. This central antioxidant vitamin can provide longer-term support of oxygen metabolism in the body if it is accompanied by flavonoids that allow it to recycle. Broccoli provides many such flavonoids in significant amounts, including the flavonoids kaempferol and quercitin. Also concentrated in broccoli are the carotenoids lutein, zeaxanthin, and beta-carotene. All three of thesecarotenoids function as key antioxidants. In the case of lutein and beta-carotene, broccoli has been shown not only to provide significant amounts of these antioxidants but to significantly increase their blood levels when consumed in the amount of three cups. Other antioxidants provided by broccoli in beneficial amounts include vitamin E and the minerals manganese and zinc considered as a group, the vitamins, minerals, flavonoids, and carotenoids contained in broccoli work to lower risk of oxidative stress in the body. The ability of these nutrients to support oxygen metabolism and avoid excess formation of overly reactive, oxygen-containing molecules makes them equally helpful in lowering risk of chronic inflammation and risk of cancer. If cancer development is compared to a 3-legged stool, the antioxidant benefits of broccoli can be viewed as weakening one leg of the stool, namely the leg called "oxidative stress." We've already seen how the glucosinolates and omega-3 fats in broccoli can be viewed as helping to weaken a second leg of the stool (chronic inflammation) *Zhang* and *Hamauzu* (2004).

Broccoli Can Enhance Detoxification

Most toxins that pose a risk to our cells must be detoxified in our body by a 2-step process. What's remarkable about broccoli is its ability to alter activity in both of these two detox steps. Isothiocyanates (ITCs) made from the glucosinolates in broccoli are well-documented modifiers of the first step in detoxification (called Phase I) *Marion* (1979). In fact, some ITCs like sulforaphane can actually help shut down the genetic machinery that produces certain Phase I enzymes. ITCs are equally capable of altering the activity of enzymes involved in the second step of detoxification (called Phase II). From research in the field of genetics, we know that ITCs can help bridge gaps in Phase II activity when it is insufficient. Taken in combination, the impact of ITCs on Phase I and II detox events is unique—and equally unique is the presence of glucosinolate compounds in broccoli that can be used to make ITCs. Glucosinolates like glucoraphanin, gluconasturtiian, and glucobrassicin are simply not found in other foods in the same combination and concentration that is offered by broccoli. By helping to promote as well as regulate detox activity in our cells, the ITCs made from broccoli can help prevent insufficient detoxification of dangerous substances that threaten our cells. Broccoli has a strong, positive impact on our body's detoxification system, and researchers have recently identified one of the key reasons for this detox benefit. Glucoraphanin, gluconasturtiian, and glucobrassicin are 3 glucosinolate phytonutrients found in a special combination in broccoli. This dynamic trio is able to support all steps in body's detox process, including activation, neutralization, and elimination of unwanted contaminants. Isothiocyanates (ITCs) are the detox-regulating molecules made from broccoli's glucosinolates, and they help control the detox process at a genetic level.

Broccoli may help us solve our vitamin D deficiency epidemic. When large supplemental doses of vitamin D are needed to offset deficiency, ample supplies of vitamin K and vitamin A help keep our vitamin D metabolism in balance. Broccoli has an unusually strong combination of both vitamin A (in the form of beta-carotene) and vitamin K. For people faced with the need to rebuild vitamin D stores through vitamin D supplements, broccoli may be an ideal food to include in the diet (*Zahra et al.*, 2012). The fiber-related components in broccoli does a better job of binding together with bile acids in digestive tract when they've been steamed. When this binding process takes place, it's easier for bile acids to be excreted, and the result is a lowering of your cholesterol levels. Raw broccoli still has cholesterol-lowering ability—just not as much.Broccoli is a particularly rich source of a flavonoid called kaempferol. Recent research has shown the ability of kaempferol to lessen the impact of allergy-related substances on our body. This kaempferol connection helps to explain the unique anti-inflammatory benefits of broccoli, and it should also open the door to future research on the benefits of broccoli for a hypoallergenic diet.

Broccoli and Cancer Prevention

The unique combination of antioxidant, anti-inflammatory, and pro-detoxification components in broccoli make it a unique food in terms of cancer prevention (*Cheng-Fang et al.*, 2013). Connections between cancer development and oxidative stress, chronic inflammation, and inadequate detoxification are so well-documented in the research that any food improving all three of these metabolic problems would be highly likely to lower our risk of cancer. In the case of broccoli, the research is strongest in showing decreased risk of prostate cancer, colon cancer, breast cancer, bladder cancer, and ovarian cancer. The risk of other cancer types will also eventually be shown to undergo reduction from regular consumption of broccoli (*Prawan et al.*, 2009). Research in this area is still in the early stages, anti-inflammatory substances found in cruciferous vegetables are becoming the topic of increasing interest with respect to heart disease. One particular focus here involves the anti-inflammatory properties of sulforaphane, one of the isothiocyanates (ITCs) derived from the glucoraphanin in broccoli. In some individuals susceptible to high blood sugar, sulforaphane may be able to prevent (or even reverse) some of the damage to blood vessel linings that can be cause by chronic blood sugar problems. Decreased risk of heart attacks and strokes may also eventually be linked in a statistically significant way to intake of broccoli and its glucoraphanin (*Muhammad et al.*, 2007).

A second area you can count on broccoli for cardiovascular support involves its cholesterol-lowering ability. Our liver uses cholesterol as a basic building block to product bile acids. Bile acids are specialized molecules that aid in the digestion and absorption of fat through a process called emulsification. These molecules are typically stored in fluid form in our gall bladder, and when we eat a fat-containing meal, they get released into the intestine where they help ready the fat for interaction with enzymes and eventual absorption up into the body. When we eat broccoli, fiber-related nutrients in this cruciferous vegetable bind together with some of the bile acids in the intestine in such a way that they simply stay inside the intestine and pass out of our body in a bowel movement, rather than getting absorbed along with the fat they have emulsified.

When this happens, our liver needs to replace the lost bile acids by drawing upon our existing supply of cholesterol, and as a result, our cholesterol level drops down. Broccoli provides us with this cholesterol-lowering benefit whether it is raw or cooked. However, a recent study has shown that the cholesterol-lowering ability of raw broccoli improves significantly when it is steamed. In fact, when the cholesterol-lowering ability of steamed broccoli was compared with the cholesterol-lowering ability of the prescription drug cholestyramine (a medication that is taken for the purpose of lowering cholesterol), broccoli bound 33% as many bile acids (based on a standard of comparison involving total dietary fiber).The B-complex vitamins in broccoli can also make a major contribution to our cardiovascular health. Especially with respect to excessive formation of homo cysteine—an event which raises our risk of atherosclerosis, stroke, and heart attack—B-complex vitamin deficiency intake can pose a major risk. Three B vitamins especially important for lowering our risk of hyper homocysteinemia (excessive formation of homo cysteine) are vitamin B6, vitamin B12, and folate. By making an important contribution to our B6 and folate intake, broccoli can help us lower our risk of excessive homocysteine formation and cardiovascular problems that are related to excess homocysteine (*Issa*, and *Wargovich* 2006).

Hepatoprotective Effect of Broccoli

The hepatoprotective effect of broccoli and red cabbage extracts against hepatocellur carcinoma induced by N- Nitrosodiethyamine (NDEA) in male rats were studied by (*Morsy et al.*, 2010). The obtained results revealed that rats with hepatocellurcarcinoma (HCC) had significant increase in serum levels of AST, ALT, ALP, total protein, albumin, total and direct bilirubin and malondialdehyide (MDA), as well as ignificant decrease in reduced glutathione (GSH), glutathione peroxidase (GPX), superoxide dismutase (SOD) and catalase (CAT) enzymes, compared to the normal control group. Liver sections of rats with HCC showed fatty infiltration of hepatocytes, cytomegaly with karyomegaly as well as vesicular active nuclei and presence of more than one nucleolus in some hepatocytes. Oral administration of broccoli extracts caused significant reduction in serum levels of AST, ALT, ALP, total protein, albumin, total and direct bilirubin as well as MDA and produced significant increase in GSH, GPX, SOD and CAT, compared to the positive group.

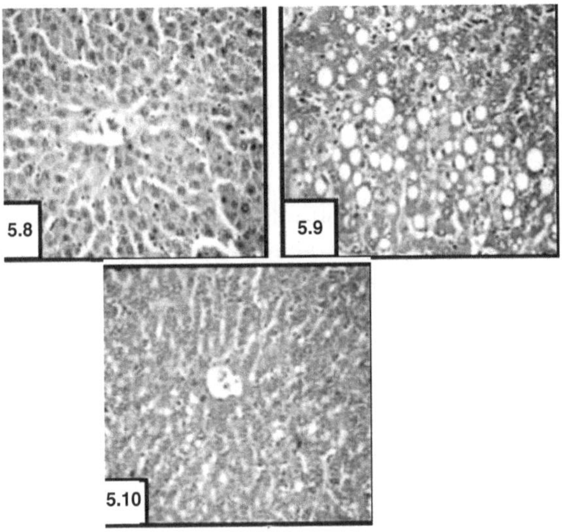

Fig. 5.8: **Liver of Control Rat, Showing the Normal Histological Structure of Hepatic Lobular. (H and E x 200)**

Fig. 5.9: **Liver of Positive Group, Showing Fatty Infiltration of Hepatocytes, Cytomegaly with Karyomegale, Viscular Active Nuclei and more Thanone Nucleolus. (H and E x 200).**

Fig. 5.10: **Liver of Rats with HCC Treated with Broccoli Extract Showing Slight Hydropic Degeneration of Heptocytes. (H and E x 200)**

Histopathological examination of the liver of normal rats revealed normal histological structure of hepatic lobule as shown in Figure (5.8 - 5.10). Liver of these rats revealed only slight hydropic degeneration of hepatocytes, while other sections showed apparent normal hepatocytes. This study concluded that broccoli and red cabbage have a protective effect against hepatocellular carcinoma in rats. These results agreed with *Wargovich,* (1999) who reported that cruciferous vegetables namely cabbage, Brussels sprouts, cauliflower and broccoli are rich in anticarcinogens. A possible mechanism of reduced activities of the tested enzymes and hepatoprotective effect of broccoli extract may be related to their antioxidant effect of the phenolic and flavonoids compounds. Previous study reported thatpolyphenols can inhibit nitrosation and flavonoides have hepatoprotective activities (*Orhan et al.,* 2007).Therefore this study recommends increased dietary intake of broccoli may be beneficial for patients with liver cancer as a preventative agent.

Hashem et al., (2013) studied the effect of Broccoli intensively for their prophylactic and therapeutic effects (Table 5.7) on rat's liver damage induced by paracetamol. The evaluation of biochemical parameters and histopathological analysis showed that broccoli extracts have prophylactic activity (Table 5.8) against liver damage. Phytochemical investigation of 80% ethanolic extract resulted in isolation of three compounds, obtucarbamate, *N*-(4-hydroxy phenyl) acetamide, and *p*-hydroxy benzoic acid, and can be considered a good candidate for the protection of liver damage induced by paracetamol.

Table 5.7: Liver function of Rats Administered Different Extracts of Broccoli and Paracetamol (Prophylactic Test)

Groups	GPT (IU/l)	GOT (IU/l)	ALP (IU/l)
Control	30.2 ± 3.8	93 ± 1.6	65.5 ± 1.2
Group VIII	112.8 ± 1.8*	183.1 ± 2.8*	195.6 ± 4.5*
Group IX	70.0 ± 1.2**	116.1 ± 6.5**	98.1 ± 20.8**
Group X	79.0 ± 4.1**	124.7± 2.9**	101.8 ± 6.1**
Group XI	69.9± 4.7**	122.1 ± 4.3**	124.1 ± 8.3**
Group XII	74.5 ± 4.2**	133.7 ± 8.4**	116.6 ± 6.1**
Group XIII	87.8 ± 5.3**	141.6 ± 6.3**	119.9 ± 3.4**

Data presented as means ± SE

Glutamte oxaloacetate transaminase (GOT)

Glutamate pyruvate transaminase(GPT)

alkaline phosphatase (ALP)

*Significant at $P < 0.05$ as compared with the paracetamol group.

Hashem et al., 2013

Table 5.8: Liver Function of Rats Administered Different Extracts of Broccoli and Paracetamol (Therapeutic test)

Groups	GPT (IU/l)	GOT (IU/l)	ALP (IU/l)
Control	30.2 ± 3.8	93.7 ± 10.6	30.2 ± 3.8
Group VIII	129.0 ± 6.8*	213.4 ± 14.4*	129.0 ± 6.8*
Group IX	71.4 ± 2.5**	126.8 ± 8.5**	71.4 ± 2.5**
Group X	88.9 ± 5.3**	131.9± 5.6**	88.9 ± 5.3**
Group XI	77.7 ± 5.2**	129.6 ± 4.9**	77.7 ± 5.2**
Group XII	80.0 ± 5.8**	134.2 ± 4.6**	80.0 ± 5.8**
Group XIII	87.8 ± 5.3**	141.6 ± 6.3**	87.8 ± 5.3**

Data presented as means ± SE
Glutamte oxaloacetate transaminase (GOT)
Glutamate pyruvate transaminase(GPT)
Alkaline phosphatase (ALP)
*Significant at $P < 0.05$ as compared with the paracetamol group
Hashem et al., 2013

Other Health Benefits Provided by Broccoli

Three other areas of health benefits are important to mention when considering broccoli and its unique combination of nutrients.

The first area is eye health. Two carotenoids found in significant concentrations in broccoli—lutein and zeaxanthin—play an especially important role in the health of the eye. In fact, no tissue in the body is more concentrated with lutein than the area in the outer portion of the retina (called the peripheral retina). Similarly, in the macula near the central portion of the retina, zeaxanthin is uniquely concentrated. Risk of problems involving the macula of the eye (for example, macular degeneration) and problems involving the lens area of the eye (for example, cataracts) have both been show to lessen with intake of foods (including broccoli) that provide significant amounts of the lutein and zeaxanthin, carotenonids (*Norman et al.*, 2003).

A second area is skin support, including support of sun-damaged skin. Here it is the glucoraphanin found in broccoli—converted into sulforaphane by the body—that has received the most research attention. Since skin cells can carry out the process of detoxification, it may be detox-related benefits of sulforaphane that are especially important in helping to counteract sun damage (*Albena et al.*, 2006).

A third area of increasing research interest involves the metabolism of vitamin D. Broccoli is not a source of this vitamin, but it is an excellent source of vitamin K and also of vitamin A (in one of its precursor forms, beta-carotene (*Weizmann, et al.*, 2008). Many individuals have large vitamin D deficiencies that cannot be remedied through diet alone, and these deficiencies require sizable amounts of vitamin D to be provided through dietary supplementation. When large supplemental doses of vitamin D are needed to offset deficiency, ample supplies of vitamin K and vitamin A appear to help keep our vitamin D metabolism in the proper balance. Assuring adequate intake of vitamins K and A alongside of vitamin D supplementation may turn out to be important in achieving optimal vitamin D supplementation results and avoiding potential problems related to supplementation. Broccoli may turn out to play a particularly helpful role in balancing this set of events by providing its unusually strong combination of both vitamin A and vitamin K (*Damon et al.*, 2005).

Broccoli Requirements for Healthy Diet

Studies have shown that even kids like broccoli and one way to ensure that they enjoy it is to cook it properly by using our Healthy Steaming method. Overcooked broccoli becomes soft and mushy, an indication that it has lost both nutrients and flavor. Begin by cutting broccoli florets into quarters and let sit for several minutes before cooking to enhance its health-promoting benefits. You'll want to include broccoli as one of the cruciferous vegetables you eat on a regular basis if you want to receive the fantastic health benefits provided by the cruciferous vegetable family. At a minimum, include cruciferous vegetables as part of your diet 2-3 times per week, and make the serving size at least 1-1/2 cups. Even better from a health standpoint, enjoy broccoli and other vegetables from the cruciferous vegetable group 4-5 times per week, and increase your serving size to 2 cups.

Broccoli is one of the very low calorie vegetables; provides just 34 calories per 100 g. Nevertheless, it is rich in dietary fiber, minerals, vitamins, and anti-oxidants that have proven health benefits. Total antioxidant strength measured in terms of *oxygen radical absorbance capacity* (ORAC) of broccoli is 1632 µmol TE/100 g. Fresh Broccoli is a store house of many phyto-nutrients such as thiocyanates, indoles, sulforaphane, isothiocy-anates and flavonoids like beta-carotene cryptoxanthin, lutein, and zea-xanthin. Studies have shown that these compounds by modifying positive signaling at molecular receptor levels help protect from prostate, colon, urinary bladder, pancreatic, and breast cancers (*Tarozzi et al.*, 2009).

Fresh vegetable is exceptionally rich source of vitamin-C. Provides 89.2 mg or about 150% of RDA per 100 g. Vitamin-C is a powerful natural anti-oxidant and immune modulator, helps fight against flu causing viruses (*Schurgers et al.*, 2004).

Further, it contains very good amounts of another anti-oxidant vitamin, vitamin-A. 100 g fresh head provides 623 IU or 21% of recommended daily levels. Together with other pro-vitamins like beta-carotene, alpha-carotene, and zea-xanthin, vitamin A helps maintain integrity of skin and mucus membranes. Vitamin A is essential for healthy eye-sight and helps prevent from macular degeneration of the retina in the elderly population (*Norman et al.*, 2003).

Broccoli leaves (green tops) are an excellent source of carotenoids and vitamin A; (provide 16000 IU of vitamin A per 100 g) contain these compounds, several times greater than that in their flower-heads.Fresh heads are an excellent source of folates; contain about 63 µg/100 g (Provides 16% of RDA). Studies have shown that consumption of fresh vegetables and fruits rich in folates during pre-conception, and pregnancy helps prevent neural tube defects in the off spring.

Source: (USDA National Nutrient data base)

REFERENCES

Agte, V.V., Tarwadi, K.V., Mengale, S., & Chiplonkar, S.A. (2000). Potential of Traditionally Cooked Green Leafy Vegetables as Natural Sources for Supplementation of Eight Micronutrients in Vegetarian Diets. Journal of Food Composition and Analysis, 13, 885-891.

Arisha, H.M.; Gad, A.A. and Younes, S.E. (2003): Response of Some Pepper Cultivars to Organic and Mineral Nitrogen Fertilizer Under Sandy Soil Conditions. *Zagazig J. Agric.Res.*, 30, 1875-1899.

Angeloni C, Leoncini E, Malaguti M, (2009). Modulation of Phase II Enzymes by Sulforaphane: Implications for its Cardio Protective Potential. J Agaric. Food Chem. Jun 24; 57(12): 5615-22.

Albena T. Dinkova-Kostova, Stephanie N. Jenkins, Jed W. Fahey, LingxiangYe,Scott L. Wehage, Karen T. Liby, Katherine K. Stephenson, Kristina L. Wade,Paul Talalay(2006). Protection Against UV-light-induced Skin Carcinogenesis in SKH-1 High-risk Mice by Sulforaphane-containing Broccoli Sprout Extracts. Cancer Letters. Volume 240, Issue 2, Pages 243-252.

Aldrich HT, Kendall P, Bunning M, Stonaker F, Kulen O, Stushnoff C (2011). Environmental Temperatures Influence Antioxidant Properties and Mineral Content in Broccoli Cultivars Grown Organically and Conventionally. J. Agron. Crop Sci. J. 2: 110.

Aml F.M. Morsy, Hodaa S. Ibrahim and M.A. Shalab (2010). Protective Effect of Broccoli and Red Cabbage Against Hepatoocellular Carcinoma Induced by Nitrosodiethylamine in Rats Journal of American Science .6(12), 1136-1144.

Anika Eva Wagner, Anna Maria Terschluesen, and Gerald Rimbach (2013). Health Promoting Effects of Brassica-Derived Phytochemicals: From Chemopreventive andAnti-Inflammatory Activities to Epigenetic Regulation Hindawi Publishing Corporation Oxidative Medicine and Cellular Longevity Volume 2013, Article ID 964539, 12 pages.

Ambrosone CB, Tang L. (2009). Cruciferous Vegetable Intake and Cancer Prevention: Role of Nutrigenetics. Cancer Prev. Res. (*Phila Pa*). Apr; 2(4): 298-300.

Bahorun, T., Luximon-Ramma, A., Crozier, A., & Aruoma, O. I. (2004). Total Phenol, Flavonoid, Proanthocyanidin and Vitamin C Levels and Antioxidant Activities of Mauritian Vegetables. Journal of the Science of Food and Agriculture, 84, 1553-1561.

Beecher, C.W.W. (1994). Cancer Preventive Properties of Varieties of *Brassica oleracea*: A Review. Amer. J. Clin. Nutr. 59(suppl): 1166S–1170S.

Bin J. (1983). Utilization of Green Manure for Raising Soil Fertility in China. Soil Sci., 135 (1983), pp. 65-69.

Bryant CS, Kumar S, Chamala S, (2010). Sulforaphane Induces Cell Cycle Arrest by Protecting RB-E2F-1 Complex in Epithelial Ovarian Cancer Cells. Molecular Cancer 2010, 9: 47.

Block, G., Jensen, C., Dietrich, M., Norkus, E. P., Hudes, M., & Packer, L. (2004). Plasma C-reactive Protein Concentrations in Active and Passive Smokers: Influence of Antioxidant Suplementation. Journal of the American College of Nutrition, 23(2), 141-147.

Brown PD, Morra MJ, (1997). Control of Soil-borne Plant Pests Using Glucosinolate Containing Plants, Advan. Agron. 61, 167-231.

Burow, M; Bergner, A; Gershenzon, J; Wittstock, U (2007). "Glucosinolate Hydrolysis in Lepidium Sativum—identification of the Thiocyanate-forming Protein". Plant Molecular Biology 63 (1): 49-61.

Cheng-Fang Tsai, Bor-Rung Ou, Yu-Chuan Liang, Jan-Ying Yeh (2013). Growth Inhibition and Antioxidative Status Induced by Selenium-enriched Broccoli Extract and Selenocompounds in DNA Mismatch Repair-deficient Human Colon Cancer Cells. Food Chemistry. Jul 2013, Vol. 139: 267-273.

Chu Y-F, Sun J, Wu X, Liu RH (2002). Antioxidant and Antiproliferative Activities of Common Vegetables. J. Agric. Food Chem. 50: 6910-6916.

Cohen JH, Kristal AR, Stanford JL (2000). Fruit and Vegetable Intakes and Prostate Cancer Risk. J. Natl. Cancer Inst. 92: 61-68.

Damon, M., Zhang, N.Z., Haytowitz, D.B., Booth, S.L. (2005). Phylloquinone (Vitamin K_1 Content of Vegetables. J. Food Comp and Analysis. 18: 751-758.

Davey, M.W., van Montagu, M., Inze, D., Sanmartin, M., Kanellis, A., Smirnoff, N., et al. (2000). Plant L-ascorbic acid: Chemistry, Function, Metabolism, Bioavailability and Effects of Processing. Journal of the Science of Food and Agriculture, 80, 825-860.

Dauda, S.N. Ajayi, F.A. Ndo E. (2008). Growth and Yield of Water Melon (*Citrullus lanatus*) as Affected by Poultry Manure Application J. Agric. Soc. Sci., 4 pp. 121-124.

De Sa, M.C., & Rodriguez-Amaya, D. B. (2004). Optimization of HPLC Quantification of Carotenoids in Cooked Green Vegetables—Comparison of Analytical and Calculated Data. Journal of Food Composition and Analysis 17, 37-51.

Farooq, M., Wahid, A., Kadambot, H., & Siddique, M. (2012). Micronutrient Application Through Seed Treatments - A Review. Journal of Soil Science and Plant Nutrition, 12, 125-142. http://dx.doi.org/10.4067/S0718-95162012000100011.

Favell, D. J. (1998). A Comparison of the Vitamin C Content of Fresh and Frozen Vegetables. Food Chemistry,62 (1), 59-64.

Franke, A.A., Custer, L.J., Arakaki, C., & Murphy, S.P. (2004). Vitamin C and Flavonoid Levels of Fruits and Vegetables Consumed in Hawaii. Journal of Food Composition and Analysis,17, 1-35.

Ferreres, F. Valentão, P. Llorach, R. Pinheiro, C. Cardoso, L. Pereira, J.A. Sousa, C. Seabra, R.M. Andrade P.B. (2005). Phenolic Compounds in External Leaves of Tronchuda Cabbage (*Brassica oleracea* L. var. *Costata* DC). J Agric Food Chem. 20; 53(8): 2901-7.

Grusak, M.A., & Cakmak, I. (2005). Methods to Improve the Crop Delivery of Minerals to Human and Livestock. In M.R. Broadley & P.J. White (Eds.), Plant Nutritional Genomics (pp. 265-286). Blackwel.

Gundgaard J, Nielsen JN, Olsen J, Sorensen J (2003). Increased Intake of Fruit and Vegetables: Estimation of Impact in Terms of Life Expectancy and Healthcare Costs. Public Health Nutr. 6: 25-30.

Gupta, A.P., Antil, S.R., Narwal, P.R., (1988). Effect of Farmyard Manure on Organic Carbon, Available N and P Contents of Soil during Different Periods of Wheat Growth. J. Indian Soil Sci. 36, 269-273.

Hashem, FA., Hemaia M. Motawea, Abdel Rahman E. El-Shabrawy, Samar M. El-Sherbini, Kamel Shaker, Abdel Razik H. Farrag,(2015). Hepatoprotective Activity of Brassica oleracea L. var. Italica. Egyptian Pharmaceutical Journal 17, 2015, IP: 195.43.5.55.

Heaton, (2001) Organic Farming, Food Quality and Human Health: A Review of the Evidence. Soil Association of the United Kingdom (2001).

Heimler, D., Vignolini, P., Dini, M.G., Vincieri, F.F., Romani, A., (2006). Antiradical Activity and Polyphenols Composition of Local Brassicaceae Edible Varieties. Food Chem. 99, 464-469.

Heinonen, M.I., Ollilainen, V., Linkola, E.K., Varo, P.T., & Koivistoinen, P.E. (1989). Carotenoids in Finnish Foods: Vegetables, Fruits, and Berries. Journal of Agriculture and Food Chemistry, 37, 655-659.

Holden, J.M., Eldridge, A.L., Beecher, G.R., Buzzard, I.M., Bhagwat, S., Davis, C. S., et al. (1999). Carotenoid Content of US Foods: An Uptade of the Database. Journal of Food Composition and Analysis,12, 169-196.

Howard, L.A., Wong, A.D., Perry, A.K., & Klein, B.P. (1999). Bcarotene and Ascorbic Acid Retention in Fresh and Processed Vegetables. Journal of Food Science, 64(5), 929-936.

Hrncirik, K., Valusek, J., & Velisek, J. (2001). Investigation of Ascorbigen as a Break Down Product of Glucobrassicin Autolysis in Brassicavegetables. European Food Research and Technology 212, 576-581.

Hussein, A., Odumeru, J.A., Ayanbadejo, T., Faulkner, H., McNab, W.B., Hager, H., et al. (2000). Effect of Processing and Packaging on Vitamin C and b-carotene Content of Ready-to-use (RTU) Vegetables. Food Research International 33, 131-136.

ISSA, S VOLATE, WARGOVICH, M. (2006). The Role of Photochemical in Inhibition of Cancer and Inflammation: New Directions and Perspectives. Journal of Food Composition and Analysis. Vol. 19: 405-419.

Kurilich, A.C., Jeffery, E.H., Juvik, J.A., Wallig, M.A., & Klein, B.P. (2002). Antioxidant Capacity of Different Broccoli (Brassica Oleracea) Genotypes Using the Oxygen Radical Absorbance Capacity (ORAC) Assay. Journal of Agriculture and Food Chemistry, 50, 5053-5057.

Lakhan SE, Kirchgessner A, Hofer M. (2009). Inflammatory Mechanisms in Ischemic Stroke: Therapeutic Approaches. Journal of Translational Medicine 2009, 7: 97.

Lampi, A.-M., Kamal-Eldin, A., Piironen, V., (2002). Tocopherols and Tocotrienols from Oil and Cereal Grains. In: J. Shi, G. Mazza, M. LeMaguer, (Eds.), Functional Food–Biochemical and Processing Aspects. Boca Raton, FL: CRC Press LLC.

Lee, S.K., & Kader, A.A. (2000). Preharvest and Postharvest Factors Influencing Vitamin C Content of Horticultural Crops. Postharvest Biology and Technology, 20, 207-220.

Lombardi-Boccia, G. Lucarini, M. Lanzi, S. Aguzzi, A. Cappelloni M. (2004). Nutrients and Antioxidant Molecules in Yellow Plums (*Prunus domestica* L.) from Conventional and Organic Productions: A Comparative Study .J. Agric. Food Chem., 52 (2004), pp. 90-94.

Lundega, R.D.H.B., Ma Rtensson, A., (2003). Organically Produced Plant Foods – Evidence for Health Benefits. Review Article. Acta Agric. Scand. Sect B, Soil Plant Sci. 53, 3-15.

Manach, C., Scalbert, A., Morand, C., Re´me´sy, C., Jime´nez, L., (2004). Polyphenol. Rhizobial inoculants had been used in legume fields

Marion Nestle(1979). Broccoli sprouts as inducers of carcinogen-detoxifying enzyme systems. Proc. Natl. Acad. Sci. USA, Vol. 94, pp. 11149-11151.

Martínez-Ballesta, M.C., Dominguez-Perles, R., Muries, B., Alcaraz-López, C., Moreno, D.A., García-Viguera, C., & Carvajal, M. (2010). Plant Mineral Content and Their Role in Promoting Human Health. *Agronomy for Sustainable Development, 30,* 295-309. http://dx.doi.org/10.1051/agro/2009022

Muhammad Jahangir, Hye K. Kim, Young H. Choi, Robert. Verpoorte (2007). Health-Affecting Compounds in *Brassicaceae* Comprehensive Reviews in Food Science and Food Safety. Vol. 8, No. 10.1111/crfs.2009.8.issue-2: 31-43

Moreno, D.A., Carvajal, M., Lopez-Berenguer, C., Garcia-Viguera, C., 2006.Chemical and Biological Characterisation of Nutraceutical Compounds of Broccoli. J. Pharmaceut. Biomed. 41, 1508-1522.

Muller, H. (1997). Determination of the Carotenoid Content in Selected Vegetables and Fruit by HPLC and Photodiode Array Detection. Zeitschrift fur Lebensmittel-Untersuchung und–Forschung A.204, 88-94.

Murcia, M.A., Lopez-Ayerra, B., Martinez-Tome, M., Vera, A.M., & Garcia-Carmona, F. (2000). Evolution of Ascorbic Acid and Peroxidase during Industrial Processing of Broccoli. Journal of the Science of Food and Agriculture, 80, 1882-1886.

Murkovic, M., Gams, K., Draxl, S., & Pfannhauser, W. (2000). Development of an Austrian Carotenoid Database. Journal of Food Composition and Analysis, 13, 435-440.

Naeem, M. Iqbal, J., Bakhsh, M.A.A. (2006). Comparative Study of Inorganic Fertilizers and Organic Manures on Yield and Yield Components of Mung Bean (*Vigna radiat* L.) J. Agric. Soc. Sci., 2 (2006), 227-229.

Naguib AEMM, El-Baz FK, Salama ZA, Hanaa HAEB, Ali HF, Gaafar AA (2012). Enhancement of Phenolics, Flavonoids and Glucosinolates of Broccoli (*Brassica olaracea,* var. *talic*) as Antioxidants in Response to Organic and Bio-organic Fertilizers. J. Saudi Soc. Agric. 11-135-142.

Norman I. Krinsky, John T. Landrum, And Richard A. Bone (2003). Biologic Mechanisms of the Protective Role of Lutein and Zeaxanthin in the Eye. Annual Review of Nutrition, Vol. 23: 171-201.

Podsedek A (2007). Natural Antioxidants and Antioxidant Capacity of Brassica Vegetables: A Review. LWT-Food Sci. Technol. 40: 1-11.

Prawan A, Saw CL, Khor TO (2009). Anti-NF-kappaB and Anti-inflammatory Activities of Synthetic Isothiocyanates: Effect of Chemical Structures and Cellular Signaling. Chem Biol Interact. 15; 179(2-3): 202-211.

Price, K.R., Casuscelli, F., Colquhoun, I.J., & Rhodes, M.J.C. (1997). Hydroxycinnamic Acid Esters from Broccoli Florets. Phytochemistry, 45, 1683-1687.

Price, K.R., Casuscelli, F., Colquhoun, I.J., & Rhodes, M.J.C. (1998). Composition and Content of Flavonol Glycosides in Broccoli Florets (Brassica olearacea) and Their Fate during Cooking. Journal of the Science of Food and Agriculture, 77, 468-472.

Rice-Evans, C., Miller, N.J., Blowell, P.G., Bramley, P.M., Pridham, J.B., (1995). The Relative Antioxidant Activities of Plant-derived Polyphenolic Flavonoids. Free Rad. Res. 22, 375-383.

Rodriguez, A.S. Rosa E.A.S. (1999). Effect of Post-harvest Treatments on the Level of Glucosinolates in Broccoli. J. Sci. Food Agric., 79 pp. 1028-1032.

Rosa, E., R.K. Heaney, C.A.M. Portas, and G.R. Fenwick. (1996). Changes in Glucosinolate Concentrations in *Brassica* Crops (*B. oleracea* and *B. napus*) Throughout Growing Seasons. J. Sci. Food Agr. 71: 237-244.

Saber K., Nahla L., Ahmed D., Chedly A. (2005). Effect of P on Nodule Formation and N Fixation in Bean, Agron. Sustain. Dev. 25, 389-393.

Schurgers LJ, Shearer MJ, Hamulyák K, Stöcklin E, Vermeer C. (2004). Effect of Vitamin K Intake on the Stability of Oral Anticoagulant Treatment: Dose-response Relationships in Healthy Subjects. Blood.; 104(9): 2682-2689.

Sørensen, H., (1990). Glucosinolates: Structure-properties-function. In: Shahidi, F. (Ed.), Canola and Rapeseed. Van Nostrand Reinhold, New York, pp. 149-172.

Sousa, C. Pereira, D.M Pereira, J.A. Bento, A. Rodrigues, M.A., Dopico-García, S. Valentão, P., Lopes, G., Ferreres, Federico Seabra, R.M. Andrade Multivariate, P.B. (2008). Analysis of Tronchuda Cabbage (*Brassica oleracea* L. var. costata DC) Phenolics: Influence of Fertilizers J. Agric. Food Chem., 56 (2008), pp. 2231-2239.

Stampfer, M.J., & Rimm, E.B. (1995). Epidemiologic Evidence for Vitamin E in Prevention of Cardiovascular Disease. American Journal of Clinical Nutrition, 62, 1365-1369.

Suresh, D. Sneh, G. Krishn, K.K. Mool C.M.(2004). Microbial Biomass Carbon and Microbial Activities of Soils Receiving Chemical Fertilizers and Organicamendments Arch. Agron. Soil Sci., 50641-647.

Tarozzi A, Morroni F, Merlicco A, (2009). Sulforaphane as an Inducer of Glutathione Prevents Oxidative Stress-induced Cell Death in a Dopaminergic-like Neuroblastoma Cell Line. J Neurochem. Dec; 111(5): 1161-71.

U.S. Department of Agriculture, Agricultural Research Service. (2014). USDA National Nutrient Database for Standard Reference, Release 27. Nutrient Data Laboratory Home Page, http://www.ars.usda.gov/ba/bhnrc/ndl

Orhan D.D., Orhan, N., Ergun, E. and Ergun, F. (2007). Hepatoprotective Effect of Vitisvinifera L. Leaves on Carbon Tetrachlorideinduced Acute Liver Damage in Rats. Ethnopharmacol 112(1) 145-51.

Vallejo, F., Tomas-Barberan, F.A., & Garcia-Viguera, C. (2002). Potential Bioactive Compounds in Health Promotion from Broccoli Cultivars Grown in Spain. Journal of the Science of Food and Agriculture, 82, 1293-1297.

Vallejo, F., Garcia-Viguera, C. Tomas-Barberan F.A. (2003). Changes in Broccoli (*Brassica oleracea* L. Var. *Italica*) Health-promoting Compounds with Inflorescence Development J. Agric. Food Chem., 51 pp. 3776-3782.

Vallejo, F., Garcia-Viguera, C. Tomas-Barberan F.A. (2003a). Changes in Broccoli (*Brassica oleracea* L. Var. *Italica*) Health-promoting Compounds with Inflorescence Development J. Agric. Food Chem., 51 pp. 3776-3782.

Vallejo, F.A. Tomas-Barberan, C. Garcia-Viguera (2003b). Effect of Climatic and Sulphur Fertilisation Conditions, on Phenolic Compounds and Vitamin C in the Inflorescences of Eight Broccoli Cultivars Eur. Food Res. Technol., 216 pp. 395-401.

Vinson, J.A., Dabbagh, Y.A., Serry, M.M., & Jang, J. (1995). Plant Flavonoids, Especially Tea Flavonols, are Powerful Antioxidants Using an *in vitro* Oxidation Model for Heart Disease. Journal of Agriculture and Food Chemistry, 43, 2800-2802.

Wilkinson, S.R. (1979). Plant Nutrient and Economic Value of Animal Manures. J. Anim. Sci., 48 (1979), pp. 121-133

Wargovich M.J., (1999). Nutrition and Cancer the Herbal Revolution. Curr Opin Clin Nutr Metab Care 2, 421-425.

Weizmann, N., Peterson, J.W., Haytowitz, D., Pehrsson, P.R., de Jesus, V.P. and Booth, S.L. (2004). Vitamin K Content of Fast Foods and Snack Foods in the US Diet. J. Food Comp. Anal. 17: 379-384.

Yoldas F, Ceylan S, Yagmur B, Mordogan N (2008). Effects of Nitrogen Fertilizer on Yield Quality and Nutrient Content in Broccoli. J. Plant Nutr. 31: 13 33-1343.

Welch, R.M., & Graham, R.D. (2004). Breeding for Micronutrients in Staple Food Crops from a Human Nutrition Perspective. Journal of Experimental Botany, 55, 353-364. http://dx.doi.org/10.1093/jxb/erh064

Williamson G, Faulkner K, Plumb GW (1998). Glucosinolates and Phenolics as Antioxidants from Plant Foods. Eur. J. Cancer Prev. 7.17-21.

Woese K., Lange, D. Boess, C. Bogl K.W. (1997). A Comparison of Organically and Conventionally Grown Foods. J. Sci. Food Agric., 74 (1997), pp. 281-293.

Wong J.W.C., Ma, K.K. Fang, K.M. Cheung, C. (1999). Utilization of Manure Compost for Organic Farming in Hong Kong Bio-resource Technol., 67 pp. 43-46.

Young, J.W. Mau, J.L. Ko, P.T. Huang L.C. (2000). Antioxidant Properties of Fermented Soybean Broth Food Chem., 71, pp. 249-254.

Zahra Bahadoran, Parvin Mirmiran, Farhad Hosseinpanah, Asadolah Rajab, Golale Asghari, Fereidoun Azizi (2012). Broccoli (Brassica oleracea var. italica) Sprouts and Extracts Rich in Glucosinolates and Isothiocyanates Affect Cholesterol Metabolism and Genes Involved in Lipid Homeostasis in Hamsters, Practice Volume, Pages 348-354.

Zhang D, Hamauzu Y (1997). Phenolics, Ascorbic Acid, Carotenoids and Antioxidant Activity of Broccoli and Their Changes during Conventional and Microwave Cooking. Food Chem. 88: 503-509.

Zhang Donglin, Hamauzu Yasunori (2004). Phenolics, Ascorbic Acid, Carotenoids and Antioxidant Activity of Broccoli and Their Changes during Conventional and Microwave Cooking Food ChemistryVolume 88, Issue 4, December 2004, Pages 503-509.

Zhao, F., Evans, E., Bilsborrow, P., Syers, J.K., (1994). Influence of Nitrogen and Sulphur on the Glucosinolate Profile of Rapeseed (Brassica napus L.). J. Sci. Food Agric. 64, 295-304.

Pages: 106-119

SEED TREATMENT, PLANT HEALTH AND AGRO-TECHNOLOGY

Edited by: Dr. Avnish Chauhan and Dr. Pawan Kumar 'Bharti'

ISBN: 978-93-5056-810-1

Edition: 2016

Published by: Discovery Publishing House Pvt. Ltd., New Delhi (India)

6

Genetic Parameters and Selection Strategies Under Changing Environmental Conditions in Wheat

Divya, R.K. Arya and I.S. Panwar

ABSTRACT

The nature and magnitude of genetic parameters like components of genetic variance (additive, dominance and epistatic), coefficient of variation, heritability and genetic advance may vary from character to character for the same population, from population to population for the same character and from environment to environment for the same population and same character. An abiotic stress may be the major cause of such variations. The magnitude of such variation may be relatively much more if there is simultaneous occurrence of two or more abiotic stresses such as drought, salt and heat stress coupled with the high seasonal and interannual variability of the environment. Many workers including author have found in their studies conducted in different years that additive genetic component and unfixable epistasis respond more to change in environment than the dominance component and fixable epistasis indicating that heterozygotes exhibit higher stability than the corresponding homozygotes i.e. superiority of hybrids.

Since the development of hybrid wheat varieties has not so far being successful at commercial scale, the best way to increase the magnitude of dominance variation in wheat is to increase magnitude of homozygous genomic heterosis (intergenomic heterozygosity) by utilizing alien gene transfer (i.e. 1B/1R and

Wheat and Barley Section, Department of Genetics and Plant Breeding, CCS Haryana Agricultural University, Hisar - 125 004, (India).

7D/7Ae. etc.).The stress affects the means adversely, causes reduction in both genotypic and phenotypic variances, but increases heritability in many cases. Degree of dominance does not vary very much between the environment. Probably this is the main reasons why yields of cereals is stressed dry land areas have increased only modestly as compared to irrigated areas. The estimation of genetic parameter should be done under the environment where selection is to be practiced. This paper briefly reviews impact of environment on character expression, genetic parameters and selection strategies for developing elite germplasm lines and/or improved wheat varieties.

Key words: genetic parameters, breeding strategies, changing environment, wheat.

Introduction

Climate change and agriculture are interrelated processes, both of which take place on a global scale. Moreover, climate change has the potential to affect agriculture through changes in temperature, rainfall (timing and quantity), CO2, solar radiation and the interaction of these elements. The effect of climate on agriculture is related to variabilities in local weather parameters rather than in global climate patterns. The Earth's average surface temperature has increased by 1 degree F in just over the last century. Consequently, agronomists consider any assessment has to be individually considering each location.

Wheat (*Triticum aestivum* L.em.Thell) is one of the most important cereal crops of the world both in terms of area and production. The wide spread cultivation of the crop all along the globe is largely due to high versatility of genome, which enable its adaptation to different agro climatic conditions and the unique property of wheat flour and dough which allows its processing into a range of food products (Kant *et al.*, 2011). Wheat is the second most important crop after rice in India and achieved a record wheat production of 84.27 million tones during 2010-11 (DWR Vision 2030). The national wheat production accounts for 12 per cent of global wheat production that made India the 2nd largest wheat producing nation with surplus wheat. Therefore, today to maintain the pace of increase in wheat production, designing of genotypes well adapted to changing climatic condition are an instant need.

In spite of poor salt tolerance of our crops, there are considerable variations among the different crops and their cultivars to tolerate salt stress (Singh *et al.*, 2009). For a tolerant line of bread wheat, one must be aware of crop genetics and physiology and develop an efficient screening system based on stable selection criteria. Grain yield is a complex trait and highly influenced by many genetic factors and environmental fluctuations. In plant breeding programme, direct selection for yield as such could be misleading. Efficiency of selection for higher yield depends upon the knowledge of trait components and their interaction with grain yield. This requires information about nature and magnitude of variability in base population and association of yield components with grain yield. There are many reports on genetic variability and characters association analysis in wheat but quite deficient on study under sodicity stress (Kumar *et al.*, 2014).

Job of plant breeder is very difficult in choosing selection criteria under biotic and abiotic stress environments for combining high yield with resistance to adverse biotic and abiotic factors. The information about the relative magnitudes of genetic parameters over a range of environments may help in making the plant breeding programme scientifically more sound. It is desirable for breeder to have a much information as possible on the genetic control of the important agronomic and yield characters of the crop. Thus knowledge of the nature and extent of variability, particularly genetic variability, present in any crop is essential for further improvement. Several genetical procedures are available to study the nature and magnitude of genetic variation, However, Triple test cross analysis has the least assumptions and, therefore, is more widely applicable for studying populations of various kinds (Eissa 1994 and Koumber 2006).

Target Environment and Breeding Strategy

Since yield is the integrated product of genotypic expression in a given environment, the production potential of the target environment can affect the decision regarding breeding strategies. Therefore, one important question arises that whether the breeding for the target environment should rely on selection under favourable conditions and subsequent testing of selected material in target environment or on direct selection under target environment, or stated differently, whether the estimates of genetic parameters (Which determine the kind of selection procedure to be adopted to maximize improvement) should be obtained from the target environment or from the favourable environment?

Falconer (1952) emphasized that the genotypes selected under favourable environment though showed their superiority over the genotypes selected under unfavourable environment when grown under good crop growing conditions, the situation was just reverse when they were grown under poor crop growing conditions, that is, the genotypes performed better in the environment under which they were selected. While discussing barley and wheat improvement for moisture-limiting area in West Asia and North Africa, Srivastava (1987) opined that if the yield production potential of the target environment is high (30 q/h and above); then selection should effectively be practised in favourable crop-growing conditions. However, if the yield potential is low (below 30 q/h), it would be more efficient to select plants directly under target environment. The estimation of genetic parameters should therefore be done under the environment where selection is to be practised.

The view of Srivastava (1987) seems to be justified because the lines selected under favourable conditions will generally be different from those selected under unfavourable conditions, that is, selection for high yield potential under good crop-growing conditions does not generally cause a carry-over effect in stress environments (Table 6.1). Similarly, direct selection under stress environments will reduce yield under favourable environments unless genetic variances in unfavourable environment considerably greater than those in favourable environments and genetic correlations are positive and close to unity.

Table 6.1: Mean Yield Performance (q/ha) of Wheat Varieties Tested Under Two Different Environmental Conditions Over Different Locations during 2008-09

Variety	Restricted Irrigated Conditions	Rank	Rainfed Conditions	Rank
WH1080	34.9	3	32.2	1
HD3013	33.5	8	32.0	2
PBW 613	32.4	11	31.7	3
WAS 315	34.1	6	31.3	4
WH 1081	35.6	1	30.8	5
C306#	26.4	13	28.7	12
PBW175#	35.1	2	29.9	8
CD	2.2	–	1.1	–

Another basis for direct selection for yield potential under target environment is provided by the fact that general adaptation to a wide range of environments representing different stresses may cost the genotype some yield sacrifice. It is therefore; better to evolve separate varieties with best fitness in separate small areas, that is, sacrificing some wide adaptability in favour of specific adaptation to cope with prevailing stresses that limit yield and stability of production. For marking a breeding programme more effective to evolve elite germplasm particularly for poor environments (production, potential below 30 q/h), varieties should be developed to meet the specific needs of a particular area.

Mean Value and Genetic Parameters

The development of high yielding wheat varieties for changing agro-climatic conditions depends upon the nature and amount of genetic variability in the germplasm collection and extent of transmissibility of characters under consideration. A breeding programme depends on proper management of genetic variability present in the material. High magnitude of variability in a population provides the opportunity of selection to evolve a variety having desirable characters. The variability in a biological population that we can see, measure or study is the result of the genetic constitution of the individuals making up that population. All measurements can only be made at phenotypic level, which is the result of interplay of a large number of genes interacting with each other and also with the environment. The phenotypic variability is thus, composed of genotypic and environmental components. In fact, the genotypic component is ultimately useful in utilizing this variability in a breeding programme (Kant *et al.*, 2011).

A number of studies have been carried out to know the effect of change in environment on the magnitude of various genetic parameters. Singh *et al.* (1987) estimated mean, coefficient of variation, heritability and genetic advance for seven metric traits in parents, F1 and F2 generations of a 9 × 9 wheat diallel grown under irrigated (normal) and rainfed (stress) conditions. They found significantly higher mean values for all the characters in normal environment than in the stress environment except 1000 grain weight. On contrary, both genotypic and phenotypic coefficients of variation were higher in stress environment for all the traits.

Similarly, the estimates of heritability were higher in stress environment than in normal environment in majority of the cases. However, the values of genetic advance showed some what different trend. Whereas, the genetic advance was higher in stress environment for days to heading and 1000 grain weight, just a reverse condition was found for plant height, tiller number, total biomass and grain yield per plant, that is, its values were higher in normal environment than in stress environment. These results clearly indicate one thing that the trait 1000 grain weight can be more easily improved in stress environment.

Dhanda and Sethi (1996) studied genetics of yield and its related traits in nine generations (P_1, P_2, F_1, F_2, F_2, F_3, F_3, B_1, B_2, B_1s and B_2s) under irrigated and rainfed conditions in wheat cross CPAN 1992 x Kharchia 65. The mean performance of all the characters was considerably lower under rainfed conditions than under irrigated conditions. Although both the additive and dominance components were involved in the expression of all the traits under both the environments, yet the dominance component, in general, suffered more than the additive component under rainfed conditions. Additive component appeared to be main source of genetic variation under both environments. The estimates of heritability and genetic advance were higher under irrigated than under rainfed conditions which may be due to better expression of genotypes under normal conditions.

Singh *et al.* (1991) determines photothermo response, by raising 50 genotypes of wheat under four photothermal environments created through alteration of sowing dates from October through December. By taking days to heading as the key diagnostic character for photothermo response, they classified the genotypes into five groups—photoperiod non-responsive and high temperature sensitive. photoperiod non-responsive and low temperature responsive, photothermo sensitive, partial photothermo-responsive, and photothermo insensitive and computed groupwise phenotypic and genotypic correlation coefficients. Grain yield showed positive correlation with grain weight, grain number and tillers per plant in all the photothermal environments and negative correlation with days to heading, maturity and flag leaf duration in E_1 and E_3 environments (sowing dates, 5th October and 5th December, respectively). In general, the magnitude and direction of correlation changed with a change in photothermal environment.

Singh and Rana (1987) conducted experiments to estimate various kinds of gene effects in six generations (P_1, P_2, F_1, F_2, B_1 and B_2) of eight bread wheat crosses for grain yield and its major components under three edaphic environments (normal, alkali and saline soils). They found a great impact of environmental conditions on trait expression as there was a lack of consistency in the significance of gene effects under different environments. This and a subsequent study conducted by Singh *et al.* (1991) led the authors to conclude that the estimation of gene effects should be carried in wide range of environments. A similar study conducted by Redhu *et al.* (1990) to quantify various gene effects in three wheat crosses (Kharchia 65 × WH 157, Kharchia 65× WH 283 and HD 2009× WH 283) grown under normal vis-a-vis saline environment, indicated differential genetic mechanism in two environments for all the three crosses in respect of the adequacy of model, the nature, magnitude and the level of significance of gene effects for yield and its component traits, Also, the duplicate type of epistasis was more pronounced in normal than in the saline environment. However, Richards (1983) has argued that since the saline soils are typically patchy in their salinity, the yields of crops growing on them are similarly patchy. But, since most of the yield from such fields comes from least saline areas, the best strategy for maximising overall yield is to select for high yield on non-saline soils.

Arya *et al.* (2005) studied variability, correlation and path coefficient for ten metric trait in 40 genotypes of wheat at two locations i.e. Hisar nd Bawal with two dates of sowing. Significant genotypic differences were observed for all the traits in all the four environments. In the present study, E_1 and E_3 (timely sown at Hisar and Bawal) appeared to be the most favourable for the genetic manifestation of yield and its components as compared to E_2 and E_4 (late sown at Hisar and Bawal) as evident from higher mean values as well as greater coefficient of variations for most of the characters i. E_1 and E_3 (Table 6.2). The genetic variability was high for grain yield per plant in all the environments followed by biological yield per plant, number of grains and tillers per plant. Grain yield was positively correlated with tillers per plant, biological yield per plant and grains per ear.

Table 6.2: Mean and Coefficient of Variation (Genotypic and Phenotypic) for Yield and Yield Components Under Different Environment in Wheat

Character	Mean				GCV				PCV			
	E_1	E_2	E_3	E_4	E_1	E_2	E_3	E_4	E_1	E_2	E_3	E_4
Tillers/plant	9.86	7.82	9.05	7.45	8.27	9.73	11.31	5.73	19.11	18.29	19.21	17.81
Grain/ear	48.33	39.77	61.15	53.40	16.70	15.31	10.68	15.60	17.56	15.87	11.07	16.10
1000-grain weight (g)	42.39	39.56	42.24	38.90	10.92	15.32	10.18	10.11	11.37	15.76	10.73	10.81
Biological yield/plant (g)	74.60	68.34	72.87	66.86	17.31	17.47	15.40	21.50	17.78	17.81	15.87	21.89
Grain yield/plant (g)	32.94	30.61	31.73	29.45	23.79	23.24	21.69	23.35	24.77	24.05	22.27	23.94

Source: Arya *et al*. (2005)

The path analysis suggested that biological yield per plant was the main contributor to grain yield per plant in all the four environments. Mohsin *et al.* (2009) also evaluated genetic variability for quantitative traits and found characters like biomass, number of spikes, spike length, grain for spike, 1000-grain weight and harvest index of utmost importance that may be used as suitable selection criteria in wheat breeding.

Kant *et al.* (2011) the highest PCV for effective tillers per plant followed by grain yield per plant, number of grains per plant, biological yield per plant, plant height, sedimentation value, days to heading, protein % and days to maturity in their study conducted in four different environments recorded. The highest heritability was recorded for days to maturity followed by biological yield per plant, number of grains per plant, days to heading, grain yield per plant and effective tillers per plant. Similar findings were also reported by Shoran (1995) for total biomass and grain yield. The highest value of genetic advance per cent of mean was observed for effective tillers per plant followed by number of grains per plant, grain yield per plant and biological yield per plant. Moderate value of heritability was observed for these traits. On the other hand, low heritability value along with lower value of genetic advance was observed for protein content (%) and sedimentation value. High heritability with high genetic advance indicates additive gene effects and, therefore, these characters can be better exploited through simple selection. The occurrence of high variability for grain yield has also been reported by Shoran (1995), for biological yield by Mehta and Dhagat (1992) and for grains per ear by Nagireddy and Jyothula (2009) and Din *et al.* (2010).

Kumar *et al.* (2014) revealed that in general the material under study had wide range of estimates for all the traits except for days to heading and maturity, thereby indicating presence of high genetic variability. The phenotypic coefficient of variation (PCV) was higher than genotypic coefficients of variation (GCV) for all the characters indicating that the visible variation in the expression of traits was not only due to genotypes alone but also due to varying influence of environment. High PCV was observed for grain yield (18.57) followed by number of tillers per meter row (18.44) and harvest index (17.30) while, GCV was highest in number of tillers per meter row (16.27) followed by grain yield (13.31) and number of grains per spike (13.26). However, days to heading and maturity exhibited least genotypic and phenotypic coefficients of variation. Similar findings were also reported by Singh *et al.* (2012) in bread wheat.

Kumar *et al.* (2014) repoted that the estimates of heritability varied from 41 per cent for biological yield to 95 per cent for days to heading whereas grain yield showed 51 per cent heritability. Singh *et al.* (2012) reported high heritability for various traits while , Abinasa *et al.*, (2011), and Kumar *et al.* (2014) reported low heritability was for grain yield and biological yield and

Verma et al., (2013) also repoted low heritability for harvest index . Genetic advance as per cent of mean was recorded maximum for number of tillers per meter row (29.59) followed by number of grains per spike (25.35) and grain yield (19.65). In general, number of tillers per meter row, number of grains per spike, 1000-grain weight and ear length revealed high estimates of heritability along with high genetic advance (Kumar *et al.*, 2014). The estimates of high heritability (broad sense) and high genetic advance (GA % of mean) indicate additive gene effects and hence improvement in these traits could be possible by direct selection (Panse, 1957). High heritability coupled with low genetic advance was observed for days to heading and maturity indicating predominance of non-additive gene action and presence of G × E interaction, simple selection may not be rewarding. In such cases hybridization followed by selecting desirable segregants in later generations will be better option. The intermediate estimates of heritability and relatively high estimates of genetic advance was observed in the present study for grain yield, harvest index, plant height and biological yield, moderate improvement through direct selection could be possible (Singh *et al.*, 2012 and Kumar *et al.*, 2014).

Triple Test Cross Approach-Some Results

Genetic analyses were performed to estimate the supremacy of additive, dominance and epistasis genetic variances following triple test cross analyses. The analysis of variance revealed highly significant difference due to genotype; hybrids, lines and testers for all studied characters, indicating the presence of considerable amount of genetic variability. The analysis of variance for the detection of epistasis indicated highly significant over all epistasis for all characters studied. Further partitioning of epistasis to its component parts, revealed that additive x additive (i) type of epistasis was significant for all characters except for no spikes/plant (Koumber, 2011).

In a set of 90 triple test cross progeny families produced by crossing 30 homozygous and genetically diverse varieties of wheat with three testers and grown in two years, Singh (1980) reported that the fixable and unfixable components of epistasis were equally sensitive to the environmental change. However, the response of dominance component to year difference was negligible as compared to that of additive genetic component which was highly sensitive to micro-as well as to macro-environmental differences. In a similar study in wheat.

Singh *et al.* (1985, 1986) recorded a higher sensitivity of unfixable component of epistasis to environmental differences (irrigated and rainfed conditions) than that of the fixable epistasis. However, the response of additive and dominance components to the two environments was almost equal. Exactly similar results were obtained by Singh *et al.* (1988, 89) regarding the sensitivity of additive, dominance and epistatic components to environmental differences in another set of 45 wheat triple test cross families raised in two environments (normal and late sowings). Higher sensitivity of additive component to environmental differences was also noted by Singh (1990) in 324 triple test cross families produced from three wheat, crosses (HD 2009 × WH 147, NP 876 × HD 2160 and Sonalika × WL 711).

Pawar *et al.* (1994) studied 60 TTC families produced by crossing 20 pure breeding varieties/strains of wheat with three testers to detect epistasis and test and estimate D and H components of genetic variation for six metric traits at two locations. Epistasis was significant for plant height, 1000-grain weight and grain yield. The component D was more important than H for almost all the character studied. In 1996, they used the data of these families to study interaction of additive, dominance and epistatic effects with environment. Additive gene effects were more sensitive to environmental differences than the domance gene effects indicating higher stability of heterozygous genotypes than the homozygous varieties. However, non-fixable epistasis was more sensitive than fixable epitasis.

Dhiman *et al.*, 1999 estimated genetic components of variance following triple test cross analysis involving 10 diverse true breeding lines of wheat for grain yield per plant, biological yield per plant, spikes per plant, 100-grain weight, grains per spike, spikelets per spike and spike length. Epistasis was found to be an integral componenet of genetic variation for all the traits except spike per plant. Additive x additive (i) type of interaction was preponderant for biological yield per plant and grains per spike. Additive × dominance (j) and dominance × dominance (l) types of interactions influenced the inheritance of rest of the traits except spike length for which only additive × additive type of interaction was associated.

Noori *et al.* (1999) produced 75 families by crossing 25 F2 plants derived from crosses between two spring wheats, Siete cerror (salt tolerant) and Axona (salt sensitive) with their parents and their F1 (testers). The above material was subject to TTC analysis for detecting epistasis, additive and dominace genetic components and their interactions with environment (control:salinity) for three physiological characters Na+, K+ and Cl- accumulation in the leaf immediately below the flage leaf on 48-day old wheat plants. Additive x dominance and dominance x dominance types of epistasis were dedected for these characters under saline conditions. Additive components were more important than dominance especially in salinity conditions. Dominance ratio was less than unity in both the environments and narrow sense heritability was moderate to high for Na+, K+ accumulation, respectively, in salinity conditions.

To study G x E interaction in wheat, Sarmah *et al.* (1997) used data from 48 TTC families and applied analysis of Perkins and Jinks (1971). They found that additive gene effects and non-fixable epistasis, were relatively more sensitive to environmental change than dominance gene effect and fixable epistasis, respectively. Relative sensitivity of additive, dominanance and epistatic gene effects to environmental change in wheat carried out by earlier research workers are given in Table 6.3.

Table 6.3: Relative Sensitivity of Additive, Dominanance and Epistatic Gene Effects to Environmental Change in Wheat

Situation		Author(s)
Additive gene effects more sensitive than dominance gene effects	:	Singh (1980,1990), Singh and Dahiya (1984), Dhindsa and Bains (1986) and Pawar *et al.* (1994, 1996).
Additive and dominanance gene effects equally sensitive	:	Singh *et al.* (1986), Singh *et al.* (1989), Singh *et al.* (1990, 1992) and Singh *et al.* (1995).
Unfixable epistasis more sensitive than fixable epistasis	:	Singh and Dahiya (1984), Pawar *et al.* (1986), Singh *et al.* (1986), Singh *et al.* (1989), Singh *et al.* (1990) and Singh *et al.* (1995).
Fixable and unfixable types of epistasis equally sensitive	:	Singh *et al.* (1980).

Consequently, Koumber (2006), Hendawy (2008) and Koumber, (2011) reporteded that selection procedure based on accumulation of additive effect would be successful for producing superior inbreds which could be utilized in hybrid breading to exploit non-additive effective.

Job of plant breeder is very difficult in choosing selection criteria under biotic and abiotic stress environments for combining high yield with resistance to adverse biotic and abiotic factors. The information about the relative magnitudes of genetic parameters over a range of environments may help in making the plant breeding programme scientifically more sound. However, while dealing with a breeding for dry areas, one must try to screen his material at the earliest segregating stage in the target environment to avoid the risk of losing highly drought resistant genotypes by selecting for one or more cycles in a favourable environment.

Conclusion

On the basis of the results discussed above regarding the sensitivity of variance components to environmental differences in wheat a few generalizations can easily be made: (1) Additive genetic component and unfixable epistasis respond more to the change in environment than the dominance component and fixable epistasis; (2) heterozygotes exhibit higher stability than the corresponding homozygotes; indicating superiority of hybrids. Since the development of hybrid wheat varieties has not so far been successful at commercial scale, the best way to increase the magnitude of dominance variation in this cereal is to increase magnitude of homozygous genomic heterosis (intergenomic heterozygosity) and (3) though the degree of dominance may vary from character to character and from material to material for the same character, it does not vary very much between the environments.

It is concluded that epistasis is an unignorable factor in the inheritance of agronomic traits. therefore, this componenet should not be ignored while formulating breeding programmes to improve wheat populations for economic traits. If the presence of epistasis is ignored in wheat population, one would not lose information about epistasis but also the estimates of additive and dominance components would be biased to an unknown extent and thus the result could be misleading. In almost all studies, epistasis played a significant role in the control of grain yield per plant. Hence, delayed selection will be effective. The information about the relative magnitudes of genetic parameters over a range of environments may help in making the plant breeding programme scientifically more sound.

REFERENCES

Abinasa M, A Ayana and G Bultosa. 2011. Genetic Variability, Heritability and Trait Associations in Durum Wheat (Triticum Turgidum L. var. durum) Genotypes. *African Journal of Agricultural Research* 6(17): 3972-3979.

Arya VD. Pawar IS and Lamba RAS (2005). Genetic Variability, Correlation and Path Analysis for Yield and Quality Traits of Bread Wheat. *Haryana Agricultural Journal of Research* 35: 59-63.

Dhanda, S.S. and Sethi, G.S. 1996. Genetics and Interrelationships of Grain Yield and its Related Traits in Bread Wheat Under Irrigated and Rainfed Conditions. *Wheat Information Service*. 83: 19-27.

Dhiman, K.C., Tabhi Dawa and Dawa, T. 1999. Genetic Architecture of Yield Traits in Bread Wheat. *Crop Improv*. 26: 193-197.

Dhindsa, G.S. and Bains, K.S. 1986. Genotype x Environment Interaction for Some Morpho-physiological Characters in Triple Test Cross Progenies of Wheat. *Crop Improv*. 13: 168-171.

Din Riaz-ud. Subhani-G-M, Naeem-Ahmad, Makhdoom-Hussain and Aziz-ur-Rehman (2010). Effect of Temperature on Development and Grain Formation in Spring Wheat. *Pakistan Journal of Botany* 42(2): 899-906.

DWR Vision (2030). Published by Project Director, DWR, Karnal.

Eissa, M.M. (1994). Triple Test Cross Analysis in Bread Wheat (*Triticum aestivum* L.) *Zagazig J.Agric.Res*. 21: 1-10.

Falconer, D.S. 1952. The Problem of Environment and Selection. *Amer. Net*. 86: 293-298.

Hendawy, H.I. (2008). Estimation of Additive, Dominance and Detection of Epistasis Using Triple Test Cross and Line Tester Analysis in Bread Wheat. *Minufiya J. Agric. Res*., 33(4): 997-1010.

Kant S, RAS Lamba, IS Panwar and RK Arya 2011.Variability and Inter-relationship Among Yield and Quality Parameters in Bread Wheat *J. Wheat Res*. 3(2): 50-55.

Koumber, R.M. (2006). Detection of Epistasis and Estimation of Additive and Dominance Components of Genetic Variation Using Triple Test Cross Analysis in Breadwheat. *Egypt J. of Appl. Sci.*, 21 (10 B): 448- 461.

Koumber, R.M.A. 2011: Estimation of Genetic Variability and Divergence Through Triple Test Analysis in Bread Wheat. *J. Agric. Res. Kafer El-Sheikh Univ.*, 37(4): 615-628.

Kumar Y, SK Sethi and RAS Lamba 2014 Genetic Analysis for Economic Traits in Wheat (Triticum aestivum L.) under Salt Affected Soil. *J. Wheat Res.* 6(1): 76-81.

Mehta, A.K. and Dhagat, N.K. 1992. Genetic Divergence in Wheat. *Advances Pl. Sci.* 5: 369-378.

Mohsin, T., Khan, N and Farzana, N 2009 Heritability, Phenotypic Correlation and Path Coefficient Studies for Some Agronomic Character in Synthetic Elite Lines of Wheat. *Journal of Food Agriculture and Environment* 7: 278-282.

Nagireddy AV and Jyothula DPB (2009). Heritability and Interrelationship of Yield and Certain Agronomic Traits in Wheat. *Research on Crops* 10(1): 124-127.

Panse V.G. 1957. Genetics of Quantitative Character in Relation to Plant Breeding. *Indian Journal of Genetics and Plant Breeding* 17: 318-328.

Pawar, I.S., Yunus, M. and Singh, V.P. 1996. Study of Interaction of Additive, Dominance and Epistatic Gene Effects with Environment in Wheat. *Haryana agric. Univ. J. Res.* 26: 17-21.

Pawar, I.S., Yunus, M., Singh, S. and Singh, V.P. 1994. Detection of Additive, Dominance and Epistatic Variation in Wheat Using Triple Test Cross Method. *Indian J. Genet.* 54: 275-280.

Redhu, A.S., Chowdhury, R.K. and Singh, R.P. 1990. Genetic Analysis for Yield and Yield Components of Bread Wheat Grown Under Normal visa-v-vis Saline Environment. *Crop Res.* 3: 291-293.

Richards, R.A. 1983. Should Selection for Yield in Saline Regions be Made on Saline or Non Saline Soils? *Euphytica* 32: 431-438.

Sarmah, P., Pawar, I.S., Yunus, M. and Sharma, S.C. 1997. Genotype x Environment Interaction Analysis of Some Triple Test Cross Families in Bread Wheat. *Haryana agric. University J. Res.* 27: 117-120.

Shoran Jag (1995). Estimation of Variability Parameters and Path Coefficients for Certain Metric Traits in Winter Wheat (Triticum aestivum L. em. Thell.). *Indian Journal of Genetics Plant Breeding* 55(4): 399-405.

Singh G, B S Tyagi, M K Singh, D Bind, M S Saharan, A Verma and I Sharma. 2012. Genetic Analysis for Economic Traits in Elite Indigenous and Exotic Lines of Bread Wheat (Triticum aestivum L.) Under Timely Sown High Fertility Conditions. *Journal of Wheat Research* 4(2): 45-48.

Singh, I, Pawar, I.S. and Singh S. 1989. Detection of Genotype x Environment Interaction in Spring Wheat Through Triple Test Cross Analysis. *Crop Improv.* 16: 34-37.

Singh, I, Pawar, I.S. and Singh S. 1995. A Study of Components of Genetic Variation and Genotype x Environment Interaction in Selfed Wheat Triple Test Cross Families. *Indian J. Genet.* 55: 324-329.

Singh, I. and Pawar, I.S. 2000. Effect of Epistasis on the Estimates of Additive and Dominance Components and Their Interactions with Environment in Bread Wheat. *Natnl. J. Pl. Improv.* 2: 93-94.

Singh, I. Paroda, R.S. and Singh S. 1986. Genotype x Environment Interaction Analysis of TTC Progenies for Some Metric Traits in Wheat. *Crop Improv.* 13: 117-121.

Singh, I., Paroda, R.S. and Singh, S. 1987. Estimation of Genetic Parameters for Some Quantitative Traits in Spring Wheat, *Haryana agric. Univ. J. Res.* 17: 364-369.

Singh, I., Paroda, R.S. and. Singh, S. 1985. Estimation of Additive and Dominance Components Through Triple Test Cross in Wheat. *J. agric. Sc Camb.* 105: 123-28.

Singh, I., Pawar I S and Singh S 1988. Detection of Additive, Dominance and Epistatic Components of Genetic Variation for some Metric Traits in Wheat. *Genet Agr.* 42: 371-378.

Singh, K.N. and Rana, R.S. 1987 Influence of Soil Alkalimity and Salimity on Estimates of Hetoersis and Gene Effects Governing Some Quantitative Trait in Bread Wheat. *Indian J. Genet*. 47: 76-78.

Singh, R., Rana, R.S. and Chaudhary, M.S. 1991. Nature of Gene Effects in the Inheritance of Grain Yield and its Components Inbread Wheat Under Normal and Sodic Soils. Golden Jubilee Symp on Genetic Research and Education: Current Trends and Next Fifty Years. Feb. 12-15, 1991, Indian Soc. Genet. & P Br., Abst. 216-17.

Singh, R.P., Kumar, K. and Singh, K.P. 1991. Golden Jubliee Symp. Indian Soc. Genet. & Pl. Br. Abst. 209-210.

Singh, S. 1980. Detection of Components of Genetic Variation and Genotype x Environment Interaction in Spring Wheat. *J. agric. Sci. Camb.* 95: 67-72.

Singh, S. 1990. Bias Caused by Epistasis in the Estimation of Additive and Dominance Components and Their Interaction with Environment in Wheat. *Indian J. Genet.* 50: 157-160.

Singh, S. and Dahiya, M.S. 1984. Dection and Estimation of Components of Genetic Variation and Genotype x Environment Interaction in Three Wheat Crosses. *J. agric. Sci. Camb.* 103: 543-547.

Singh, S., Kumar, S., Pawar, I.S. and Singh, I. 1992. Detection and Estimation of Additive and Dominance Components and Their Interaction with Sowing Data in Presence and Absence of Epistasis in Wheat. *Haryana agric. Univ. J. Res.* 22: 165-169.

Singh, S., Kumar, S., Pawar, I.S. and Singh, I. 1990. Interaction of Gene Effects with Environment in Wheat. *Haryana agric. Univ. J. Res.* 20: 201-205.

Singh, S. and Pawar, I.S. 2006. Trends in Wheat Breeding. CBS Publishers and Distributors, New Delhi.

Srivastava, J.P. 1987. "Proc. Internat Workshop on Drought Tolerance in Winter Cereals, Capri (Italy). J.P. Srivastava *et al* (Eds). John Wiley & Sons: 65-78.

Verma PN, BN Singh and RK Yadav. 2013. Genetic Variability and Divergence Analysis of Yield and its Contributing Traits Under Sodic Soil Condition in Wheat (*T. aestivum* L.). *International Journal of Agricultural Science* 3(2):395-399.

Pages: 120-144

SEED TREATMENT, PLANT HEALTH AND AGRO-TECHNOLOGY

Edited by: Dr. Avnish Chauhan and Dr. Pawan Kumar 'Bharti'

ISBN: 978-93-5056-810-1

Edition: 2016

Published by: Discovery Publishing House Pvt. Ltd., New Delhi (India)

7

Cisgenic Breeding Approach for Crop Plants

R.R. Dhutmal[1], S.R. Maloo[2] and A.W. More[3]

Introduction

Breeding of crops, is becoming complicated. As number of requirements for new varieties increasing day by day. In general wild species are utilized as a source of new traits through introgression breeding. In allopolyploid crops e.g. wheat, even more complicated, induced translocation breeding has to be applied (Friebe *et al.* 1996). Introgression breeding is relatively easy in self-pollinating crops such as tomato, barley and rice, but is more complicated in allopolyploid wheat. Interspecific hybridization followed by back cross breeding is most commonly adopted breeding method for transfer of new traits from wild species into an existing variety in sexually propagating crops. But the main drawback in such an approach is linkage drag of unwanted gene along with the gene of interest. However in case of self-incompatible, vegetatively propagated crops such as potato and apple, there is an additional bottleneck, i.e. the heterozygous nature of varieties (Jacobsen and Schouten 2007). To overcome such problems associated with classical breeding, genetic transformation has become a promising tool for improvement of a variety of crop species. Transgenic is commonly adopted genetic transformation system. But food, feed and environmental safely are the issues which limits its

1 Ph.D Scholar (PBG), Rajasthan Collage of Agriculture, MPUAT, Udaipur. Pin: 313 001. (Rajasthan) (India).

2 Professor and Dean, Rajasthan Collage of Agriculture, MPUAT, Udaipur, 313 001 (Rajasthan)

3 Asstt. Breeder, Sorghum Research Station, Vasantrao Naik, Marathwada Krishi Vidyapeeth, Parbhani. Pin - 431 401 (M.S.) (India).

applicability. Schouten, *et al.* (2006) introduced the term cisgenesis. A cisgenic plant is a crop plant that has been genetically modiûed with one or more genes (containing introns and ûanking regions such as native promoter and terminator regions in a sense orientation) isolated from a crossable donor plant'. Cisgenic plants contain only genes from within the same species or from sexually compatible species as used in traditional breeding.

Conventional Plant Breeding Approaches

The following conventional breeding techniques are considered most relevant for the comparison with cisgenic plants as in both techniques, the incorporated genes keep their native promoters intact (Fig. 7.1). The different steps in introgression breeding, induced translocation breeding and cisgenesis are illustrated in Table 7.1.

(i) Sexual crosses within species

Crossing closely related parental line to produce viable progeny is the most commonly used breeding method. Promising progenies are then selected on the basis of objectives set by the breeder. Almost homozygous breeding lines with desired characteristics are developed by backcrossing to the original parents and self fertilization Once the homozygous lines are developed they are crossed to combine the desired traits in the F1 seed.

(ii) Bridge crosses

Bridge crosses allows the transfer of new trait which is present in cross compatible spacies. When F1 progeny is sterile, in such situation a third species which is compatible with both the species is used to bridge the crossing barrier is known as bridge cross (Van der Wiel *et al.* 2010). Suppose parent A and B are cross compatible then third parent C which can cross with both A and B is used to transfer desired trait from A to B. A is first crossed with C then a resulting hybrid is the crossed with B For example genes in *Solanum bulbocastanum conferring* resetance to potato late blight have been transferred to *S. tuberosum* by "double-bridge" crosses between four different *Solanum* species {[*S. acaule* × *S. bulbocastanum*] × *S. phureja*} × *S. tuberosum*. (Hermsen and Ramanna, 1973).

(iii) Wide crosses using embryo rescue

Interspecific incompatibility in plants can occur for many reasons, usually leading to embryo abortion (Reed, 2005). Crossing between distantly related spacies (wide hybridization) results in F_1 sterility due to embryo abortion. To overcome this barrier embryo rescue technique involving in vitro culture techniques are used to assist in the development of plant embryos to become viable plants (Cisneros and Tel-Zur, 2010). Embyo rescue plays an important role in the development of viable interspacific and intergeneric F_1s. Immature abortive embryos are grown on culture medium applying tissue culture techniques facilitating survival. Embryo culture is widely used embryo rescue technique used to develop fertile interspecific and intergeneric crosses (Miyajima, 2006).

(iv) Translocation breeding

When two species are distantly related such as wild relative and cultivated spacies, nomal chromosome pairing and genetic recombination during sexual reproduction is not observed. Which hinders transfer the desired gene(s) from the chromosome of wild to cultivated plant. When the wild relative's chromosome is distantly related to its equivalent in the cultivated species, ordinary cannot be relied upon to transfer the desired gene(s) from the chromosome of wild to cultivated plant. Use of chromosome addition and substitution line i.e. chromosome manipulation techniques can be used to incorporate the desired gene(s), and these are confined to allopolyploids tolerant of chromosome addition and substitution (Chu and Zhang, 1985; Rayburn and Carver, 1988). Physical mutagenic agents such as X-rays and gamma rays, are used to break chromosomes more or less randomly. If a translocated fragment contains the desired gene but no other genes with undesirable effects, and no undesirable position effects the new recombinant chromosome can be incorporated in the genome of the cultivated species. For example the transfer of tobacco mosaic virus resistance from *Nicotiana glutinosa* to *N. tabacum* rust resistances from rye and wild diploidsin wheat (Ko *et al.* 2002; Lewis *et al.* 2005).

(v) Somatic Hybridisation (Protoplast Fusion)

Somatic hybridisation is excluded from the GMO legislation when it involves the fusion of plant cells of organisms which can exchange genetic material through conventional breeding methods. Such *in vitro* cell fusion techniques can increase the efficiency of generation of hybrids that can be developed by sexual crossing only with difficulty (Liu *et al.* 2005). The fusion is induced chemically (e.g. polyethylene glycol) or electrically. The technique has been applied to many species, e.g. carrot, tobacco, rapeseed and potato. In potato a polyploid fusion product between tetraploid *S. tuberosum* and wild diploid *S. brevidens* has been developed to obtain virus resistance. Somatic hybridisation can be used to combine specific nuclear and organellar (plastid and mitochondrial) genomes in an efficient manner, avoiding lengthy backcrossing.

(vi) Somaclonal variation

The term describes the variation seen in plants that have been produced by plant tissue culture. This variation is particularly common in plants regenerated via a callus phase. Chromosomal rearrangements are an important source of this variation. Somaclonal variation has been observed in many plant species and is an alternative way to create variants and expand the germplasm pool (Evans, 1989; Larkin and Scowcroft, 1981).

Table 7.1: The Different Steps in Introgression Breeding, Induced Translocation Breeding and Cisgenesis

Introgression Breeding	Induced Translocation	Cisgenesis Breeding
Interscacific crossing with wild source containing the desired gene	Interspacific crossing with wild source	Isolation of the desired gene from wild source
Backcross procedure and transformation removal of disturbing linkage drag	Back cross procedure resulting in monosomic addition line	Back bone free transformation and selection for cisgegene expression
Crossess with breeding parent for variety selection	Irradiation and selection for useful translocations in offsrings	Selection of cisgenics variety without linkage drag
Resistant variety with linkage drag	Crossess with induced translocation line for variety selection	–
–	Resistant variety with linkage drag	–

New Plant Breeding Techniques

In the past two decades, applications of biotech and molecular biology in plants have emerged, with the potential to further enlarge the plant breeder's toolbox.

Table 7.2: Terminology of Different New Breeding Technologies

Sl. No.	Technology	Gene or Region to Transfer	Introgressed Region/ Linkage Drag
	Xenogenesis	Foreign gene including artificial	Highly defined/no linkage
1.	Transgenesis	Across spacies boundaries	Highly defined/no linkage
2.	Cisgenesis	Within species of related or/ breeders pool (no further rearrangement)	Highly defined/no linkage
3.	Intragenesis	Different parts from the genome of same or s-related organisms*	Highly defined/no linkage
4.	Transplatomics	Xeno or transgenesis of plastid genome	Highly defined/no linkage
5.	Cisplantomics	Within specie plastid genome	Highly defined/no linkage
6.	MASPB	Region between markers from sexually compatible	Low to medium linkage/ yes linkage
7.	Classical PB i.e., mutant allele transformed to another cultivars or breeders gene pool	Region associated to traits from sexually compatible	Low resolution/ yes linkage

A brief description of important novel technologies is given describing their area of application and importance in crop improvement (Maria Lusser, *et al.*, 2012)

1. ZFN technology

ZFNs are synthetic restriction endonucleases, custom designed to cut DNA at specific sequences. They consist of a zinc-finger domain that recognizes specific DNA sequences and a nuclease domain. Genes encoding the ZFNs are delivered to plant cells in an expression plasmid. Depending on the method, the expression plasmid may additionally contain a short template sequence or a stretch of DNA to be inserted. The ZFNs create a double-strand break (DSB) at a specific site in the DNA. The double-strand break stimulates the cell's repair mechanism, the process of homologous recombination and the insertion of DNA.

2. Oligonucleotide directed mutagenesis (ODM)

Also known as targeted gene repair, oligonucleotide-directed gene targeting, genoplasty and chimeraplasty. Oligonucleotides are chemically synthesized to share homology with a target sequence, with the exception of a few nucleotides. Oligonucleotides induce site-specific mutation at the target sequence. The genetic changes include the introduction of a new mutation (replacement of one or a few base pairs), the reversal of an existing mutation or the induction of short deletions.

3. Cisgenesis and intragenesis

Cisgenic and intragenic plants are produced by the same transformation techniques as transgenic plants, but the DNA transferred belongs to the same species of the transformed plant, or to a cross-compatible species. In cisgenesis, the DNA sequence includes the gene of interest flanked by its own promoter and terminator. In intragenesis, the gene of interest can be combined with regulatory elements from the species itself or from a cross-compatible species. Both approaches aim to confer a new property to the modified plant. By definition only cisgenics could achieve results also possible by traditional breeding methods, whereas intragenesis offers more options for modifying gene expression and trait development. Intragenesis can also include the use of silencing approaches, for example, RNA interference, by introducing inverted DNA repeats.

4. RNA-dependent DNA methylation (RdDM)

RdDM induces transcriptional gene silencing by methylation of promoter sequences. Genes encoding RNAs homologous to promoter regions are delivered to the plant cells. These genes give rise to the formation of small double-stranded RNAs that induce methylation and silencing of the homologous sequences. RdDM allows breeders to produce plants that do not contain foreign DNA sequences and in which no changes or mutations are made in the nucleotide sequence but in which gene expression is modified epigenetically.

5. Grafting

A chimeric plant is produced by grafting a nongenetically modified scion on a genetically modified rootstock. Consequently, the fruits of the plant do not contain the inserted DNA sequence. The rootstock can be modified to improve its rooting capacity or resistance to soil-borne diseases, resulting in a substantial increase in the yield of harvestable components. The rootstock can also be modified for obtaining gene silencing through the technique of RNA interference. In grafted plants, the small RNAs can also move through the graft so that the silencing signal can affect gene expression in the scion.

6. Reverse breeding

Homozygous parental lines of a selected heterozygous plant are reproduced. The genes involved in the meiotic recombination process are silenced through transgenesis. Consequently, nonrecombined haploid lines are obtained from the heterozygous plant and their chromosomes are doubled through the double-haploid technique. The doubled haploids obtained are screened to find a pair that, would reconstitute the original heterozygous plants. Only nontransgenic plants are selected, thus the offspring of the selected parental lines would not carry any additional genomic change.

7. Agro-infiltration

Three types of agro-infiltration can be distinguished:

'Sensu stricto,' nongermline tissues, mostly leaves, are infiltrated with a liquid suspension of Agrobacterium carrying a gene of interest. The gene is locally expressed at a high level, without being integrated into the plant genome; Agro-infection, nongermline tissues, typically leaves, are infiltrated with a full-length virus vector containing a gene of interest. Through the virus vector, the expression of the gene of interest is spread in the entire plant.

The floral dip technique involves immersion of germline tissues, typically flowers, into a suspension of Agrobacterium carrying a gene of interest so as to obtain stable transformation. Transformed embryos are then selected at the germination state.

Agro-infiltration can be used to screen for plants with valuable phenotypes that can then be used in breeding programmes, for instance, with specific genes from pathogens to evaluate plant resistance. The technique has also been developed as a production platform for high-value recombinant proteins. However, the technique is mostly used in a research context, for example, to study plant-pathogen interaction in living tissues (leaves) or to test the functionality of regulatory elements in gene constructs.

Cisgenesis, Intragenesis and Transgenesis

Cisgenesis and intragenesis make use of the same transformation techniques as transgenesis. Commonly used methods will result in random integration of the gene in the plant genome although in the future site-directed integration might become more widely available.

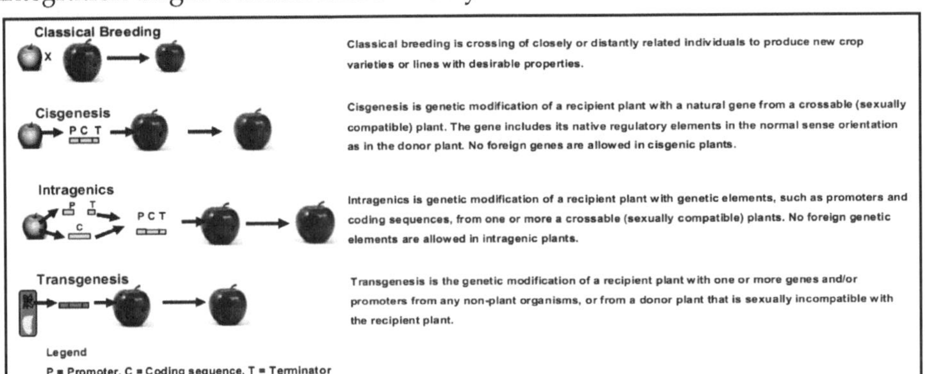

Fig. 7.1: **Different Breeding Methods and Their Characteristics (Joshi, *et al.* 2009)**

(i) Cisgenesis

Main drawback associated with conventional breeding is linkage drag which leads to the development of product with some undesirable traits linked with gene of interest or may take long period to develop desired product. Cisgeneic is a method of genetic modification in which desired alleles/genes (without any change to the DNA sequence of original gene i.e. promoters, introns, coding sequences and terminator sequences) found in crossable species are incorporated in host plant. This technique is most useful for fruit tree species with long life cycle or for species with complex genetics (polyploidy, vegetative propagated), e.g. potato or banana.

(ii) Intragenesis

Like cisgenic plants, intragenic plants contain genetic elements from the breeders' gene pool. Basic difference between cisgenics and intragenics is that source of promoters, coding sequences and terminator sequences may have different origin but only from breeders gene pool. Gene is no more original gene as in case of cisgenics. Intragenesis therefore offers considerably more options for modifying gene expression and for trait development. Intragenesis can also include hairpin gene silencing approaches (Rommens *et al.* 2007).

(iii) Transgenesis

In this case transgene originating from outside the breeders' gene pool is incorporated into the plant. Recombinant nucleic acid techniques are used to form new combinations of genetic material. Transgenic plants can contain genetic elements, e.g. coding and regulatory sequences, from any organism (eukaryotic, prokaryotic) as well as novel synthetic sequences

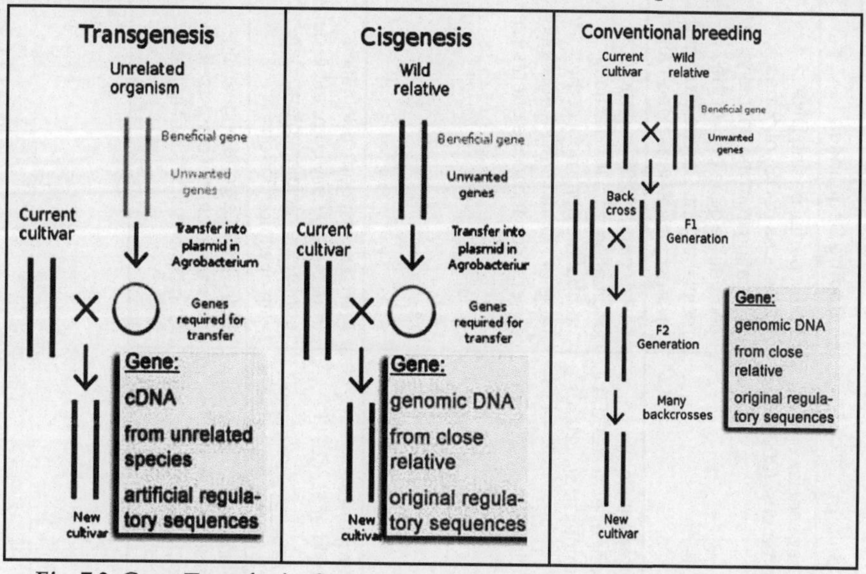

Fig. 7.2: **Gene Transfer in Conventional, Transgenic and Cisgenic Method**

Table 7.3: Changing Definitions of Cis/Transgenics

Concept	Coding Sequences	Promotor/Terminator/Spacer	Borders	Vector-Backbone
Intragenesis Rommens, (2004)	Full or partial coding DNA sequences (CDS) of genes originating from the sexually compatible gene pool of the recipient plant. Can be arranged in sense or antisense orientation	Promoter, spacer and terminator originating from sexually compatible gene pool of the recipient plant	P-DNA	Vector-backbone of bacterial origin
Intragenesis Conner *et al.*, (2007); Conner *et al.*, (2010)	Full or partial CDS of genes originating from the sexually compatible gene pool of the recipient plant. Can be arranged in sense or antisense orientation	Promoter, spacer and terminator originating from sexually compatible gene pool of the recipient plant	P-DNA	Construction of backbone using DNA fragments from the sexually compatible DNA pool of the recipient plant, arranged to fulfil the requirements of a vector-backbone. Alternatively, the backbone can be eliminated before P-DNA transfer to the plant cell through the use of DNA mini-cycles.
Intragenesis Joshi *et al.*, (2011)	Full CDS of a gene originating from the sexually compatible gene pool of the recipient plant. Can be with or without introns	Promoter and terminator originating from sexually compatible gene pool of the recipient plant	T-DNAa	Vector-backbone of bacterial origin
Cisgenesis (first definition) Jochemsen and Schouten, (2000)	Full CDS of a gene originating from the recipient plant itself. Can be with or without introns	Promoter and terminator originating from the recipient plant itself	T-DNAa	Vector-backbone of bacterial origin

(Table Contd...)

Concept	Coding Sequences	Promotor/Terminator/Spacer	Borders	Vector-Backbone
Cisgenesis (present definition) Schouten *et al.*, (2006)	Full CDS including introns of a gene originating from the sexually compatible gene pool of the recipient plant	Coding regions linked to gene's own promoter and terminator	T-DNAa	Vector-backbone of bacterial origin
Cisgenics Bajaj *et al.*, (2008)	Full CDS of a gene originating from the sexually compatible gene pool of the recipient plant. Can be with or without introns	Promoter and terminator originating from sexually compatible gene pool of the recipient plant	P-DNA	Vector-backbone of bacterial origin

Table 7.4: Major Characteristics of Different GM Concepts

Cisgene	Contigeous gene from the plant itself or from any croosable spacies is used Gene with all native comonants including promoter, introns, and terminator regions.Use of *Agrobacterum* sequences for gene transfer (T-DNA)Selection markers are removed.
Intragene	Coding sequences, regulatory sequences and marker gene obtained from same or any crossable spaciesGene elements may be rearrangedUse of plant-derived sequences for gene transfer (P-DNA) via *Agrobacterium*Selection markers are removed from transformed plants
Transgene	Gene is obtained from outside of the sexually incompatible groupIt could be obtained from any organismSelection marker gene may originate from any living organism

Method for the development of cisgenic plant (Krens *et al.* 2004)

The steps required for the production of marker-free GM plants are

8. Inoculation of explants with *Agrobacterium* carrying the appropriate vectors as binary plasmids, according to established protocols.
9. Selection of transgenic material by growth on antibiotic-containing media, according to existing protocols. (Positive selection).
10. Induction of recombinase activity by applying a DEX treatment.
11. Selection for marker-free plantlets by applying regeneration protocols in the presence of FC as a negative selectable agent for non-successful recombination events. (Negative selection).
12. A thorough molecular characterization of the end products should confirm the transgenic and marker-free nature of the plants produced.

Transformation with *Agrobacterium*

Cisgenic are prepared through the process of genetic modification. *Agrobacterium*-mediated transformation is the preferred method for gene transfer. Host plant cells are inoculated with the bacterium which facilitates the introduction of genes into the plant cell genome, the transformed cells are multiplied and regenerated into entire plants with their newly acquired traits. In cisgenesis any genes derived from other, sexually non-compatible organisms are no permitted, in the final product. However, selectable marker genes are usually added for esy identification of transformed cells (Komari *et al.* 2007). For example genes conferring resistance to antibiotics such as kanamycin or hygromycin, or tolerance to herbicides, e.g. phosphinothricin or glyphosate are commonly used selectable markers. Kanamycin resistance has been most frequently used. This selection gene has a bacterial origin and cannot be left behind in cisgenic plants. These genes must be removed from transformed plants.

Methods to Generate Marker Free Transformed Plants

Krens *et al.* (2004) discussed different methods to develop marker free transformed plants.

Clean Vector Technology

Clean vector technology aims to produce GM plants with only the gene-of-interest as newly introduced gene function without any superfluous gene sequences. Primarily, the goal is to avoid the use or the continued presence of antibiotic resistance genes as selectable markers. Four approaches to achieve this can be followed.

(i) No selectable marker

In this case, selectable marker gene i.e. resistance to antibiotics or tolerance to herbicides is not used to identify transformed or non-transformed cells. After a successful inoculation with *Agrobacterium* and regeneration on suitable culture media, the number of plants are developed, majority of which are non-transgenic. However depending upon the gene transfer frequencies, some plantlets will be transgenic which are identified by a PCR screening on DNA of several sets of pooled plants. A prerequisite is regeneration/trans-protocol of high efficiency. This method is limited to model species and a low number of specific crop cultivars, e.g. in potato.

(ii) Cotransformation

This method relies on segregation which plays a vital role in the physical separation of gene of interest from selectable or gene of diverse origin. Different T-DNA, one carrying gene of interest and other carrying selectable marker genes which may be on the same or on separate binary vector(s) are used. The separate binary vectors can be present in the same or in separate *Agrobacterium* strains. There are chances that these separate T-DNAs should become integrated in two genetically unlinked loci in the host plant genome. The next step is selection for the GM plants are the selected by growth on antibiotic or herbicide-containing media. As a rule only transformed plant survive, these plants are raised. Sexual crossing between these transformed, fully raised plants facilitates subsequent recombination and segregation. This should result in GM plants equipped only with the gene-of-interest. A prerequisite here is that the crop can be sexually propagated without losing too many traits or cultivar identity and this within a reasonable time frame. This approach can be practiced in vegetatively propagated crops or crops with a very long sexual cycle, such as tulip or apple. In case of apple, two T-DNAs are co-transferred, one carrying a marker gene and the other containing the gene-of-interest. There are chances of integration of T-DNA with the gene-of-interest while the other T-DNA with the selection gene will only be transiently expressed and active without integration into nuclear or plastid DNA (Rommens *et al.* 2004).

(iii) Non-antibiotic-based selection

Herbicide tolerance is the most well-known example. However, also in this case there might be aspects linked to it that can be considered undesirable by certain consumer groups. An alternative system that was developed recently is based on metabolic processes, more particularly, on carbohydrate metabolism. The phospho-mannose isomerase (PMI) system is based on the fact that plant cells in tissue culture cannot metabolize mannose and therefore cannot grow on medium with this compound as a sole source of carbon. By providing GM cells with a gene converting mannose into fructose this barrier is overcome and GM plantlets can be obtained. As a consequence, however, they then still carry this bacterium-derived selectable marker gene at a stage where it is actually no longer needed, i.e. in crop cultivation.

(iv) Transformation with a foreign selection gene and elimination of the selection gene

This approach makes use of site-specific recombination systems for removal of the selection gene after the transformation step (Dale and Ow 1991). Recombinase enzyme working on two specific recombination sites is used. T-DNA carrying a selectable marker gene, placed between two recognition sequences specific for a recombinase, whose activity can be controlled is used for transformation. After the successful T-DNA integration regenerants are selected, follows the recombinase is activated and it excises the selectable marker gene.

The gene construct which has to be removed is placed between the recombination sites ensures that in the final GM plant product only the gene of interest remains. Control over the recombinase activity is the prime need of this method. This can be achieved by regulating or inducing expression of the recombinase gene or by inducing recombinase enzyme activity. Leakiness of the recombinase regulation, effectiveness of the induction process and recovery of 100% homogeneous recombined GM plants are the problems associated with this technique. A negative selection marker system is adopted to recognize non-recombined cells or plantlets so that plantlets carrying the negative selection gene will die or show an aberrant phenotype. Ebinuma *et al.* (1997) used the *ipt* gene as a phenotypical negative selection marker, the presence of which results in an aberrant phenotype. Another system i.e., R/Rs system (Schaart *et al.* 2004) uses ligand-binding domain (LBD) combined with R (recombinase, which excise the DNA segment lies between two recognition sites). LBD, at first, inhibit the activity of R so that excision does not take place. The recombinase activity can be induced by the addition of dexamethasone (DEX).

At Plant Research International (PRI) a synthetic copy of the recombinase (R) gene of *Zygosaccharomyces rouxii*, developed and is fused to the ligand-binding domain (LBD) of a corticosteroid receptor. The R gene is continuously expressed, but the protein is inactive due to the translational fusion to LBD. Dexamethasone DEX is added to establish the activity. Further dual positive-negative selectable marker consisting of a fusion between the *nptII* gene (positive) and the *codA* gene (negative) are also used. *ntpII* gene confers resistant against antibiotic kanamycin. The cells carrying ntpII gene can to grow on medium supplemented with e.g. the antibiotic kanamycin, i.e. positive selection. The other selection gene i.e. cytosine deaminase *codA* converts nontoxic fluorocytosine (FC) into toxic fluorouracil (FU). Hence cells carrying this coda gene will die on medium supplemented with FC, i.e. negative selection. All of these elements are placed between the two Rs recombination sites. The model construct has been successfully applied in potato, strawberry and apple (Schaart *et al.* 2004).

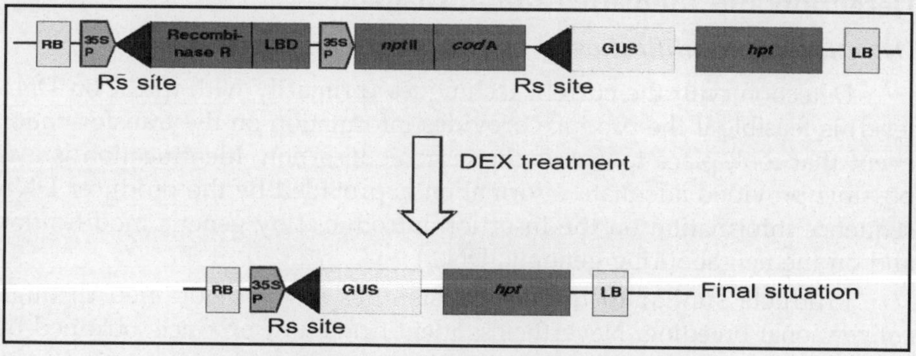

Fig. 7.3: **A Model Vector, pRCNG (Krens *et al.* 2004))**

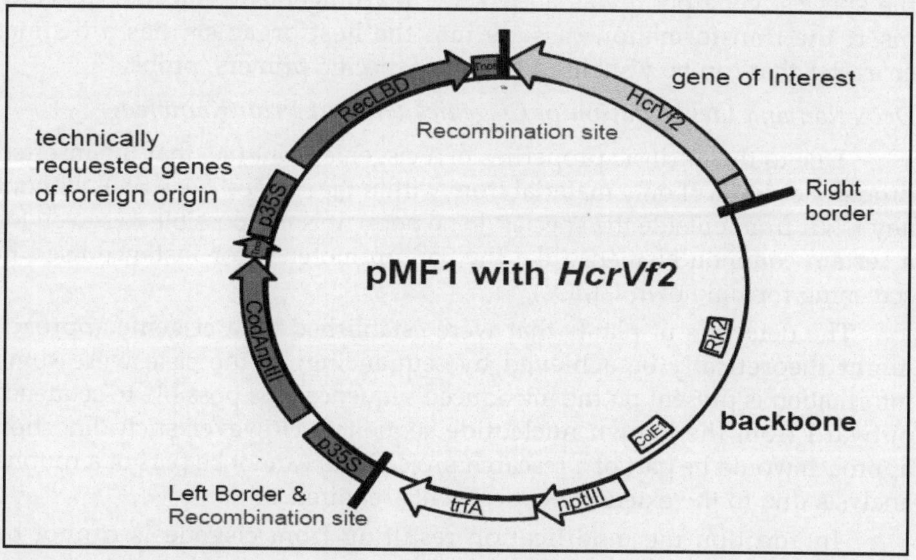

Fig. 7.4: **pMF1 Vector Containing HcrVf2 Apple Scab Resistant Gene from Apple cv. Florina (Joshi *et al.* 2008)**

T-DNA borders or plant-derived T-DNA borders (P-DNA borders)

When using *Agrobacterium*-mediated transformation, intragenic and Cisgenics plants should as defined by Rommens (2004), Conner *et al.* (2007) and Bajaj *et al.* (2008) be generated with border sequences isolated from the sexually compatible gene pool (Table 7.1). Suitable plant transfer DNAs (P-DNAs) resembling T-DNA borders have been identified in several species (Rommens *et al.*, 2005). In contrast, cisgenic and intragenic plants as defined by Schouten *et al.* (2006a), Jochemsen and Schouten (2000) and Joshi *et al.* (2011) have no specific requirements for P-DNAs and T-DNA borders from *Agrobacterium tumefaciens* can be used.

Detection and Identification of Cisgenics

Detection and Identification of Cisgenics with Prior Knowledge

Detection with the current techniques (primarily with qPCR on DNA level) is feasible if the produce provides information on the transformation event that took place to enable the cisgenic insertion. Identification is also possible provided adequate information is provided by the producer DNA sequence information on the insertion introduced by genetic modification and on the neighbouring genomic DNA).

Products similar to the cisgenesis ones may be obtained through conventional breeding. Nevertheless identification of products obtained by cisgenesis is still possible due to the unique event-specific transitio in nucleotide sequence: although no novel material (i.e. present only outside the species' gene pool) was added, the rearrangement that took place to insert the transformation cassette into the host organism has a distinct character that can be visualised by event-specific primers/probe.

Detection and Identification of Cisgenics without Prior Knowledge

Due to the intrinsic properties of a cisgenic plant (i.e. that the inserted property consists of only material from within the species' gene pool without any DNA from outside the species' gene pool), it is not possible to screen for a certain common element (like the 35S promoter is for instance used in screening for unknown GMOs).

The detection of plants that were established by a cisgenic approach might theoretically be achieved by sequencing: in the case were some information is present on the introduced sequence, it is possible to sequence outward from the known nucleotide sequence. However such detection approach would be part of a research project, and cannot be part of a routine analysis due to the extensive experiments required.

In addition the modification resulting from cisgenesis cannot be identified as such without prior knowledge from the producer. A genome analysis by means of transcriptome sequencing or even whole genome sequencing could possibly detect the insert, although the success rate is unknown. The prerequisites are the presence a pure reference material and knowledge on the comparators that can be used as a baseline, although the sequencing process is not easy.

Cisgenic/intragenic plants harbor genes that were derived from within the gene pool of the same species. Cisgenic/intragenic plants can be detected and identified as such when the event is known beforehand i.e. when adequate information about the cisgenesis/intragenesis modification is made available. Event-specific primers can be developed to create a detection and identification method. In the case of unknown alterations, sequencing (genome or transcriptome) could in theory support the detection of plants but the method has not been validated yet for this purpose. Therefore it can be concluded that without prior knowledge, the detection and the identification of cisgenic and intragenic plants is not feasible at this moment.

High-amylopectin Potatoes

The granule bound starch synthase gene (*GBSS*) is responsible for the synthesis of amylose in potato. This gene was silenced by a GBSS-silencing construct composed of only potato *GBSS* sequences (de Vetten *et al.*, 2003). The construct was controlled by the promoter of the *GBSS*-potato gene but terminated by the nopaline synthase gene terminator (*nos*) isolated from *Agrobacterium tumefaciens*. The high-amylopectin potato can therefore not be considered fully intragenic due to the presence of the *nos*-terminator.

Potatoes with Improved Processing Qualities

Intragenic approaches have been applied for the silencing of unwanted genes causing enzymatic browning (Rommens *et al.*, 2004). Enzymatic browning of potatoes is caused by polyphenol oxidases (PPO's) that leak from damaged plastids. A *Ppo* gene predominantly expressed in mature tubers was silenced with a silencing construct consisting exclusively of potato DNA and controlled by the *GBSS* promoter and the *Ubi-3* terminator, both isolated from potato. The resulting intragenic potatoes showed reduced browning and increased black spot bruise tolerance in the tubers.Another intragenic potato lines were developed by Rommens *et al.* (2006) using silencing construct containing fragments of the *Ppo*, the *R1* and the *PhL* genes in sense and antisense orientation. The resulting tubers with low levels of glucose and fructose and a significant decrease (30%) in acrylamide level.

Disease Resistance Approaches

Modification of disease resistance through both intragenic and cisgenic approaches has been attempted in potato, apple, strawberry and grapevine. The resistance has been obtained either through transfer of resistance genes from related wild species or through overexpression of already existing resistance genes present within the crop itself.

Applications of Cis/Intragenics

Potato, apple, strawberry and grapevine are some of the crops that are difficult to breed by classical methods, and these were among the first crops in which the intragenic/cisgenic approaches were implemented Some of these are described below.

Table 7.5: Applications of Cis/Intragenics

Sl. No.	Intra/Cis-genesis	Type	Gene	Traits	References
1.	Potato (Intra)	Silencing	*GBSS**	High amylopectin	de Vetten, *et al.* 2003
2.	Potato (Intra)	Silencing	*Ppo*	Preventing black spot bruise	Rommens *et al.* 2004
3.	Potato (Intra)	Silencing	*Ppo, R1, PhL*	Limiting degradation of starch. Limiting acryl- amide formation	Rommens *et al.* 2006
4.	Potato (Intra)	Silencing	*StAs1,StAS2*	Limiting acrylamide formation	Rommens *et al.* 2008
5.	Potato (Intra)	Silencing	*StAs1*	Limiting acrylamide formation	Chawla *et al.* 2012
6.	Potato (Cis)	Genes from related spacies	*R-genes*	Late blight resistance	Haverkort *et al.* 2009
7.	Apple (Cis)	Genes from related spacies	*HcrVf2*	Scab resistance	Vanblaere *et al.* 2011
8.	Strawberry (Intra)	Genes from related spacies	*PGIP*	Gray mould resistance	Schaart (2004)
9.	Grapevine (Cis)	Overexpression	*VVTL-1****	Fungal disease resis-tance	Dhekney *et al.* 2011
10.	Poplar (Cis)	Overexpression	Genes involved in growth**	Different growth types	Han *et al.*2011
11.	Perennial ray grass (Intra)	Overexpression	*Lpvp1****	Drought tolerance	Bajaj *et al.* 2008
12.	Alfalfa (Intra)	Silencing	*Comt*	Reduced levels of lignin	Weeks *et al.* (2008)
13.	Durum wheat(Cis)	Genes from related spacies	*1Dy10*	Improved baking quality	Gadaleta, *et al.* 2008
14.	Barley (Cis)	Overexpression	*HvPAPhy_a*	Improved grain phytase activity	Holme *et al.* 2012

Crops with asterisks are only partially intragenic or cisgenic: * - Contains the nos terminator originating from Agrobacterium. ** - Still contains a selection marker gene. *** - Still contains selection marker genes, promoters and terminators from unrelated species.

Potatoes with Resistance to Late Blight

The most important disease in potato throughout the world is late blight caused by the fungus-like microorganism *Phytophthora infestans*. Various *R*-genes conferring resistance to late blight, recognizing different avirulence genes, are currently identified and isolated from wild potatoes (Zhu *et al.*, 2012a). Two or more *R*-genes conferring resistance have been identified, they are inserted into into potato genome in two stage i.e., first with selection marker genes to quickly assess the resistance and second, using a marker-free transformation method (de Vetten *et al.*, 2003).

Apple with Increased Resistance to Scab

Scab is the most destructive fungal disease in apple (Joshi *et al.*, 2011). The disease is caused by the ascomycete *Venturia inaequalis*. *Vf* locus from the wild apple *Malus floribunda* 821 is the most commonly used resistance in conventional breeding of apple (Szankowski *et al.*, 2009). But transfer through classical procedure is extremely long and is associated with undesirable linkage drag. The *Vf* locus consists of a gene cluster of four paralogues but only one (*HcrVf2*) provides resistance against avirulent isolates of *V. inaequalis* (Joshi *et al.*, 2011). A cisgenic apple with resistance to scab was developed through the transfer of the *HcrVf2* genomic clone having its own promoter and terminator into apple cv Gala (Vanblaere *et al.*, 2011).

Table 7.6: Several Apple Scab Resistance Genes

Sl. No.	Reported Genes	Reported by
1.	*HcrVf* (Homologues of *Cladosporium fulvum* resistance genes of *Vf* region)	Patocchi *et al.*, 1999
2.	*Va*	Hemmat *et al.*, 2003
3.	*Vr2*	Patocchi *et al.*, 1999
4.	*Vbj*	Gygax *et al.*, 2004
5.	*Vb*	Erdin *et al.*, 2006
6.	*Vd3*	Soriano *et al.*, 2009

Strawberry with Increased Resistance to Grey Mould

Grey mould caused by the fungus *Botrytis cinerea*. The fungus breaks down the cell wall using the polygalacturonase (PG) enzyme to enter the cell. Schaart (2004) attemted overexpression of *PGIP*-genes (PG inhibiting proteins, produced by cell as a defence mechanism) having high-affinity binding to fungal enzyme, PG (polygalacturonase, actual cause of disease) in strawberry, controlled by promoter gene from strawberry, *Exp2*, which is active in ripe fruits.

Grapevine with Enhanced Fungal Disease Resistance

Pathogenesis-related (PR) proteins are produce in response to pathogen attack.This VVTL-1 (*Vitis vinifera* thaumatin-like protein) PR protein inhibits spore germination and hyphal growth of disease causing fungus. genomic DNA encoding this protein was isolated along with 35S-CMV promoter, terminator and selection marker (Dhekney *et al.*, 2011). The resulting transformants showed delay in powdery mildew disease development and decreased severity of black rot.

Alfalfa with Reduced Levels of Lignin

The forage quality of alfalfa is lowered by the high levels of the indigestible fibre component lignin. Intragenic alfalfa with reduced levels of lignin was developed by transformation with an intragenic construct, silencing the caffeic acid o-methyltransferase gene (*Comt*) (Weeks *et al.*, 2008).

Cisgenic Barley with Improved Phytase Activity

Phytase are enzymes which releases phosphate in barley bound in the form of phytic acid. only about 30% of the phosphate in the grains is absorbed by the animals. In order to release maximum phosphate the cisgenic approach is used in barley in which extra copies of the phytase gene (*HvPAPhy*_a) preferentially expressed during seed development and responsible for the preformed phytase in the mature grain were inserted into barley with its native promoter and terminator (Holme *et al.*, 2012)

Durum Wheat with 1Dy10 HMW Glutenin Subunit from Bread Wheat

The glutenin subunit 1Dy10 from hexaploid wheat (not present in tetraploid durum wheat) plays an important role in bread making. A cisgenic approach was successfully used to transfer the *1Dy10* HMW glutenin subunit gene from bread wheat to durum wheat (Gadaleta *et al.*, 2008). Biolistic transformation was performed with two separate linear gene cassettes containing the *1Dy10* gene with its native promoter and terminator and a selection marker gene, respectively. Plants without selectable marker but with an expressed *1Dy10* subunit were identified in the next generations. The baking quality of the cisgenic durum wheat was not evaluated in this study.

Bottlenecks for the practical use of cisgenesis

1. Major bottleneck may be the identification of genes encoding for the desired traits. Genes need to be fully characterised, including potential interactions.
2. Many important traits in plants constituting major breeding goals result from the interaction of several genes.
3. To ensure that new resistances are not broken rapidly, a combination of genes should be inserted into the recipient plant (gene stacking,).

4. Isolated genes and their regulatory elements are introduced into a different genetic background. It has to be proven whether they retain their anticipated function in an altered genetic background.
5. Plant transformation remains a tedious procedure, in particular in fruit trees.
6. The same limitations (e.g. random integration) as for transgenic plants apply.
7. Current plant transformation methods rarely lead to the desired results and the selection of an appropriate plant is costly as many plants have to be thoroughly analysed.
8. The complete removal of selection markers is, by definition of cisgenesis, indispensable; the efficiency depends on the method applied and needs to be verified individually.
9. Native promoters may altered native expression level of a gene (Szankowski *et al*. 2009). The altered expression can alter the environmental behaviour of the plant and also render considerations concerning exposure of potential consumers necessary.

Objections/Drawbacks and Clarification

1. *Unknown insertion site*

A frequently mentioned drawback is the fact that cisgenes will be inserted at unknown places of the plant genome, which could bring unforeseen risks.

Clarification: The phenomenon of random insertion of pieces of alien DNA into the plant genome occurs also in traditional plant breeding. The most prominent examples are induced translocation breeding in wheat (Friebe *et al*. 1996). Another example of gene insertion is the naturally occurring transposon activity in many plant species. The most well known crop plant with this phenomenon is maize.

2. *Mutation at insertion site*

Another theoretical drawback that is mentioned regarding cisgenesis is the mutation made at the insertion site of the cisgene and the unexpected accompanying phenotypic changes that might result from this.

Clarification: It has seen that induced translocations and especially naturally occurring transposons can cause mutations in the crop genome, which even can be used. Usually, mutations are inherited recessively and represent loss of function. These mutations have never been accompanied with additional risks. This is also true for the over 2,700 varieties which have been obtained in mutation breeding by using induced or spontaneously occurring mutations (Ahloowalia *et al*. 2004).

3. *Food safety*

The use of wild Solanum species as source of genetic variation is bringing back different kinds of glycoalkaloids that have been removed during the breeding process in the past. The use of wild species as new source of genetic variation is accompanied by the re-introduction of these compounds (Van Gelder, *et al.* 1989). Before release for food safety, new varieties have, therefore, always to be tested for the amount of glycoalkaloids that has to be below a certain threshold in the potato tuber.

Challenges/limitations of cisgenic

1. Only those of the traits in sexually compatible gene pool can be transferred to a crop.
2. The gene of interest or fragment of genes may not be readily available but need to be isolated from the sexually compatible gene pool
3. Development of marker and vector backbone –free plants
4. Position effects

Cisgenic Crops should not be Under the European GMO Regulation

Cisgenic crops should not be under the European GMO Regulation for the following reasons:

1. **Cisgenic crops are as safe as conventionally bred crops.** On 16 February 2012 EFSA published its thorough study on safety of cisgenic crops.[1] EFSA confirmed that cisgenic crops are as safe as conventionally bred crops for environment, food and feed. Intragenic and transgenic crops, however, can lead to additional risks.
2. **Cisgenic micro-organisms are already excluded from the GMO Regulation.** The current GMO regulation for contained use excludes cisgenic micro-organisms from this regulation. Products from cisgenic micro-organisms are used widely for more than 15 years throughout the Food and Feed industry. Cisgenesis of micro-organisms is named 'self-cloning'. As self-cloning is excluded from the GMO Regulation, all experts of the European Working Group on New Breeding Techniques (see below) indicated that it makes sense to exclude also cisgenic crops from the GMO Regulation.
3. **Cisgenesis is well accepted by a majority of European consumers.** The latest Eurobarometer compared consumers' willingness to buy cisgenic apples and transgenic apples. The willingness to buy cisgenic apples was far higher than for transgenic apples in all member states (Gaskell, G. *et al.* 2010).

Table 7.7: The Public is Considerably more Comfortable with the Idea of a Cisgenic Crop when Compared with a Transgenic Crop

Country	Cisgenic	Transgenic	Crop
Mississippi	81 %	14-23%	Vegetable
United States	52-77%	17-25%	Vegetable
Denmark	75%	25%	Bread Flour
Europe (32 countries)	55%	33%	Apple

(Viswanath *et al.* 2010 and Holme, 2013)

Cis genenics can bring out Second Green Revolution

According to Jacobson and Nataraja (2008) cisgenesis is better than traditional introgression and translocation breeding because of the absence of linkage drag and the reduced number of steps. While transferring gene of interest from wild species possibility of acquiring unrelated traits/toxic compounds is observed most of the times. In cisgenesis would be a better option to over come these problems as the desired traits can be incorporated by gene stacking. For example, cisgenic apple varieties are being evolved by stacking resistance genes from crossable *Malus* plant for durable résistance to apple scab. A second green revolution is needed in India to overcome the challenges related to yield, quality traits and healthy vegetables and fruits. Similar approach can be attempted for developing cisgenic crop plants for quality traits and biotic/abiotic stress tolerance in India.

Conclusion

Despite success, the Classical methods of alien gene transfer have disadvantages and difficulties, particularly linkage drag, that require time-consuming backcrosses and simultaneous selection steps. Cisgenesis is a powerful alternative, a single-step gene transfer without linkage drag only wanted alleles inserted. Stacking of (resistance) genes is more feasible so that existing varieties can be improved directly using genes from the gene pool of breeders. Final product is more referred by consumers compared to transgenics.

REFERENCES

Ahloowalia, B.S., Maluszynski, M., Nichterlein, K. (2004): Global Impact of Mutation-derived Varieties. *Euphytica*, 135: 187-204.

Bajaj, S., Puthigae, S., Templeton, K., Bryant, C., Gill, G., Lomba, P., Zhang, H., Altpeter, F. and Hanley, Z. (2008): Towards Engineering Drought Tolerance in Perennial Ryegrass Using its Own Genome. 6th Canadian Plant Genomics Workshop, Abstract p. 62.

Chawla R, Shakya R and Rommens CM. (2012) Tuber-specific Silencing of Asparagine Synthetase-1 Reduces the Acrylamide-forming Potential of Potatoes Grown in the Field Without Affecting Tuber Shape and Yield. Plant Biotechnol. J. 10, 913-924.

Chu, Q.R. and Zhang, L.N. (1985): Cytogenetics of Aneuploids Derived by Anther Culture in Rice. *Acta Genetica Sinica*, 12: 51-60.

Cisneros, A, and Tel-Zur, N. (2010): Embryo Rescue and Plant Regeneration Following Interspecific Crosses in the Genus Hylocereus (Cactaceae). *Euphytica*, 174: 73-82.

Conner, A., Pringle, J., Lokerse, A., Jacobs, J., Barrell, P., Deroles, S. and Boase, M. (2010): Plant Transformation Using DNA Minicycles. WO Patent Application. WO 2010/09536 A2.

Conner, A., Barrell, P., Baldwin, S., Lokerse, A., Cooper, P., Erasmuson, A., Nap, J.-P., Jacobs, J. (2007): Intragenic Vectors for Gene Transfer Without Foreign DNA. *Euphytica* 154, 341-353.

Dale, E.C. and Ow, D.W. (1991): Gene Transfer with Subsequent Removal of the Selection Gene from the Host Genome. Proceedings of the National Academy of Sciences 88: 10558-10562.

de Vetten N, Wolters, A, Raemakers, K, van der Meer, I, ter Stege, R, Heeres, E, Heeres, P. and Visser, R. (2003): A Transformation Method for Obtaining Marker-free Plants of a Cross-pollinating and Vegetatively Propagated Crop. Nat. Biotech. 21, 439-442.

Dhekney, S.A., Li, Z.T. and Gray, D.J. (2011): Grapevines Engineered to Express Cisgenic Vitis Vinifera Thaumatin-like Protein Exhibit Fungal Disease Resistance. In Vitro Cell. Dev. Biol.-Plant 47, 458-466.

Ebinuma, H., Sugita, K., Matsunaga, E. and Yamakado, M. (1997): Selection of Marker-free Transgenic Plants Using the Isopentenyl Transferase Gene. *Proc Natl Acad Sci* USA 94: 2117-2121.

EFSA. (2012): Guidance for Risk Assessment of Food and Feed from Genetically Modified Plants. *EFSA Journal*, 10(2): 2561.

Evans, D.A. (1989): Somaclonal Variation - genetic-basis and Breeding Applications. *Trends in Genetics*, 5: 46-50.

Friebe, B., Jiang, J., Raupp, W.P., McIntosh, R.A. and Gill, B.S. (1996): Characterization of Wheat-alien Translocations Conferring Resistance to Diseases and Pests: Current Status. *Euphytica* 91: 59-87.

Gadaleta, A., Giancaspro, A., Blechl, A.E. and Blanco, A,. (2008): A Transgenic Durum Wheat Line that is Free of Marker Genes and Expresses 1DY10. J. Cereal Sci.48, 439-445. Gadaleta A, Giancaspro A, Blechl AE and Blanco A. (2008) A Transgenic Durum Wheat Line that is Free of Marker Genes and Expresses 1DY10. J. Cereal Sci. 48, 439-445.

Gaskell, G., Allansdottir, A., Allum, N., Castro, P., Esmer, Y., Fischler, C., Jackson, J., Kronberger, N., Hampel, J., Mejlgaard, N., Quintanilha, A., Rammer, A., Revuelta, G., Stares, S., Torgersen, H. and Wager, W. (2011): The 2010 Eurobarometer on the Life Sciences. *Nat. Biotechnol.*, 29: 113-114.

Han, K.M., Dharmawardhana, P., Arias, R.S., Ma, C., Busov, V. and Strauss, S.H. (2011): Gibberellin-associated Cisgenes Modify Growth, Stature and Wood Properties in Populus. Plant Biotechnol. J. 9, 162-178.

Haverkor, T A.J., Struik, P.C., Visser, R.G.F. and Jacobsen, E. (2009): Applied Biotechnology to Combat Late Blight in Potato Caused by Phytophthora Infestans. Potato Res. 52, 249-264.

Hermsen, J.G.T. and Ramanna, M.S. (1973): Double-bridge Hybrids of Solanum Bulbocastanum and Cultivars of Solanum Tuberosum. *Euphytica*, 22: 457-466.

Holme, I.B., Dionisio, G., Brinch-Pedersen, H., Wendt, T., Madsen, C.K., Vincze, E. and Holm, P.B. (2012): Cisgenic Barley with Improved Phytase Activity. Plant Bio-technol. J. 10, 237-247.

Holme, I.B., Wendt, T. and Preben, Bach Holm, P. B. (2013): Current Developments of Tragenic and Cisgenic Crops. ISB News Report, July 2013.

Jochemsen, H. and Schouten, H.J. (2000): Ethische Beoordeling van Genetische Modificatie. In: 'Toetsen en Begrenzen. Een Ethische en Politieke Beoordeling van de Moderne Biotechnologie' (Jochemsen, H. ed), pp. 88–95. Amsterdam, Netherlands: Buijten and Schipperheijn.

Jacobson, E. and Nataraja, K. N, (2008): Cisgenics Facilitating the Second Green Revolution in India by Improved Traditional Plant Breeding. Current Science, 94 (11): 1365-1366.

Jacobsen, E. and Schouten, H.J. (2008): Cisgenesis, A New Tool for Traditional Plant Breeding, should be Exempted from the Regulation on Genetically Modified Organisms in a Step by Step Approach. *Potato Research*, 51: 75-88.

Jacobsen, E. and Schouten, H. (2007): Cisgenesis Strongly Improves Introgression Breeding and Induced Translocation Breeding of Plants. *Trends in Biotechnology*, 25: 219-223.

Joshi Sameer, Jose Miguel Soriano, Jan Schaart, Giovanni Antonio, Lodovico Broggini, Iris Szankowski, Evert Jacobsen, Frans Krens, Henk Schouten (2009): Approaches for Development of Cisgenic Apples. Transgenic Plant Journal 3 (Spacial issue 1).

Ko, J.M., Seo, B.B., Suh, D.Y., Do, G.S., Park, D.S. and Kwack, Y.H. (2002): Production of a New Wheat Line Possessing the 1BL.1RS Wheat-rye Translocation Derived from Korean rye cultivar Paldanghomil. *Theoretical and Applied Genetics*, 104: 171-176.

Komari T, Imayama T, Kato N, Ishida Y, Ueki J, Komari T (2007): Current Status of Binary Vectors and Superbinary Vectors. *Plant Physiology*, 145, 1155-1160.

Krens, A., Koen, T.B, Pelgrom, Jan G., Schaart, Ton P.M. Den Nijs and Gerard J.A. Rouwendal (2003): Clean Vector Technology for Marker-free Transgenic Crops. Tuberosa R., Phillips R.L., Gale M. (eds.), Proceedings of the International Congress "In the Wake of the Double Helix: From the Green Revolution to the Gene Revolution", 27-31 May 2003, Bologna, Italy, 509-515, 2005 Avenue Media, Bologna, Italy.

Larkin, P.J. and Scowcroft, W.R. (1981): Somaclonal Variation - A Novel Source of Variability from Cell-cultures for Plant Improvement. Theoretical and Applied Genetics, 60, 197-214.

Lewis, R.S., Milla, S.R. and Levin, J.S. (2005): Molecular and Genetic Characterization of Nicotiana glutinosa L. chromosome segments in Tobacco mosaic virus-resistant Tobacco Accessions. *Crop Science*, 45: 2355-2362.

Liu, J.H., Xu, X.Y. and Deng, X.X. (2005): Intergeneric Somatic Hybridization and its Application to Crop Genetic Improvement. Plant Cell Tissue and Organ Culture, 82, 19-44.

Maria Lusser, Claudia Parisi, Damien Plan and Emilio Rodríguez-Cerezo. (2012): Deployment of New Biotechnologies in Plant Breeding. *Nature Biotechnology*, 30(3): 231-239.

Miyajima, D. 2006. Ovules that Failed to form Seeds in Zinnia (Zinnia violacea Cav.). *Scientia Horticulturae*, 107: 176-182.

Rayburn, A.L. and Carver, B.F. (1988): Cytological Identification of 1b/1r Wheat-rye Translocations in Winter-wheat Breeding Lines. *Euphytica*, 38: 237-240.

Reed, S.M. (2005): Embryo Rescue. *Plant Development and Biotechnology*, 235-239.

Rommens, C.M., Haring, M.A., Swords, K., Davies, H.V. and Belknap, W.R. (2007): The intragenic Approach as a New Extension to Traditional Plant Breeding. *Trends in Plant Science*, 12: 397-403.

Rommens, C.M., Yan, H., Swords, K., Richael, C. and Ye, J. (2008): Low-acrylamide French Fries and Potato Chips. Plant Biotechnol. J. 6, 843-853.

Rommens, C.M., Ye, J., Richael, C. and Swords, K. (2006): Improving Potato Storage and Processing Characteristics Through all-native DNA Transformation. J. Agric. Food Chem. 54, 9882-9887.

Rommens, C.M., Humara, J.M., Ye, J., Yan, H., Richael, C., Zhang, L., Perry, R. and Swords, K. (2004): Crop Improvement Through Modification of the Plant's Own Genome. *Plant Physiology*, 135: 421-431.

Schaart, J.G. (2004): Towards Consumer-friendly Cisgenic Strawberries which are Less Susceptible to Botrytis Cinerea. Ph.D. Thesis, Wageningen University, Wageningen, the Netherlands.

Schouten, H.J., Krens, F.A. and Jacobsen, E. (2006): Cisgenic Plants are Similar to Traditionally Bred Plants. *EMBO Reports* 7: 750-753.

Szankowski, I., Waidmann, S., Degenhardt, J., Patocchi, A., Paris, R., Silfverberg-Dilworth, E., Broggini, G. and Gessler, C. (2009): Highly Scab-resistant Transgenic Apple Lines Achieved by Introgression of HcrVf2 Controlled by Different Native Promoter Lengths. *Tree Genetics & Genomes*, 5(2): 349-358.

Vanblaere, T., Szankowski, I., Schaart, J., Schouten, H., Flachowsky, H., Broggini, G.A.L. and Gessler, C. (2011): The Development of a Cisgenic Apple Plant. J. Bio-technol. 154, 304-311.

Van der Wiel, C., Schaart, J., Niks, R. and Visser, R. (2010): Traditional Plant Breeding Methods. Report 338, (Wageningen UR Plant Breeding) Available Frop http://edepot.wur.nl/141713.

Van Gelder, W.M.J., Tuinstra, L.G.M.T., Van der Greef J, Scheffer, J.J.C. (1989): Characterization of Novel Steroidal Alkaloids from Tubers of Solanum Species by Combined Gas Chromatography - mass Spectrometry. Implications for Potato Breeding. J Chromatogr 482: 13-22.

Weeks, J.T., Ye, J. and Rommens, C.M. (2008): Development of an in Planta Method for Transformation of Alfalfa (Medicago sativa). Transgenic Res. 17, 587-597.

www.en.Wikipedia.org/wiki/cisgenic

Pages: 145-167

SEED TREATMENT, PLANT HEALTH AND AGRO-TECHNOLOGY

Edited by: Dr. Avnish Chauhan and Dr. Pawan Kumar 'Bharti'

ISBN: 978-93-5056-810-1

Edition: 2016

Published by: Discovery Publishing House Pvt. Ltd., New Delhi (India)

8

Retrospective and Perspectives of the Strongest Natural Fibre Crop *Ramie*

Kanti Meena* and **Asit B. Mandal**

ABSTRACT

Fibers are used in our daily life for various domestic purposes, in course of time they dominated industrial sector for diversified product development. However, with the development and large-scale utilization of synthetic fibres drastic decline in fibre crop cultivation in spite of their eco-friendly and non-biodegradable nature. Among the fibre yielding plants ramie provides strongest fibre. Being orphan crop much emphasis has not been given, which is the major bottle neck for genetic improvisation of the varieties and product diversification in spite of its bright prospect. In this chapter retrospective and perspectives of Ramie is represented based on the available data.

Key words: Ramie, Ramie degumming, *In vitro* culture, Molecular breeding, Ramie fibre.

Introduction

Ramie (*Boehmeria*) is the name used to designate a stingless nettle plant and also the textile bast fiber obtained from the plant. The fibre plant has attracted an unusual amount of attention and financial exploitation. The interest in ramie is mainly due to its beautiful laster possessed by the fibre and its reported durability and great strength. It ranks first among all the vegetable fibre with respect of its strength. Itis a genus containing of about 100 species with basic chromosome number $2n=2X=24$. However chromosome

Central Research Institute for Jute and Allied Fibres, Barrckpore, Kolkata - 700 120 (WB), (India)

number of polyploids of ramie and its hybrid varies from 12 to 84 with plenty of abnormal chromosomal behaviors (Sixiang *et al.*, 1996).

The plants are perennial (hardy, small shrubs, herbs and tree) flowering plant belongs to the nettle family or Urticaceae (but without stinging nettles). So far only two species are cultivated for multipurpose use. The species *Boehmeria nivea* commonly known as white ramie or Chinese ramie is named so due to distinct white abaxial surface of the leaf. This species grow best under temperate and subtropical regions (Ray *et al.*, 2014) and is believed to have originated in the Malay Peninsula. It appears bushy shrub with numerous branches arising from the base with round leaves. Whereas *Boehmeria nivea* var. *tenacissima* commonly known as *rhea* or green ramie (Indian ramie) is named due to green abaxial and adaxial leaf surface. It grows luxuriantly under typical tropical conditions (Cobley, 1957) and is believed to be a native of eastern Asia. It requires warm humid climate with well distributed annual rainfall of about 1000 mm and prefers loamy or sandy loam soil for its luxuriant growth. The crop is harvested 5-6 times a year with a life span of about 6-20 years and grows up to 1.5-2 m in height with profuse and deep rooting system. The leaves are thick, broadly ovate, petiolate, velvety abaxial surface owing to presence of non-stinging tomentose hairs and alternate with serrated margins. The species is highly vulnerable to water-logging and submergence.

It is a monoecious plant producing separate inflorescence bearing male (at lower part of the stem) and female (at the terminal region of the stem) flowers (very small) on the same plant and there number may vary according to the species. The flowers appears drooping clusters growing from the angles between leafstalks and stems. The female flowers (green and smaller in comparison to male) appear first than male and the flowering occurs once or twice depending upon the environment. The female flower contain single ovule with one ovule, whereas the male flower contain four anthers. The have a capacity to generate plants with either male or female under certain environmental conditions or by external hormone treatment.

The fruit (0.5-0.7 mm long) is very small, develop in clusters on the twigs back from the leaves containing seeds (small, oval, coffee coloured), which can be used as a planting material.

Origin and Distribution

Ramie is one of the oldest textile fibre evident to be used in the mummy cloths in Egypt during 5000-3000 BC. The crop was grown for centauries in China, thus believed to be the homeland of ramie where its origin, domestication and diversification took place (*Vavilo*, 1951). Farmers in ancient China were reported to use the fibre to weave clothing. Brazil began its production in late 1930s, however, area under cultivation steadily declined due to the introduction of other crops and synthetic fibres. About 90% of the ramie cultivated in the world comes from China and exported mainly to Japan and Europe. Other countries like Japan, Taiwan, Indonesia, Vietnam, Korea, The Philippines, Brazil Columbia, Malaysia and France have also started cultivating ramie (Dempsey, 1954; Bally, 1957; Kirby, 1963; Greenhalgh, 1978). In India, ramie cultivation is mainly restricted to the regions of north-eastern hill (NEH) region (Seven sister states viz. Assam, Arunachal Pradesh, Meghalaya, Manipur, and Sikkim), parts of Western Ghats and northern parts of West Bengal. About 19 species of ramie have been reported so far from India, most of which are distributed in the NEH region. Some species have been reported from Western Ghats, northern parts of West Bengal, a few from low lying parts of Odisha and Uttaranchal (Satya *et al.*, 2010). This crop has also been successfully tried in other parts of India like Nilgiri hills (Tamil Nadu), Maharashtra, Goa etc (Sinha *et al.*, 2009).

Propagation of Ramie

Ramie grows well in areas with good rainfall (annual rainfall of 1500-2500 mm) and a warm humid climate with fertile loamy or sandy loam soils (pH 6-7). The optimum temperature for ramie growth ranges between 25 to 31° C up to 35° C and relative humidity (RH) up to 80%. The crop is highly sensitive to waterlogging, frost and strong wind. For commercial plantation, rhizomes or cuttings of ramie are the means for cultivation with a spacing of 60 cm (row to row) × 30 cm (plant to plant).

Ramie is generally propagated through rhizome cuttings, plantlets, stem cuttings, waste stalk plantings, seed (Mitra*et al.*, 2013). However, it is conventionally propagated by rhizome cuttings for commercial production globally. Rhizomes are obtained from the roots of about 3-4 year old healthy and disease-free plants, cut into 10 to 15 cm pieces in length with 1.5 to 2.5 cm diameter. The cut rhizome should be plated as early as possible, before they lose their viability. The practice of propagation through rhizomes ensures good sprouting, clonal purity and is reported to be economic (Singh, 1996). Ramie can be propagated by seed, but the resulting plants take 1-2 years to become productive and are often inferior to their parents, plausibly owing to their highly heterozygous, heterogeneous nature like trees. Indeed it needs study why genetic homeostasis gets disrupted when plants grown from naturally set seed.

Other alternate sources reported for planting material like plantlets (mature canes (more than one year) < 10 cm attached with 2-5 cm underground stem) were found affective. Stem cutting (mature stem (2/3rd length), which is unsuitable for fibre extraction (brownish, > 1m in length) can be cut into small pieces with 2-3 nodes for planting. Another source is waste stalk

Pest and Disease of Ramie

The soil temperature and moisture have great impact on disease occurrence. Generally speaking, drought, flooding and low temperature are helpful to alleviate the disease. The infestation of insect's pests and diseases in this crops has not been so alarming in India, however some of the disease and there casual organisms has been reported in India and China. Among the insects, hairy caterpillar has been reported to infect the ramie plants moderately. Ramie leaf roller and leaf eating caterpillar have also been observed from time to time (Ghosh and Ghosh, 1971, Mustafee, 1977). Some of the pest infecting and disease caused by different organisms in ramie crop are mentioned below (Table 8.1).

Table 8.1: Pest and Diseases of Ramie Crop

Disease	Causal Organism
Ramie root rot nematode disease	(Root lesion nematode)
Ramie mosaic disease	(Ramie mosaic virus)
Ramie white root rot	(*Rosellinianecatrix*)
Ramie brown spot	(*Rhizoctoniasolani*)
Ramie leaf spot	(*Phytophthoraboehmeriae*)
Ramie angular leaf spot	(*Cercosporaboehmeriae*)
Ramie anthracnose	(*Colletotrichumcorchori*) (*Colletotrichumgleosporides*)
Collar rot	(SclerotiumrolfsiiSacc.)
Pest	**Causal Organism**
Hairy caterpillar	*(Spilosomaobliqua)*
Ramie leaf roller	*(Syleptra derogate)*
Leaf eating caterpillar	*(Spodopteraexigua)*
Indian red admiral	*(Vanessa indicaHerbst.)*
Leaf beetle	*(PachnephrousbretinghamiBaly.)*

Unique Fibre

Ramie is regarded as the "King of all fibres". It produces the longest, strongest and finest vegetable fibres from the outer part of the stem. The fabrics made up of blends of ramie and diverse synthetics are considered to be ideal for clothing under tropical climates (Baily, 1949; Kirby, 1963). Owing to its excellent fibre properties, such as high tensile strength, (which slightly increases when made wet (Fontanelli, 1998), excellent thermal conductivity, coolness, ventilation function, moisture absorption (this makes comfortable to wear), and antibacterial properties, which makes it one of the best plant fibre for textile industries (Kirby, 1963; Wood and Angus, 1974; Batra and Bell, 1975; Dempsey, 1954; Jarman*et al.*, 1978; Goda*et al.*, 2006). Other merits of this fibre lie in its resistance to bacteria, mildew, alkalis, rotting, light and insect attacks. The fibre has great ability to hold shape, reduce wrinkling and introduce a silky lustre to the fabrics. It can be coloured with dye like cotton easily and can also be bleached. It has good strength and durablility (Its tensile strength reported to be eight times more than that of cotton and seven times greater than silk). To the contrary because of its high molecular crystallinity, ramie is stiff and brittle and generally breaks if folded repeatedly in the same place; it lacks resiliency and is low in respect of elasticity and elongation potential. It wrinkles easily and fibre extraction and cleaning is a difficult and labour-intensive process, which need special treatment (tedious, cost effective). Despite its strength, ramie possess limited acceptance in the textile industry too. At the interface of 100% biodegradability, it is emerging as a promising "ecological" fibre or "green fibre" for use in textile industries in the days to come.

Applications

Ramie contains triterpenes, polyphenols, flavonoids, chlorogenic acid, quercetin, ursolic acid and other ingredients (Zhang *et al.*, 2002), some of which were shown to exert different properties viz. antitumor (Cai *et al.*, 2006, Yan *et al.*, 2006; Luo *et al.*, 2003), antiviral (Huang *et al.*, 2006, 2009; Chang *et al.*, 2010), antibacterial (Semwal *et al.*, 2009), hepatoprotective, glucose-lowering (Sancheti *et al.*, 2010) and antioxidant effects (Lin *et al.*, 1998). Very recently phytochemical profile (phenols and flavonoids) and antioxidant property from the leaf of six ramie species was generated (Chen *et al.*, 2014) and *a*nti-hepatitis B virus activity of ramie leaves in human HepG2.2.15 cells (Wei *et al.*, 2014). One US patent (No. 7431946) for the production of *Boehmerianivea* extracts for the treatment of hepatitis is existing. Ethanol based root extract of ramie exhibited anti-hepatitis B virus (HBV) activity *in vitro* and *in vivo* (Huang *et al.*, 2006, 2009), whereas methanol based root extract showed in vivoantidiabetic, antihyperlipidaemic and antioxidant effects in rats. Ethylacetate leaf extracts showed free radical scavenging activity, inhibitory effects on angiotensin I-converting enzyme and in vitro anticancer activity. An aqueous leaf extract showed antimicrobial properties against the fungus Acremoniumkiliense and the bacteria Bacillus cereus and Bacillus subtilis. Other uses involvesantiphlogistic, demulcent, diuretic, febrifuge, haemostatic, antiabortifacient, cooling and uterosedative properties. It is commonly used to prevent miscarriages and promote the drainages of pus.

Young shoots of ramie are excellent source of nutrients, thus used as feed for cattle. They are enriched with protein (16.4% dry matter), digestible fibre (25% dry matter), Ca (31.8g/kg dry matter), K (18.7 g/kg dry matter) and with high metabolic energy (6.4 MJ/kg dry matter) (INFIC, 1978). A new variety was bred by Institute of BastFibre Crops (IBFC), which named Zhongsizhu No.1 as first ramie variety used as forage in the world. The leaves are found to be astringent and resolvent, used in treating fluxes and wounds. Roots contain the flavonoid rutin. Due to high cellulose content in ramie makes it potential raw source for high quality paper like currency notes. Gradually growing demands of newsprint paper cannot be met alone with forest resources due to increasing effects on environment. Ramie cores can be used as raw materials for paper pulp and newsprint making, to manufacture plywoods. Due to its high biomass production, high content of N source and good physical performance it is being used as an optional crop for preparing media for mushroom cultivation. Since it absorbs CO_2 @3.4 to 4.5 tonnes/ha/year, ramie is a perspective species for carbon sequestration, and a country like India can earn huge foreign exchequer from carbon trading from large-scale cultivation of ramie under the aegis of UNO/World Bank.

A good volume of ramie waste is generated from huge quantity of biomass during the process of ramie decortication and incorporation of waste. Application of ramie composite @ 40 t/ha reported to supply adequately nutrient required for ramie plant for maximum fibre yield (14.7 q/ha), which saves the consumption of chemical fertilizers (Mandal and Goswami, 1999). The feasibility to use ramie and spanish broom in composite materials showed both fibres as potential replacement for manmade fibres in composite materials (Angelini *et al.*, 2013).

Value Added Products of Ramie

Because of high luster, strength, durability and ability to be blend with other natural and synthetic fibres ramie fibre is highly suitable for textile purposes. The various useful properties of ramie fibre and other parts are capitalized nowadays in diverse ways (Greenhalgh 1978). Practically all the end products, which are manufactured from cotton, hemp, flax or silk can also be made from ramie (Petruszka, 1977), which are easily blended with almost all the fibres (including wool, *munga, endi* and polyester fibres successfully) and are considered as an ideal ingradient for clothing in tropical climates (Baily, 1949; Kirby, 1963). The fibre can be blended in various proportions like 30:70, 33:67, 35:65 and 40:60, with polyesters and 50:50 mixture with wool is reported to be stronger than even the carpets (Singh, 1996). Its fibre is resistance to bacterial action and enhancement in the strength when wet, which makes it more suitable for the manufacture of curtains and toweling materials, twines, threads, pullybelts, ropes and cordages, fishing nets, fire hoses, water carrying bags, ammunition belts, camouflage nets, cartridge cloths, industrial packing, canvas upholstery fabrics, furnishing materials, parachute chords, designing of the shirting and suiting materials, table cloths, bed sheets, bed covers and curtain cloths etc. It is also used for the manufacture of shoes, shoe sewing threads, for special papers (cigarette papers and even used as papers for making currency notes). Manufacture of fibre hoses, water carrying bags and other impermeable fabrics. Used to manufacture products, which require high strength like twines, threads, pully belts, ropes and cordages and fishing nets, for manufacturing gas mantles, roving for electric batteries and used for industrial packing, canvas, upholstery fabrics, paper pulp, anchoring ropes of ships etc.

Ramie the strongest and stiffest bastfibre?

Ramie fibre is prosenchymatous in origin (Maiti, 1997), which develops from procambium by repetitive cell division followed by extensive cell elongation. The fibre is regarded as primary in origin as it is not differentiated from the secondary activity of cambium (Hazra and Karmakar, 2008) as compared to jute and mesta, which are developed by secondary activity of cambium. Ramie fibre is a typical lingo-cellulose bastfibre with very high cellulose content. It would be logical to compare with other fibres in terms of fibre filament strength, length and breadth ratio of final cells and fibre fineness. High length and breadth ratio, which indicates better fibre quality, is found to be exceedingly high in ramie in comparison to cotton (1000-3000) (Kim, 2001). This is an important unique property of fibre accounts for high durability, pliability, uniformity and absorbance of ramie fabrics. Since ramie is stiff, brittle with low elasticity (Singh, 1996), it is always blended with other fibres most commonly with cotton.

The secondary cell wall of bastfibre in general is composed of cellulose, hemicellulose and lignin. Lignin is the most important component that provides the mechanical supports to the plant but not to fibre strength. Ramie possess strongest bastfibre, but with very low lignin content in comparison to other fibre crops. High cellulosic content in ramie compared to other fibres may be the plausible reason for maximum fibre strength. But it possess low elasticity and resilience, despite the presence of high percentage and proportion of cellulose. It is to be noted that high cellulose-hemicellulose ratio possibly favour a high degree of cellulose crystalinity, which perhaps attributes strongest and stiffest natures bastfibre (Sarkar *et al.*, 2010).

Chemical Composition of Ramie Fibres and Gum Content

The physical and chemical properties of ramie fibre presented (Table 8.2) in comparison to some of the other dominating fibre crops. Ramie fibre possesses pure cellulose as main structural component, accounting for about 86.9% in comparison to other vegetable fibres (Table 8.2). The non-cellulosic constituents, e. g, hemi-cellulose, pectin, lignin, fats and waxes, being termed as gummy material, also play key role in imparting structural properties of this fibre. Decorticated ramie obtained from the stem of the plant *Boehmerianivea* contains about 19-30% gummy material (Kirby, 1963; Dasgupta *et al.*, 1966). The gum content of ramie varies along its fibre length (Table 8.3) and decreases while degumming and bleaching (22-29 % gum content) as reported (Ahmed *et al.*, 2004) chemical composition of ramie fibre after degumming and bleaching is presented (Table 8.4).

Table 8.2: Physical and Chemical Properties of Ramie Fibre in Comparison to Other Predominant Fibres

	Parameter	Ramie	Cotton[a]	Jute[b]	Flax
A.	**Physical characteristic of Fibre**				
	Ultimate fibre cell length (mm)	200-250	16-52	0.8-6.0	26-65
	Ultimate fibre cell breadth (μm)	15-80	15-20	5-25	10-35
	L/B ratio	3500	2500	110	1700
	Cell wall thickness (μm)	9-16		3-9	8-17
	Gravimetric fineness (tex)	0.4-0.8	0.1-0.3	1.25-5.0	4-10
	Fibre filament tenacity (g tex^{-1})	40-65	30-35	30-45	45-55
B.	**Mechanical Properties of Fibre**				
	Fibre diameter (mm)	0.034			
	Fracture load (N)	0.467			
	Tensile strength (MPa)	560			
	Fracture strain (%)	0.025			
C.	**Chemical composition of Fibre (%)**				
	α-Cellulose	86.9	88-96	61.0	80.0
	β-Cellulose	5.0	–	–	–
	Hemi-cellulose	3.9	–	15.9	4.4
	Lignin	0.5	–	13.5	5.5

[a]Average of four cotton species; [b]Average of C. *capsularis* and C. *olitorius*; Source: (Goda *et al.*, 2006; Sarkar D *et al.*, 2010; Pratik Satya *et al.*, 2010)

Table 8.3: Gum Content of Ramie Fibre at Different Plant Heights

Condition	Gum content (%)			
	Position Along Plant Height			
	Bottom	Middle	Top	Average
Decorticated	21.50	22.10	24.50	22.70
Degummed	2.25	2.33	2.48	2.35
Bleached	1.70	1.83	1.94	1.82

Source: Ahmed *et al.*, 2004.

Table 8.4: Chemical Composition of Ramie Fibres[a] After Degumming and Bleaching

	Constituent (%)						
Condition	Holo-cellulose	∝-cellulose	Hemi-cellulose	Lignin	Pectin	Ash	Fats and wax
Decorticated ramie	89.80	80.27	9.53	1.16	1.82	1.40	0.36
Degummed ramie	98.19	95.35	2.84	0.38	0.63	0.25	0.27
Bleached ramie	98.43	96.42	2.01	0.03	0.41	0.16	0.21

[a] Percentage of dry raw material, Source: (Ahmed *et al.*, 2004).

Degumming of Ramie Fibre

As the ramie fibre contains high amount of colloidal substances collectively termed as gum-hinders, the microbial retting as used in case of jute and other vegetable fibre crops found to be not efficient and effective. Those substances are insoluble in water but soluble in alkaline solutions (Kirby, 1963). Thus, extraction through simple microbial retting in water is not completely possible. The process of degumming (removal of gums) requires specific chemical or microbial treatment associated with the degradation of the constituents, which is performed under controlled conditions at commercial level, which is not possible for resource-poor farmers to practice individually. However, the use of chemicals for degumming is the most appropriate and unadvisable method to be adopted as it adds huge hazardous chemical components as remnants into the environment, thus damages the ecosystem. It is also reported that chemical treatment of ramie fibre leads to reduction of bastfibre length, spinnability and fibre productivity in addition to other harmful effects (Zheng *et al.*, 2001). An array of degumming methods are available and most of the companies keep the protocols as trade secret. The ramie fibre is extracted from the stem mechanically by a decorticator machine. The most common methods used for degumming are chemical, enzymatic and biological processes.

Chemical degumming: Traditional chemical degumming uses aqueous alkaline solution (Satya *et al.*, 2010) for dissolving pectinaceous substances (Cobley, 1957). The widely accepted chemical degumming method is reported (Petruszka, 1977) is very intresting. In India widely accepted degumming process is available in the public domain (Das Gupta *et al.*, 1976), whereas reports with minor modifications are also available in the public domain. The gum holding ramie filaments together are mainly composed of cutose, pectose, vasculose and fibre composed of fibrose, cellulose and its derivatives (Das Gupta *et al.*, 1976). In the majority of cases alkaline oleates or caustic alkalis are used to remove the gum without effecting the cellulose part. A novel chemical degumming process for ramie fiber was developed by using Na_2CO_3 solution with poly (vinyl alcohol) (PVA) as an auxiliary surfactant and $Na.3PO_4$.

Microbial degumming: Different microbes have been exploited for degumming the ramie fibres and certain mixed bacterial cultures were found capable of utilizing ramie gums as a source of carbon and energy (Singh,1996). *Clostridium coralliumis* a pectinolyitc anaerobic bacterium used for retting ramie in France. Similarly in *Bacillus subtilis*var. pectinovorous were used to decompose pectins from ramie ribbons in Japan. Lack of specific microbial strains, difficulties in isolation of these microbes, their culture and maintenance, cost of microbial formulations (consortia) (Saikia*et al.*, 2009) and low rate of success (Cobley, 1957). Microbial degumming process is restricted to 7 days beyond, since the fibre quality starts deteriorating thereafter. Theseare some of the serious bottlenecks of microbial degumming method to be used at commercial level. Some of the microorganisms like *Sclerotium* sp., *Aspergillusfumigatus, Fusariumoxysporum, Penicillum* spp., *Amylocota*spp. and *Curvularia* spp. producing pectinolytic enzymes have immense potential for degumming of ramie fibres(Bruhlmann*et al.*, 2000; Saikia*et al.*, 2009). Immobilization of *Agrobacterium larrymoorei* A1, a potent extra-cellular cellulase producing bacteria, in Ca-alginate followed by application to ramie fibre showed increased smoothness and orientation of surface structure of the fibers after 19.5 h and reported to be an effective methodology for treatment of natural fibers containing cellulose (Amit Bera *et al.*, 2014)

Enzymatic degumming: Pectinolytic enzymes (protoectinases, esterases and depolymerases) are the major components of gum and many microbes are able to produce proteolytic enzymes, which have been exploited for degumming with no success. The most commonly used fungal species for pectinolytic enzyme production at industrial level is *Aspergillusniger* (Barnby *et al.*, 1990; Kotzekidov 1991; Naidu and Panda, 1998). Pectatelyase is critically more important in comparison to xylanase for degumming (Kapoor *et al.*, 2001), whereas combination of pectinases and xylanases provide an eco-friendly alternative method for degumming (Naidu and Panda, 1998).

Application of enzyme mixture for degradation of gum from ramie fibre has been reported to degrade gum more effectively in comparison to chemical method (Ding *et al.*, 2014).

Genetic approach: Apart from the major (mechanical and chemical) methods of degumming, conventional breeding methodologies have been applied to reduce gum content in ramie fibres. However, those methods have not been found very successful so far through development of low-gum containing or gum-free varieties or genetic stocks.

Germplasm of Ramie and Conventional Breeding

Ramie is a clonal crop, so the breeding methods applied are similar to other vegetatively prorogated crops like sweet potato, sugar cane, potato etc. Selection work on ramie has been carried out in various countries time to time. In China, the Institute of BastFibre Crops had selected and distributed more than 30 elite accessions, whereas in Brazil a protocol has been developed for the genetic modification of ramie and experiments are being carried out to improve the amino acid composition to enhance the fodder value of ramie through genetic modification.

In India, 150 ramie germplasm and its wild species have been collected and maintained at Regional Research Station (RRS), Sorbhog, Assam under CRIJAF, a constituent institute of Indian Council of Agricultural Research (ICAR), New Delhi. Among the five elite lines (R 1452, R 1449, R 1412, R 1411 and R 6734) were selected on the basis of yield, gum content, fertilizer response and resistance to stress. The most popular among these -'Kanai' (R 6734) has been released, which is a superior selection from E56-76, preferred for its high yielding ability. The selection 'Hazarika' (R 1411) from Florida Commercial has been recommended for release after multi-location testing, which is a combination of high yield and low gum content (20-22%).

Seed derived seedlings are mostly very inferior in quality and for development of elite varieties deployment of pure stock of parents, their hybridization, followed by long term clonal selection of superior types over years across locations, which is a difficult task. Important considerations in ramie selection are: adaptation to ecological conditions, decortication characteristics, leaf and branching characteristics, resistance to diseases and insect pests, tendency to lodge and fibre characteristics (uniformity, strength, fineness and colour). Natural seed set is highly heterozygous and heterogeneous. Seed set in ramie have been reported to be environment dependent. Asynchrony in male and female flower induction with no clear knowledge on pollination behavior is one of the serious constraints to have seeds from hybridization involving superior stocks. Presence of complex genome structure with meagre understanding about inter and intra species relationship and the occurrence of polyploidy, has limited the advancement in traditional breeding to improve ramie.

Further research in ramie should be directed in days to come for germplasm exploration, collection extensively (indigenous and exotic), characterization, conservation, evaluation and utilization for genetic enhancement involving both conventional and frontier approaches. Exotic genetic stock and their wild relatives deemed to be promising since they may constitute new alleles in this crop with extremely less genetic variation (which builds the foundation of a strong breeding programme). It demands creation of *de novo* synthesis of variations enroute various methods used in conventional plant breeding like mutation breeding, TILLING etc. Characterization of germplasm at morphological, agronomic, biochemical and molecular levels need to be undertaken to develop "molecular ID cards" to delegate countries sovereign rights to Indian genetic stocks and thereby halting bio piracy, to safeguard IPR protection under TRIPS agreement (Kumar and Mandal, 2009).

Biotechnology

Tissue Culture for Ramie

Regeneration of plantlets may occur either through direct organogenesis or somatic embryogenesis. *In vitro* plant regeneration is mainly dependent upon the manipulation of organic and inorganic salt mileu in artificially prepared synthetic medium, as well as the type of explants and the species used for culture. In most of the plants, successful regeneration from callus or directly from explants takes place after a series of sub-cultures on different growth media fortified with synthetic plant hormones sequentially, which is often specific to species, variety or the genotype used. The plant regeneration determining factors are different combination and concentrations of growth promoting and retarding synthetic chemicals in the medium, the physiological status and the competence of the cells and their capability for morphogenetic expression in nutshell (Christianson and Warnick, 1985) Once the *in vitro* culture protocol is standardized, it would provide added advantage in case of vegetatively propagated plants for large–scale production of ramie by using bioreactor, which is deemed to spearhead the multiplication rate at a much faster rate.

Shoot organogenesis in ramie was first reported from callus culture followed by regeneration of shootlets from hypocotyls (Huang *et al.*, 1980) and leaf explant (Guo *et al.*, 1998) however, whole plant regeneration was found to be very low. Similarly ramie leaf tissue culture was first reported (Zhao *et al.*, 1984), which prospects mass multiplication of ramie plantlets. Micropropagation of ramie through axillary bud was successfully reported *in vitro* (Sut *et al.*, 2004; Wang *et al.*, 2008). Cotyledons and hypocotyls from 4-day-old seedlings and leaves, petioles and stems from 15-day-old seedlings were reported to be most suitable explants, with maximum regeneration efficiency on MS salts on Gamborg's B_5 vitamins fortified with 2.27 ìMthidiazuron (TDZ) and 0.054 ìMnaphthaleneacetic acid (NAA). A photoperiod of 16:8 h (light/dark) reported to be most suitable to obtain maximum plantlet regeneration with TDZ followed by shoot elongation on hormone-free medium and rooting on 1/2 MS containing 0.134 ìM NAA, the plants were successfully transferred to green house (Wang *et al.*, 2008). Multiple-shoots were reported from shoot-tip and nodal segments of 7 week old *in vitro* grown seedlings on modified medium fortified with 1.5 mg/l BAP (6-Benzylaminopurine) and root development on MS supplemented with 0.5 mg/l BAP and 2.0 mg/l IBA (Indole-3-butryic acid) (Sut *et al.*, 2004). Cotyledons excised from 4-day-old seedlings cultured on TDZ and IAA (Indoleacetic acid) supplemented medium resulted adventitious shoots at varying percentage (Wang *et al.*, 2007) as a feasible proposition.

Successful dedifferentiation was reported from calli developed from stem, leaf and hypocotyl on MS containing 6-BA@2-3mg/l medium followed by whole plantlet regeneration on ½ MS fortified with 0.2 mg/1 NAA with vigrous rooting on with 0.1ppm IAA and 0.2 ppm NAA (Qinghua, 1982). Whereas leaf explants of var. Xiangzhu No. 3 showed rapid response on 1/2 MS with low concentrations of NAA (0. 1 - 0. 2mg/l). Leaf dedifferentiation, callus formation and bud regeneration was stimulated considerably with BA (2. 0~ 3. 0mg/l), however, high dose of BA found to inhibit growth of calli and buds, but high dose of BA in combination with NAA found to increase production of buds. Interaction of NAA and BA was found to adversely affect by different light and temperature regimes. Calli developed from leaf explants pretreated at low temperature and short photoperiod found to increase dedifferentiation ratio of buds per explants (Guo *et al.*, 1998).

Ramie plants obtained via clonal propagation (callus formation on IAA alone or in combination with BAP, Kinetin or isopentenyladenine, shoot induction on NAA) showed 100 % survival in experimental glass house (Del Rosario and Corcolon, 1991). Sterilization is an important step in any *in vitro* culture experiment. Disinfection of ramie leaf with 75% ethanol, 0.1% mercuric chloride ($HgCl_2$) for 8 minutes, dipping in 1-2 drop of 1% HCl was reported to be optimum for occurrence of adventitious buds and roots. Best ramie leaf callus induction medium was found to be ½ MS. The most efficient leaf induction medium was 1/2MS+0.05mg/L TDZ+0.01mg/L IAA+0.03mg/L 2, 4-D; injury differentiation medium 1/2MS+0.5mg/L TDZ+0.02mg/L 2, 4-D+0.03mg/L IAA; rooting medium: 1/2MS+0.02mg/L TDZ+0.05mg/L NAA+0.02mg/L IAA with maximum plantlet regeneration rate till date found to be 26% (Wu *et al.*, 2009). *In vitro* culture when applied to the polyploids in ramie (Zheng *et al.*, 1995), showed diploid status having 2X=24 chromosome number, which indicates that direct organogenesis is predominant in case of ramie *in vitro* culture. Somatic embryogenesis would be the choice for large-scale production of plantlets, however, some sporadic reports on somatic embryogenesis of ramie are available, which are found to be non-reproducible. Very recently genome wide gene expression profiling of ramie reported differential transcription and phytohormone during the process (*in vitro* organogenesis) in two different genotypes with very high (Huazhu No. 5) and extremely low (Dazhuhuanhbaima) shoot regeneration abilities (Huang *et al.*, 2014).

Transgenic Research in Ramie

Although several efforts have been made to improve ramie fibre quality, because of complex genetic background of this plant and insufficient knowledge about the genetics governing major agronomic and quality traits, deployment of traditional breeding for genetic enhancement found to be extremely slow and even often misfired (Mou *et al.*, 1995). Genetic improvement of this crop may be achieved more efficiently and effectively through deployment of modern biotechnological approaches such as *Agrobacterium*-mediated genetic transformation, microprojectile bombardment, floral-dip transformation etc for development of value added transgenic plants. Some transgenics in ramie have already developed and published from China (Dusi *et al.*, 1993; Chen *et al.*, 2005). It is known that successful *Agro*-mediated transformation involving *in vitro* plantlet regeneration methods is largely dependent upon the prior development of reliable whole plant regeneration protocol. Some efforts have been made in this endeavour to regenerate shoots from ramie (Huang *et al.*,1980; Huang and Mo, 1981; Pan *et al.*,1995; Guo *et al.*,1998; Wang *et al.*, 2003). All those reports reported callus induction followed by redifferentiation of shootlets with regeneration efficiency lower than 50%, which is not sufficient to allow development of effective transgenic development with diverse alien gene/s for value addition. It demands elaborate experiments and understanding of the cell technology and molecular biology holistically. Lack of a reliable and efficient *in vitro* regeneration system has therefore limited the development of further biotechnological applications for ramie.

An efficient *Agro*-mediated genetic transformation system was developed for ramie (Wang *et al.*, 2009). It has been found to be successful in ferrying alien gene/s into ramie for the development of transgenic plants. Transgenic *Bt* ramie has recently been developed (Fu *et al.*, 2009) to control serious insect pest *Pyrameisindica*(leaf caterpillar). Successful tailoring of *cry1A* and *CPTi* (Cowpea trypsin inhibitor) gene into ramie displayed substantial resistance (Wang *et al.*,2007; 2008). They observed 33.3% plantlet regeneration from transfected calli derived from hypocotyls. Whereas, cotyledon derived calli produced 25% regenerated plantlets after transformation. The working group suggested that 2 days co-cultivation with *Agrobacterium* led to 31% of transient GUS expression in hypocotyls. Other reports showing expression of *gfp* confirms amenability to transient gene expression (Ma *et al.*, 2010a, 2010b). One of the major bottleneck of ramie *in vitro* culture is its recalcitrance towards plant regeneration. Though many reports have shown successful transformation using *A. tumefaciens* the transformation efficiency found to be exceedingly low. Transformation efficiency in ramie using *gfp* as reporter was reported to be 3.6 % (Wang *et al.*, 2007), whereas 6% kanamycin resistant explants were obtained in another study (Dusi*et al.*, 1993), however, transformation efficiency was low, which warrants further fine tuning of the protocol to upgrade transformation efficiency.

Ramie as such is found to be *in vitro* culture responsive that offers ample scope for optimization of *in vitro* culture system for prolific plantlet regeneration and development of transgenics with diverse important transgenes available in the public domain. Bright possibility is discernible in qualitative changes of the ramie fibre and also to down-regulate gum synthesis by interrupting the metabolic grid of gum biosynthesis, which is a major hassle in quality fibre extraction from decorticated plant parts either through gene silencing by various techniques. As the genetic structure of the crop has been unzipped to a very small extent, identification of major genes involved in pectin biosynthesis pathway from heterologous sources and their modification would be alternative short-cut approach to understand the pectin biosynthesis pathway and development of transgenic ramie genotypes with low pectin deposition in the fibre. Recently a key gene involved in pectin biosynthesis pathway, *galat* (α-1,4-galacturonosyltransferase), has been isolated from ramie and cloned (986-bp cDNA) (Liu *et al.*, 2009) on the basis of *Arabidopsis gaut1* gene, which showed low expression of the genes and is expected to reduce pectin content in the fibre. Thus, cloning the full gene and incorporating the gene into the ramie system should be one of the major target. Bioprospecting of new genes, their cloning and integration and ramie genomics (both the structural and functional) offers an exciting domain of research using frontier science to develop highly productive value added lines in ramie. Recently an efficient regeneration and transformation protocol was reported (An *et al.*, 2014), which involved study on different factors affecting the ramie transformation efficiency, including leaf age, *Agrobacterium* concentration, length (time) of *Agro* infection, acetosyringone concentration in the co-cultivation medium, and the co-cultivation duration involving ramie leaf midrib.

Molecular Biology and Innovative Frontier Research in Ramie

Two-dimensional electrophoresis for the proteome analysis of various parts (roots, stems and leaves) of ramie's was developed by optimizing the traditional TCA/acetone protein extraction method, which is an effective method of removing non-protein impurities and better understanding of higher yield, premium quality, stress tolerance, and disease resistance (Gang *et al.,* 2013), holistically. Some of the approaches mentioned possess immense scope and need to be deployed for ramie crop genetic improvement in the days to come.

Application of Molecular Markers in Ramie

Application of molecular markers in ramie crop is very less due to meagre efforts mounted with less number of molecular markers and availability of this crop in extremely limited localities across the globe. Some of the reports on molecular marker involves discrimination of 19 cultivars of ramie by SSR and ISSR and reported high polymorphism and low PIC with SSR (Zhou *et al.,* 2005), potential of SRAP markers to study the genetic relationship among ramie inbred lines and wild types (Liu *et al.,* 2008), utility of RAPD and ISSR (Liu *et al.,* 2009) as efficient markers for taxonomic analysis of wild genetic stocks of ramie and for genetic diversity from various geographical regions of West China provided valid guidelines for collection, conservation, and characterization of *Boehmeria* genetic resources. Ramie based EST-SSR marker were developed with immense potential for construction of fine genetic and physical maps, quantitative trait loci mapping, genetic diversity studies, association mapping and cultivar fingerprinting (Chen *et al.,* 2011; Liu *et al.,* 2013).

Mapping populations need to be developed for important traits like higher productivity, low pectin, tolerance to drought and submergence and QTL mapping for quality genes etc is essential. Suitable molecular markers need to be identified for MAS in tackling important traits to improve the productivity at early segregating generation to telescope the time requirement for elite variety development as well as in gene pyramiding/stacking. Ramie genomic studies with the deployment of most modern phenotyping by genotyping would be a gold mine to understand the genetic architecture of this important fibre crop and also in gene prospecting for crop improvement. Different molecular markers viz. RAPD, SCAR, SNP and CAPS were found (Li *et al.,* 2010) to be highly potential for rapid identification of two closely related *Boehmeria* species. Very recently core collection of 22 ramie germplasm (highly diverse) based on 21 SSR marker combinations has been developed (Luan *et al.,* 2014).

Genetic Enhancement of Ramie: Perspective

At the interface of discernible change in the climate, it is obvious that new biotic (insect pest and diseases) and abiotic stress would emerge with changed vigour and dynamics to make heavy destruction in crop productivity. In this endoveour attempts may be made to develop varieties, lines tolerant and resistant to these stress either by conventional or biotechnological approaches. Development of elite plants with enhanced productivity and enhanced biotic and abiotic stresses through conventional plant breeding and pooling of all desirable genes in a superior stock is practically impossible though spectacular achievements have been made in the past in the endoveour. Many alternatives are looming large, which are touched upon very briefly.

In vitro cultured micropropagated plantlets should be developed on large-scale, which would be logical to use since those are generally robust (as grown under balanced nutritional milieu) and free from pests (pathogens, disease causing organism or insects). Important abiotic stress tolerant genes like *Rab16A*, *SOD* family gene, *dehydrin, osmotin, glycine-betaine*, bacterial chaperone, aquaporin (drought), submergence stress tolerance genes like *adh, pdc, Sub1*, which also avert salinity and alkalinity. For fibre quality improvement Silkworm *fibronin, Elastin, PBA* producing genes are suitable. *Chitinase, phloroglucinol gene, NPRI orthologs, glucanases, plant defensins AFP-Ca* can provide tolerance towards bacterial, fungal, whereas genes like sense coat protein, antisense coat protein and antisense Rep genes for viral pathogens. To impart tolerance to insect especially lepidopteran *Cry1A(b), Cry1A(c)* are very effective. In ramie diseases and insects pests are not very rampant, however in near future if they appears these tools and techniques may be implemented.

Since ramie is a crop with narrow diversity variation can be introduced by different approaches.Techniques for gene silencing especially for silencing the gene/s involved in the biosynthesis pathway of gum synthesis can be attempted. Development of diverse randomly mated population like magic population, training population, bulk segregation population, deemed to be advantageous for genome wide selection to flag desirable plant types endowed with high productivity and premium fibre quality. Identification of suitable markers for construction of linkage map need to address in future.

Whole genomics (structural and functional), need to be unzipped to know the genome in detail as well as to mimic genes (bio prospecting of novel genes). Transcriptomics study has been initiated in ramie and microarray may be restored to study expression profiles of diverse genes during fibre development, across different developmental stages and to understand up and down regulation of the genes involved. Manipulation at nano level have immense potential in ramie alike all other crops (to dispense nutrient solution into germinating embryos or by clogging the cell membrane pores, which would halt entry and dispersal of disease causing pathogens/ insect pests/nematodes etc with special reference to seed borne disease, those often epidemics very often).

Screening the entire ramie genetic stock, applying genetic engineering approaches like silencing/blocking or inhibiting the genes/enzymes involved in gum formation or reducing the endogenous content of gum for reduced gum and pectin content, should be undertaken more aggressively in order to eliminate the hazardous process of degumming. Development of low pectin ramie genotypes offers a robust solution to increase ramie cultivation, fibre productivity and quality. Development of an efficient transformation system to incorporate desirable gene/s for trait enrichment especially for enhanced yield and fibre quality by reducing the lignin content and degumming of ramie. Lack of high density genetic linkage map, genome information or detailed report on pectin biosynthesis pathway in ramie are the major bottlenecks handicapping ramie research to a considerable extent. However, genes involved in pectin biosynthesis grid have been identified in other crops. Identification of key genes involved in pectin biosynthesis in ramie by utilizing genomic information from heterologous sources seems to be an appropriate approach in gene identification and pathway characterization in ramie.

It is found that hemi-cellulose is the key component to be modified to improve the bastfibre properties. Identifying and characterization of the genes involved in the biosynthetic pathway of hemi-cellulose development may allow to manipulate the hemi-cellulose content in bastfibre crops, which may increase the elasticity and resilience or help in reducing the stiffness or brittleness of ramie fibre. Successful regulation of this key gene vis-à-vis identification of other genes involved in pectin biosynthesis is expected to open up a new vistas in ramie cultivation by eliminating or reducing the current hazardous degumming process, which has presently crippled farmers and industry from using the finest and strongest plant fibre, especially for product diversification.

Conclusion

Ramie has untapped potential, as it possess immense potential especially in the NEH states of Indian republic and China, endowed with congenial agro-climatic conditions of these regions. To the contrary of eco offensive nature of synthetic fibres natural fibres like ramie is potential to be used by producing biodegradable products, which we popularly call "green technology". Important and diverse uses of ramie fibre as well as diverse pharmaceutical importance of the crop has attracted the scientists towards ramie research, which remained as 'orphan crop' to the geneticist and biochemists over centuries. Many successful reports on ramie tissue culture, molecular markers, transgenic and pharmaceutical application have been reported mainly from China. However, it represents tip of the ice berg since majority of the biology especially at genetic level is unknown. Climate change and global warming have considerable effect on life, and the effect on local weather is the changing of dry and wet season periods. The classifi-cation of region on rainfall types has been not accurate and valid any more. Climate change was observed to have changed the regional andlocal climate inclusively in the experimental sites. It was recorded in the localtemperature and air relative humidity. Therewas a very efficient dosage of waterw3=35%-40% of Field Capacity affectingsufficient growth on plant. The minimumdosage at which plant survives to produceyield is representing the most efficient inputof production. Water supply for ramie plantcould be designed to the most efficientvolume to maintain the need of metabolism Nitrogen and potassium were significantly support plant to growth in the limited volume of water supply, and potassium showed good effect on quality of fibre. In order to make ramie a worldwide popular crop and its successful launch into the natural fibre platform research need to be more focused.

REFERENCES

Ahmed M, Chattopadhyay SK, Chaphekar AK, Gaikwad RS, Dey SK (2004) Characteristics of Degummed Ramie Fibre and its Cotton Blended Yarns. Indian J Fibre Text Res, 29: 362-365.

Amit Bera,Abhrajyoti Ghosh, Asis Mukhopadhyay, Dhrubajyoti Chattopadhyay, Krishanu Chakrabarti (2014) Improvement of Degummed Ramie Fiber Properties Upon Treatment with Cellulase Secreting Immobilized *A. larrymoorei* A1.Bioprocess and Biosystems Engineering, DOI: 10.1007/s00449-014-1274-6.

Angelini LG, Lazzeri A, Levita G, Fontanelli D, Bozzi C (2000) "Ramie (Boehmerianivea (L.) Gaud.) and Spanish Broom (*Spartiumjunceum* L.) Fibres for Composite Materials: Agronomical Aspects, Morphology and Mechanical Properties," Industrial Crops and Products 11(2-3): 145-161.

An X, Wang B, Liu L, Jiang H, Chen J, Ye S, Chen L, Guo P, Huang X, Peng D (2014).Agrobacterium-mediated Genetic Transformation and Regeneration of Transgenic Plants Using Leaf Midribs as Explants in Ramie [*Boehmerianivea* (L.) Gaud]MolBiol Rep41(5): 3257-69.

Baily LH (1949) Manual of Cultivated Plants, Macmillan and Company.

Bally W (1957) Ciba Review #123 Ramie. Publisher Ciba Review, Basle. p. 2-31.

Barnby FM, Morpeth FF, Pyle DL (1990) Endopolygalacturonse Production from Kluyveromycesmarxianus. I. Resolution, Purification and Partial Characterization of the Enzymes. Enzyme Microbiol Technol 12: 891-897.

Batra SK, Bell C (1975) On the Efficient Utilization of Natural (Vegetable) Fibers. A Technology Adaptation Programme Report. Massachusetts Institute of Technology, Cambridge, MA.

Bruhlmann F, Leupin M, Erismann KH, Fiechter A (2000) Enzymatic Degumming of Ramie Bastfibres. J Biotechnolo 76: 43-50.

Cai XF, Jin X, Lee D, Yang YT, Lee K, Hong YS, Lee JH, Lee JJ (2006) Phenanthroquinolizidine Alkaloids from the Roots of *Boehmeriapannosa* Potently Inhibit Hypoxia-inducible Factor-1 in AGS Human Gastric Cancer Cells. J Nat Prod 69: 1095-1097.

Chang JM, Huang KL, Yuan TT, Lai YK, Hung LM (2010) The Anti-hepatitis B Virus Activity of *Boehmerianivea* Extract in HBV-viremia SCID Mice. Evid Based Complement Alternat Med 7: 189-195.

Chen Jian-Hua, Luan Ming-Bao, Song Shu-Feng, ZouZi-Zheng, Wang Xiao-Fei, Xu Ying, Sun Zhi-Min (2011). Isolation and Characterization of EST-SSRs in the Ramie. Afr J Microbiol Res 5(21): 3504-3508.

Chen JR, Zhang XW, Guo QQ, Tang XS, Yang YC (2005). Construction of CCoAOMT Antisense Expression Vector and Transformation of Ramie. J Nat Sci Human Norman University, 28: 75-78.

Chen Y, Wang G, Wang H, Cheng C, Zang G, XinboGuo, RuiHai Liu (2014) Phytochemical Profiles and Antioxidant Activities in Six Species of Ramie Leaves. PLoS ONE 9(9): e108140. doi:10.1371/journal.pone.0108140.

Christianson ML, Warnick DA (1985). Temporal Requirement for Phytohormone Balance in the Control of Organogenesis. *In vitro* DevBiol112(2): 494-497.

Cobley SL (1957) An Introduction to the Botany of Tropical Crops. Longman, Green and Co., London, 293-301.

Dasgupta PC, Sen K, Senm SK (1996) Annual Report, J T R L, Calcutta, p. 9.

Das Gupta PC, Sen K, Sen SK (1976) Degumming of Decorticated Ramie for Textile Purposes. Cellulose Chemical Technol 10: 285-291.

Del Rosario AG, Corcolon BM (1991). Clonal Multiplication of Ramie by Tissue Culture. Fibre Res J 1: 28-35.

Dempsey JM (1954) Survey of Ramie Operations in Philippines, Fibre Inspection Service, Manila.

Dinesh and mandal.

Ding RY, Zhang ZQ, Yu CW (2014) Optimization of Enzyme Mixture Degumming of Ramie Fiber. Journal of Natural Fibers 11(1): 13-24.

Dusi DMA, Almeida MDERP, Caldas LS, Gander ES (1993). Transgenic Plants of Ramie (Boehmerianivea Gaud.) Obtained by Agrobacterium Mediated Transformation. Plant Cell Rep 12: 625-628.

Fontanelli D (1998) Proprieta' meccaniche e morfologia di fibre di Spartiumjunceum L. (Ginestra). Thesis, Department of Chemical Engineering, University of Pisa (Italy).

Fu Jia-Ping, Wang Bo, Liu Li-Jun, Yang Jin-Yu, Wang Xu-Xia, Xing Xiu-Long, Peng Ding-Xiang (2009). Transgenic Ramie with Bt gene Mediated by Agrobacterium Tumefacien and Evaluation of its Pest-resistance. ActaAgron Sin35(10): 1771-1777.

Gang, Deng G, Liu L, Wang H, Lao C, Wang B, Zhu C, Peng D (2013). Establishment and Optimization of Two-dimensional Electrophoresis (2-DE) Technology for Proteomic Analysis of Ramie. Int J AgriBiol 15: 570 574.

Goda K, Sreekala MS, Gomes A, Kaji T, Ohgi J (2006) Improvement of Plant Based Natural Fibres of Toughening Green Composites- Effect of Load Application during Mercerization of Ramie Fibres. Compos: Part A 37: 2213-2220.

Greenhalgh P (1978) Report, Tropical Products Institute, London.

Guo QQ, Chen JR, Yang RF, Hu RS (1998). Callus Induction and Shoot Regeneration from Leaves of Ramie (*Boehmerianivea* Gaud). China's Fibre Crops 20: 1-4.

Hazra SK, Karmakar PG (2008) In Jute and Allied Fibres Updates (eds. Karmakar PG *et al.*), Central Research Institute for Jute and Allied Fibres, Kolkata, p 38-45.

http://en.wikipedia.org

http://www.innovateus.net

http://www.fibrafp7.net

http://www.prota4u.org

Huang KL, Lai YK, Lin CC, Chang JM (2006) Inhibition of Hepatitis B Virus Production by *Boehmerianivea* Root Extract in HepG2 2.2.15 Cells. World Gastroenterol. 12: 5721-5725.

Huang KL, Lai YK, Lin CC, Chang JM (2009) Involvement of GRP78 in Inhibition of HBV Secretion by *Boehmerianivea* Extract in Human HepG2 2.2.15 Cells. J Viral Hepat16(5): 367-375.

Huang JS, Mo RD, Ye CJ (1980). Research Note on *in vitro* Plant Regeneration from Cotyledon and Hypocotyls of Ramie (*Boehmerianivea* Gaud). Guangxi Agriculture Science 7: 27.

Huang X, Chen J, Bao Y, Liu L, Jiang H, An X, Dai L, Wang B, Peng D (2014). Transcript Profiling Reveals Auxin and Cytokinin Signaling Pathways and Transcription Regulation during *in Vitro* Organogenesis of Ramie (Boehmerianivea L. Gaud). PLoS ONE 9(11):e113768. doi:10.1371/journal.pone.0113768 64.

Huang JS, Mo RD (1981). De novo Shoot Organogenesis from Hypocotylsof Ramie (*Boehmerianivea* Gaud). ActaBiolExp Sin 14: 111-114.

INFIC (1978) Data from International Network of Feed Information Centres. Rome, FAO.

Jarman CG, Canning AJ, Mykoluk S (1978) Cultivation, Extraction and Processing of Ramie Fibre: A Review. Tropical Sci 20(1): 91-116.

Kapoor M, Beg QK, Bhusan B, Singh K, Dadich KS, Hoondal GS (2001) Application of Alkaline and Thermostablepolygalacturonase from Bacillus sp MG-cp-2 in degumming of Ramie (*Boehmerianivea*) and Sunn Hemp (*Crotolariajuncia*) Bast Fibres. Process Biochem 36: 803-807.

Kim HJ, Triplett B (2001) Cotton Fiber Growth in Planta and *in vitro*. Models for Plant Cell Elongation and Cell Wall Biogenesis. Plant Physiol 127: 1361-136.

Kirby RH (1963) Vegetable fibres. World Crops Books, Leonard Hill, London, p 464.

Kotzekidov P (1991) Production of polygalacturonases by Byssachlamysfulva. J Indian Microbiolo 7: 53-56.

Li CI, Chiou SJ, Tong TS, Lee CY, Lee LT, Cheng CM (2010). Development and Validation of Molecular Markers for Characterization of *Boehmerianivea* var. *nivea* and *Boehmerianivea* var. *tenacissima*. *Chinese Medi* 5: 40.

Lin CC, Yen MH, Lo TS, Lin JM (1998) Evaluation of the Hepato Protective and Antioxidant Activity of *Boehmerianivea* var. *nivea* and *B. nivea* var. *tenacissima*. J Ethnopharmacol 60: 9-17.

Liu Li-jun, PENG Ding-xiang, Wang Bo (2008). Genetic Relation Analysis on Ramie [*Boehmerianivea* (L.) Gaud.] Inbred Lines by SRAP Markers. AgricSci China 7(8): 944-949.

Liu Li-jun, MengZu-Qing, Wang Bo, Wang Xu-xia, Yang Jin-Yu, Peng Ding-xiang (2013). Genetic Diversity Among Wild Resources of the Genus Boehmeria Jacq. From West China Determined Using Inter-Simple Sequence Repeat and Rapid Amplification of Polymorphic DNA Markers. Plant Prod Sci 12(1): 88-96.

Luan MB, Zou ZZ, Zhu JJ, Wang XF, Xu Y, Ma QH, Sun ZM, Chen JH (2014). Development of a Core Collection for Ramie by Heuristic Search Based on SSR Markers. Biotechnol Biotechnolog Equ (November 2014).

Liu J, Yu C, Tang S, Zhu A, Wang Y, Zhu S, Ma X, Xiong H (2009). Cloning and Expression of Key Enzyme Gene GalAT in Ramie Pectin Biosynthesis. Agric Sci China 8(6): 664-670.

Luo Y, Liu Y, Luo D, Gao X, Li G, Zhang G (2003) Cytotoxic Alkaloids from *Boehmeriasiamensis*. Planta Med 69: 842-845.

Maiti RK (1997) World Fibre Crops, Science Publishers, Enfield, p. 208.

Mandal BC, Goswami KK (1999). Transformation of Ramie Waste to Wealth in Ramie Fibre Production. Jute and Allied Fibres: Agriculture and Processing, Edited by P Palit, S Pathak and DP Singh, Central Research Institute for Jute and Allied Fibres, Barrackpore, 743101, India.

Ma X, Yu C, Tang S, Guo S, Zhang R, Wang Y, Zhu A, Zhu S, Xiong H (2010a). Genetic Transformation of the Bast Fiber Plant Ramie (*Boehmerianivea* Gaud.) via Agrobacterium Tumefaciens. Plant Cell Tiss Org Cult 100: 165-174.

Ma Xiong-Feng, Yu Chun-Ming, Tang Shou-Wei, Guo San-Dui, Zhang Rui, Wang Yan-Zhou, Zhu Ai-Guo, Zhu Si-Yuan, Xiong He-Ping (2010b). Transgenic of Ramie with Synthetic CryIA+ CpTI Gene by *Agrobacterium tumefaciens*-Mediated. Acta Agron Sin 36(5): 788-793.

Mitra Sabyasachi, Saha Suprakash, Guha Biswajit, Chakrabarti Krishanu, Satya Pratik, Sharma AK, Gawande SP, Kumar Mukesh, Saha Monidipta (2013) Ramie: The Strongest Bastfibre of Nature, Technical Bulletin No. 8, Central Research Institute for Jute and Allied Fibres, ICAR, Barrackpore, Kolkata-120, p. 38.

Mou Q, Chen RX, Wu JH, Ge H, Yang F (1995). Summary on Breeding of Ramie (*Boehmerianivea* Gaud) in China. GuizhouAgricSci 5: 57-60.

Naidu GSN, Panda T (1998) Production of Pectinolytic Enzyme - A Review. Bioprocess Engineering 19: 3555-3561.

Pan CL, Li SC, Li YJ (1995). Factors Influencing Plant Regeneration Efficiency of Ramie (*Boehmerianivea Gaud*). China's Fibre Crops 17: 1-6.

Patruszka M (1977) Ramie Fibre Production & Manuring FAO Industrial Service, Rome.

Qinghua YCZ (1982). Study on Tissue Culture and its Application for the Rapid Propagation of Ramie. SciAgricSinica,72: 25-28.

Ray DP, Satya P, Mitra S, Banerjee P, Ghosh RK (2014) Degumming of Ramie: Challenge to the Queen of Fibres. International Journal of Bioresource Science 1(1): 37-41.

Saikia R, Boruah H, Samanta R (2009) Microbial Degumming of Decorticated Ramie and its Fibre Characteristics. Indian J Fibre Text Res 34: 187-190.

Sancheti S, Sancheti S, Seo SY (2010) Evaluation of Antiglycosidase and Anticholinesterase Activities of *Boehmerianivea*. Pak J Pharm Sci23: 236-240.

Sarkar D, Sinha MK, Kundu A, Kar CS, Saha A, Kharbikar LL Mahapatra BS (2010) Why is Ramie the Strongest but Stiffest of Bastfibres? Current Sci 98(12): 1570-1572.

Satya P, Sarkar D, Kar CS, Mitra J, Sharma HK, Biswas C, Sinha MK, Mahapatra BS, Maiti RK (2010) Possibilities for Reducing Gum Content in Ramie, the Strongest and Finest Bast Fibre. IJAEB 3(3): 261-264.

Semwal DK, Rawat U, Semwal R, Singh R, Krishna P, Singh M, Singh GJ (2009) Chemical Constituents from the Leaves of *Boehmeriarugulosa* with Antidiabetic and Antimicrobial Activities. J Asian Nat Prod Res 11: 1045-1055.

Singh DP (1996) Ramie (Boehmerianivea), Central Research Institute for Jute and Allied Fibres, Kolkata, p 11.

Sinha MK, Mitra Sabyasachi, Rama Subramanian T, Mahapatra BS (2009). Crop Diversification for Profitiblity in Jute and Allied Fibre Crops. Indian J Agro 54(2): 221-225.

Sixiang Z, Chuntao W, Chungeng Y, Guoxian C, Yaochu C, Zongdao L (1996) Ramie Research Institute, Hunan Agricultural University. Changsha 410128, Hunan; China. Journal of Hunan Agricultural University 22(3): 245-248.

Sut, D, Talukdar P, Singh S (2004). Micro-propagation of Ramie {Boehmerianivea (L) Gaud} Through Shoot-tip and Nodal Segment Culture. Indian J Agric Res 38: 131-4.

Vavilov NI (1951) The Origin, Variation, Immunity and Breeding of Cultivated Plants. Chronica Botanica1 3: 21-26.

Wang B, Peng D, Liu L, Sun Z, Zhang N, Gao S (2007) An Efficient Adventitious Shoot Regeneration System for Ramie (*Boehmerianivea* Gaud) Using Thidiazuron. Bot Stud 48: 173-180.

Wang B, Peng DX, Sun ZX, Zhang N, Gao SM (2008). *In vitro* Plant Regeneration from Seedling-derived Explants of Ramie [*Boehmerianivea* (L.) Gaud]. *In Vitro* Cell DevBiolo - Plant 44(2): 105-111.

Wang B, Liu L, Wang X, Yang J, Sun Z, Zhang N, Gao S, Xing X, Peng D (2009). Transgenic ramie [*Boehmerianivea* (L.) Gaud.]: Factors Affecting the Efficiency of *Agrobacteriumtumefaciens*-mediated Transformation and Regeneration. Plant Cell Rep 28(9): 1319-1327.

Wang XL, Peng DX, Chen XH (2003). Effects of Different Basal Mediafor Different Explants on Induction and Differentiation of Ramie. J Huazhong Agric Univ 22: 431-435.

Wei J, Lin L, Su X, Qin S, Xu Q, Tang Z, Deng Y, Zhou Y, He S (2014) Anti-hepatitis B Virus Activity of *Boehmerianivea* Leaf Extracts in Human HepG2.2.15 cells. Biomed Rep 2(1): 147-151.

Wood IM, Angus JF (1974) A Review of Prospective Crops for the Ord Irrigation Area. II Fibre Crops. CSIRO Australian Division of Land Use Research Technical Paper 36: 1-27.

Wu Xudong, Xing Hucheng, JieYucheng, Xum Qingguo (2009). Study on Regeneration Plants by Tissue Culture Used Leaf Explant in Ramie. Chinese AgricSci Bull 25(23): 86-89.

www. swicofil.com

www.wikipedia.org

Yan J, Luo D, Luo Y, Gao X, Zhang G (2006) Induction of G1 Arrest and Differentiation in MDA-MB-231 Breast Cancer Cell by Boehmeriasin A, a Novel Compound from Plant. Int J Gynecol Cancer 16: 165-170.

Zhang GG, Zhao LN, Cheng JH (2002) Medicinal Value and Development Prospects of Ramie. Plant Fiber Sci China, 24.

Zhao QH, Yan CJ, Pan CL, Yang MQ, Wang CT, Li ZD (1984). A Study on Leaf Tissue Culture of Ramie. China's Fibre Crops Zhongguo Mazuo 4: 9-12.

Zheng L, Du Y, Zhang J (2001) Degumming of Ramie Fibers by Alkalophilic Bacteria and Their Polysaccharide Degrading Enzymes. Bioresource Technol 78: 89-94.

Zheng Sixiang, Luo Huiming, Dong Yanyu, Hong Yahui, Wang Chuntao, Li Zongdao, Cheng Yaochu, Liu Guomin (1995). The Application of Tissue Culture to the Study of Ramie Polyploidy. J Human AgricUniv 21(4): 361-365.

Zhou Jianlin, JieYucheng, Jiang Yanbo, Zhong Yingli, Liu Yunhai, Zhang Jian (2005). Development of Simple Sequence Repeats (SSR) Markers of Ramie and Comparison of SSR and Inter-SSR Marker Systems. Prog Natural Sci 15(2): 137-142.

Pages: 168-188

SEED TREATMENT, PLANT HEALTH AND AGRO-TECHNOLOGY

Edited by: Dr. Avnish Chauhan and Dr. Pawan Kumar 'Bharti'

ISBN: 978-93-5056-810-1

Edition: 2016

Published by: Discovery Publishing House Pvt. Ltd., New Delhi (India)

9

A New Plant Breeding Technique

Reverse Breeding

R.R. Dhutmal[1], **S.R. Maloo**[2] and **H.V. Kalpande**[3]

Introduction

Reverse breeding is a novel breeding techniques which uses the approach of genetic engineering. One common feature of the new plant breeding techniques *viz.* agro infiltration, virus induced gene silencing, cisgenics, Oligonucleotide-mediated mutation, combining of genetically modified and non-genetically modified plant parts by grafting, and reverse breeding is that they all lead to end products (plants or plant parts) that are free of foreign genes. This means that we can achieve the end the new breeding techniques using conventional plant breeding techniques, but it will take much longer time with more difficulties (Schaart, 2009).

Traditional F_1 hybrid development is a tedious process. First step is the development of true breeding homozygous lines which eventually takes much longer time for selfing or close inbreeding and selection generation after generations and subsequently they are crossed in various combinations to study their combining ability. The best combiners are crossed in various fashion followed by evaluation to get desirable commercial hybrid variety. Perotti *et al.* (2004) proposed apomixis as a technique to fix heterozygosity but has not yet lead to breeding application. Dirks *et al.* (2003) demonstrated

1 Ph.D. Scholar (PBG), Rajasthan Collage of Agriculture, MPUAT, Udaipur. Pin: 313 001. (Rajasthan) (India).

2 Professor and Dean, Rajasthan Collage of Agriculture, MPUAT, Udaipur, 313 001 (Rajasthan) (India).

3 Sr. Breeder, Sorghum Research Station, Vasantrao Naik Marathwada Krishi Vidyapeeth, Parbhani -431 401 (M.S.) (India).

a novel technique of reverse breeding, for fixation of complex heterozygous genomes by constructing complementing homozygous lines. Reverse breeding approach is invented to provide an alternative method for developing homozygous parental lines for the production of hybrids. The second object is to use this method to provide even more flexibility in combining desirable parental traits in heterozygous off spring.

Classical Plant Breeding

Classical plant breeding relies on the manipulation of the combination of chromosomes. Manipulation of plant chromosome combination is achieved mainly through selection, hybridization, polyploidy and mutation breeding techniques.

(i) Selection

Selection is the most ancient and basic procedure in plant breeding. It generally involves three distinct steps. First, a large number of selections are made from the genetically variable original population. Second, progeny rows are grown from the individual plant selections for observational purposes. After obvious elimination, the selections are grown over several years to permit observations of performance under different environmental conditions for making further eliminations. Finally, the selected and inbred lines are compared to existing commercial varieties in their yielding performance and other aspects of agronomic importance.

(ii) Hybridization

Hybridization is practiced when there is limited genetic variability in a species and improvement is not possible by pureline selection. Hybridization is useful in three main ways first one to combine several desirable traits from different sources into single genotypes secondly, to create vast genetic variability in a population and third to develop hybrid varieties for commercial cultivation. One basic requirement for hybridization is development of homozygous inbred lines. Once a pure line is generated, it is outcrossed, *i.e.* combined with another inbred line. Then the resulting progeny is selected for combination of the desired traits. In case of transfer of desirable traits e.g. resistance against a disease from wild species, most of the times it was found that some unwanted characters (like low yield, low nutritional value) linked with desirable are also transferred to the crop it is known as genetic drag.

These unfavorable traits must be removed by time-consuming back-crossing, *i. e.* repeated crossing with the crop parent. There are two types of hybrid plants: interspecific and intergeneric hybrids. Beyond this biological boundary, hybridization cannot be accomplished due to sexual incompatibility, which limits the possibilities of introducing desired traits into crop plants. Heterosis is an effect which is achieved by crossing highly inbred lines of crop plants.

(iii) Polyploidy

Plants having more than two basic sets of chromosomes are referred as polyploid and such condition is known as polyploidy. They can occur naturally or can be produced artificially by applying the chemical colchicine, which leads to a doubling of the chromosome number. Generally, the main effect of polyploidy is increase in size of plant parts and genetic variability. On the other hand, polyploid plants often have a lower fertility and grow more slowly.

(iv) Mutation

Another breeding technique is mutation breeding. The occurrence of genetic mutations is a natural biological phenomenon creating new genetic variation. Mutation can be induced artificially to create new genetic variability using physical mutagens e.g. ionizing radiation or chemical mutagens e.g. EMS, MMS and other mutagenic chemicals to produce a high number of genome-wide mutations. Subsequent selection of favorable mutant plants and introducing these in breeding programmes has lead to a development of many commercial varieties in variety of crop plants (Ahloowalia *et al.* 2004). Because the most of mutants carry undesirable traits, this method has not been widely used in breeding programmes. Recently, the development of a molecular biological technique called 'tilling' has attracted breeders attention, which allows rapid identification of mutations in genes of interest (Comai and Henikoff, 2006) leading to a more focused application of mutation breeding.

Crop Improvement by Genetic Modification

Genetic modification methodology is recently invented technology which is based on recombinant DNA technology. Several methods have been developed with an object to develop a rapid method of crop improvement, overcoming crossing barriers and evolution of new genotype. Direct gene transfer (DGT) techniques whereby 'naked' DNA is introduced into plant cells were the first to be used. Direct DNA transfer involves electroporation i.e. transfer of DNA to protoplasts by using electric currents or chemical fusagens such as Poly Ethylene Glycol (PEG) with calcium phosphate. The plasmid DNA can also be delivered into host cell by mechanical means i.e. by microscopic needles (microinjection) or through high velocity metal particles i.e. gold or tungsten (called particle bombardment or ballistic method) .The DNA that is released will integrate into the plant cell genome and subsequent selection of genetically modified cells and regeneration of plants from these cells will result in the ultimate genetically modified plant lines. Of all these DGT techniques only particle bombardment is used extensively and with success and is especially applied for transformation of monocots like wheat, rice and corn.

Agrobacterium Mediated DNA Transfer

The most commonly used genetic modification (or transformation) technique makes use of the natural DNA-vector *Agrobacterium*. Large Plasmids in these *Agrobacteria* are called Tumor inducing plasmids (Ti), a recombinant Ti plasmid with target gene inserted in the T-DNA can be integrated into the plant DNA and made to be expressed. On infection of the plant cell by members of this bacterium genus foreign gene/DNA inserted into 'T-DNA' region is integrated into plant genome. After integration a partial Right Border (usually 3 base pairs) and Left Border (21-22 base pairs) of T-DNA are usually present in the genome that confers stability to inserted T-DNA in host genome. An unintentional transfer of additional DNA plasmid (vector backbone) to the plant genome has been observed. Recently the occasional transfer of *Agrobacterium* chromosomal DNA has been reported (Ulker *et al.* 2008).

Other Novel Technologies

Table 9.1: Different Classes of New Breeding Techniques and Accompanying Techniques are Listed in this Table

New breeding Technique	Accompanying Technique
Genetically (partial) modified plant lines are created and these plant lines are subsequently used to create derivatives that are in the end completely free of the genetic material that was used in the initial genetic modification.	Agro-infiltration
	Virus Induced Gene Silencing (VIGS)
	Reverse breeding
	Accelerated breeding following induction of early flowering
Combining genetically modified and non-genetically modified plants by grafting. From these chimeric plants only the non-genetically modified-part is used for harvesting of food or feed products.	Grafting of a non-genetically modified scion on a genetically modified rootstock
	Grafting of a genetically modified scion on a non-genetically modified rootstock
Use of genetic modification as a direct tool to introduce new, but to the germplasm belonging characteristics to a plant. The genetic material used for the modification is originating from the same or a sexual compatible species.	Cisgenesis
	Intragenesis
Genetic modification is used as a tool to make specific mutations. These techniques introduce site-directed mutations to native genes, leading to a knock-out of gene expression or to changes in the gene-expression pattern or in gene-product properties.	Oligo-induced mutation induction
	Zinc finger nuclease induced mutation
	Mutation through homologous recombination
Genetic modification is used to introduce proteins that lead to homologous recombination.	Zinc finger nuclease induced gene replacement
	Chloroplast transformation (homologous recombination)
	Homologous recombination
Epigenetic modification.	Gene-inactivation through DNA-methylation

Noevel Techniques Techniques for Crop Improvement

Some of the important new techniques are briefly described here:

(a) Zinc finger nuclease technology 1: Genes encoding for Zinc Finger Nucleases (ZFN) are delivered to plant cells without a repair template. The ZFN binds to the DNA and generates a site-specific double strand break (DSB). The natural DNA-repair process through non-homologous end-joining (NHEJ) leads to site-specific random mutations, which consist of changes of single or few base pairs, short deletions or insertions.

(b) Zinc finger nuclease technology 2: Genes encoding for Zinc Finger Nucleases (ZFN) are delivered to plant cells along with a short repair template. The ZFN binds to the DNA and generates a site-specific double strand break (DSB). Gene repair mechanisms generate site-specific point mutations like changes of single or few base pairs through homologous recombination.

(c) Zinc finger nuclease technology 3: Genes encoding for Zinc Finger Nucleases (ZFN) are delivered to plant cells along with a large stretch of DNA, whose ends are homologous to the DNA sequences flanking the cleavage site. As a result, the DNA stretch is site-specifically inserted into the plant genome.

(d) Oligonucleotide-directed mutagenesis: Also known as Targeted Gene Repair, Oligonucleotide-directed Gene Targeting, Genoplasty, Chimeraplasty, etc. oligonucleotides target homologous DNA and induce site-specific nucleotide substitutions, insertions or deletions through repair mechanisms. The following types of oligonucleotides are used: Single stranded DNA oligonucleotides, chimeric oligonucleotides, triple helix-forming oligonucleotides (TFOs) and RNA oligonucleotides.

(e) Cisgenesis/Intragenesis: A DNA fragment from the species itself or from a cross compatible species is inserted into the plant genome. In the case of cisgenesis, the inserted gene is unchanged and flanked by its own introns and regulatory sequences. In the case of intragenesis, the inserted DNA can be a new combination of DNA fragments from the species itself or from a cross compatible species.

(f) RNA dependent DNA methylation *via* RNAi/siRNA: Genes encoding for RNAs which are homologous to plant sequences, like promoter regions, are delivered to the plant cells. These genes, once transcribed, give rise to the formation of small double stranded RNAs. They induce methylation of the homologous sequences and consequently inhibit their transcription.

(g) Grafting on a genetically modified rootstock: A chimeric plant is produced by grafting a non-genetically modified scion on a genetically modified rootstock.

(h) Reverse breeding: Homozygous parental lines are produced from selected heterozygous plants by suppressing meiotic recombination. This suppression is obtained through RNA interference-mediate down regulation of genes involved in the meiotic recombination process. Subsequently, the obtained homozygous lines are hybridized, in order to reconstitute the original genetic composition of the selected heterozygous plants.

(i) Agro-infiltration: Plant tissues, mostly leaves, are infiltrated with a liquid suspension of *Agrobacterium* sp. containing a genetic construct. The genetic construct is locally expressed at high level, without being integrated into the plant genome.

Table 9.2: Most Relevant Crops and Traits Resulting from the Use of New Plant Breeding Techniques, According to Literature Findings

Technique	Crop	Traits	No. of Research Papers
ZNF	Maize	Herbicide tolerance	1
	Tobacco	Herbicide tolerance	3
ODM	Maize	Herbicide tolerance	2
	Rice	Herbicide tolerance	1
	Tobacco	Herbicide tolerance	3
	Oilseed rape	Herbicide tolerance	1
Cisgenesis/Intragenesis	Potato	Fungal resistance, black sot bruise tolerance, low acrylamide levels	5
	Apple	Fungal resistance	3
	Melon	Fungal resistance	1
Reverse breeding	Arabidopsis	—	1
RdDM	Maize	Male sterility	1
	Potato	Modified starch content	1
	Petunia	Reduced flower pigmentation	1
Grafting on GM rootstock	Grapevine	Resistance against bacteria, fungi and virus, rooting ability	6
	Potato	Resistance against fungi and changed composition	5
	Apple	Rooting ability	4
	Watermelon	Robust growth, virus resistance	4
	Orange	Fungal resistance, osmotic control	2
	Cucumber	Virus resistance	1
	Tomato	Insect resistance	1
	Plum	Resistance against fungi and nematodes	1

(Table Contd...)

Technique	Crop	Traits	No. of Research Papers
	Walnut	Rooting ability	1
	Pea	Virus resistance	1
	Rose	Rooting ability	1
	Tobacco	Resistance against bacteria	1
Agro-infiltration	Tomato	Production of vaccines (hepatitis B), screen for virus	2
	Tobacco	Production of vaccines(hepatitis B, HIV, diabetes, influenza, toxoplasma, tetanus, tuberculosis, SARS, New Castle disease, Norwalk virus), antibodies (HIV, hepatitis, cancer, blood typing, crinivirus), therapeutic proteins and enzymes; screen for resistance against fungi and virus	23
	White clover	Production of vaccines (bovine pasteurellosis)	1
	Lettuce	Production of vaccines (SARS)	1
	Rice	Screen for virus resistance	2
	Bean	Screen for virus resistance	1
	Potato	Screen for resistance against fungi and virus	3

Table 9.3: Leading Institutions Developing New Plant Breeding Technologies

Institution	Location	Number of Publications	Techniques
Wageningen university	Wageningen, The Netherlands	21	C, R, G, B, A
niversity of California, Riverside	Riverside, CA, uSA	11	O, R, G, A
John Innes Centre	Norwich, uK	9	C, R, G, A
J.R. Simplot *	Boise, Idaho, uSA	9	C
Austrian Academy of Sciences	Salzburg, Austria	9	R
university of Amsterdam	Amsterdam	6	Z, O, C, R
Iowa State university	Ames, Iowa, uSA	6	Z
Max-Planck Institute	Koln, Germany	4	O, R, G
University of Michigan	Ann Arbor, Michigan, uSA	4	C, Z
Institute of Plant Genetics and Crop Plant Research (IPK)	Gatersleben, Germany	4	O, G

*C, cisgenesis/intragenesis; R, RdDM; G, grafting; B, reverse breeding; A, agro-infiltration. *Private institution.*

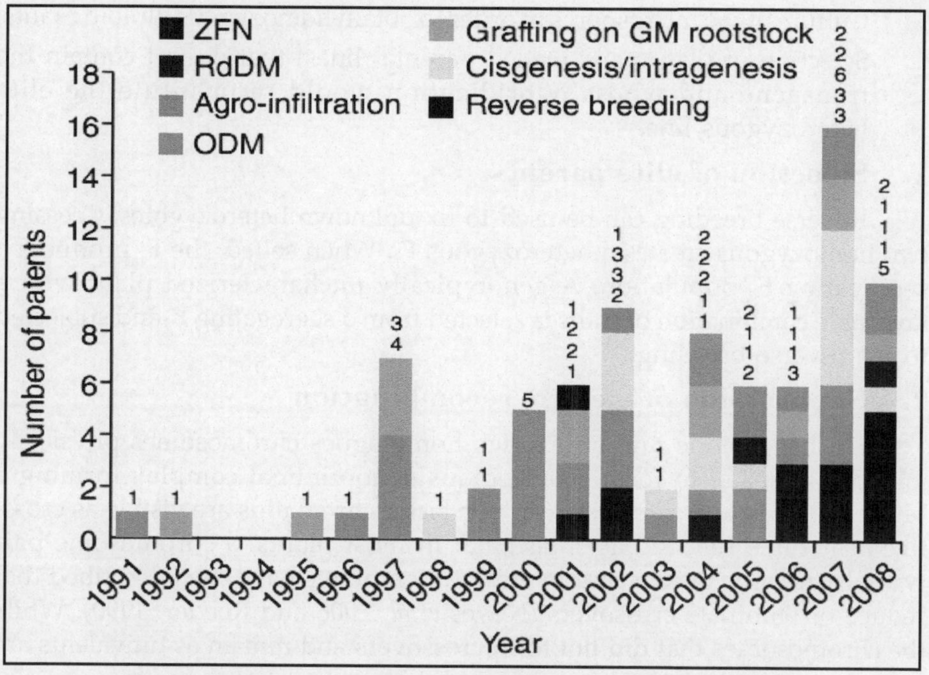

Fig. 9.1: **Patents on New Plant Breeding Technologies 1991-2008**

Reverse Breeding

Reverse breeding is a novel breeding technique that makes use of genetic modification to facilitate breeding of F1-hybrids by suppression of meiotic recombination. In the final breeding steps the genes used for the genetic modification are crossed out, resulting in end-products that are completely free of genetic modification-related DNA sequences. In these techniques, (partial) genetically modified plant lines are created and these plant lines are subsequently used to create derivatives that are in the end completely free of the genetic material that was used in the initial genetic modification.

The method of reverse breeding includes the following steps. (JRC technical and scientific report, 2011)

1. Selection of an elite heterozygous line that has to be reproduced;
2. Suppression of meiotic recombination in the elite heterozygous line through silencing of genes such as *dmc1* and *spo11* following plant transformation with transgenes encoding RNA interference (RNAi) sequences;
3. Production of haploid microspores (immature pollen grains) from flowers of the resulting transgenic elite heterozygous line;
4. Use of doubled haploid (DH) technology to double the genome of the haploid microspores and to obtain homozygous cells;

5. Culture of the microspores in order to obtain homozygous diploid plants;
6. Selection of plant pairs (called parental lines) that do not contain the transgene and whose hybridization would reconstitute the elite heterozygous line.

1. Selection of elite parents

Reverse breeding can be used to fix unknown heterozygotes. Crossing two homozygous creates a heterozygous F_1. When selfed, the F_1 produces a segregating F_2 population. A genotypically uncharacterized plant with a favorable combination of traits is selected from a segregating F_2 and subjected to the reverse breeding.

2. Suppression of meiotic recombination

During meiotic prophase I two homologues chromosomes physically joined (synopsis) to form a protenious synoptinimal complex forming a bivalent. Cross over sites between non sister chromatids are visible as cross-like structures referred as chiasmata. In most plants, a chromosome pair typically has one or two crossovers. Many mutants have been described that reduce or eliminate crossovers (Noyes *et al.* 2006 and Roeder, 1990). While the chromosomes that did not form crossovers and remain as univalents are referred as achiasmatic chromosome.

In reverse breeding suppression of meiotic recombination in the elite heterozygous line is a key step. The genes like *dmc1* and *spol1* are known to involve in meiotic recombination. Hence the selected heterozygous line is genetically modified by the introduction of gene silencing constructs to down-regulate the expression of these genes. The approaches used for gene silencing includes dominant transgenic approaches, dominant negative mutation or treatment with a chemical. first method deals with the prevention or suppression by interfering with one or more target genes involved in recombination. The target genes can be involved in double strand breaks, chromosome pairing, crossing-over and separation of sister chromatids. Gene silencing is practiced for those genes which are involved in crossover formation without interfering the chromosomal integrity. Caryl *et al.* 2000 and Nonomura *et al.* 2004 observed such genes in the Arabidopsis, *ASY1* and the rice, *ASY1* homologue *PAIR2,* the mutants of which display univalents at metaphase I. Other mutants with similar phenotypes are *dmc1, sds, ptd* and *spo11* (Couteau *et al.* 1999)

(i) RNAi technology

In reverse breeding RNA interference (RNAi) technology is used for down regulation of target genes (genes involved in meiotic crossover) is a general term which refers to a phenomenon in which double stranded RNA (dsRNA) molecules very effectively mediate gene silencing of genes with homology to the dsRNA. Silencing of an endogenous gene triggered by dsRNA is the result of post transcriptional gene silencing which is a phenomenon in which an RNA transcript is synthesized and rapidly and specifically degraded. RNAi has initially been demonstrated to operate in *Caenorhabditis elegans* (Fire, A. *et al*, 1998). RNAi has also been demonstrated to be effective in other organisms including plants (Chuang and Meyerowitz, 2000).

(ii) Construction of RNA Interference (RNAi)

DNA fragments of the *DMC1* and *SPO11* of *Brassica carinata* and the *MSH5* gene of *Arabidopsis thaliana* are inserted into pKANNIBAL (Wesley *et al.*, 2001) such that upon expression in plants an RNA molecule is formed which folds back upon itself thus forming a hairpin structure that triggers the specific degradation of homologous RNA.

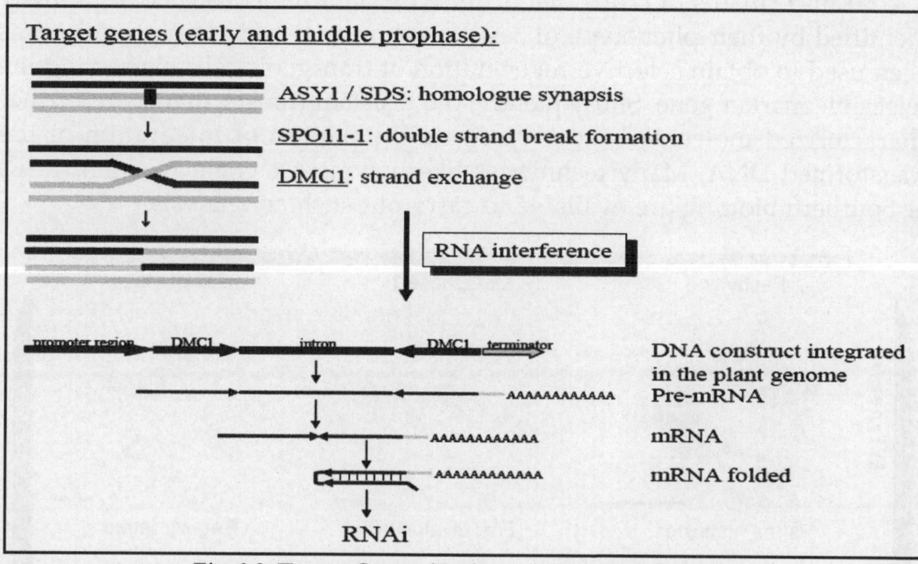

Fig. 9.2: Target Genes (Early and Middle Prophase)

(iii) Other methods for gene silencing

Dominant Negative Mutation

This mutation has altered gene product that acts antagonistically to the wild type Result in an altered molecular function (often inactive) and are characterized by a dominant or semidominat type. This method is applied in crop plants, in which stable transformation is difficult or impossible to achieve,

Virus-induced Gene Silencing (VIGS)

In this method a viral nucleic acid sequence is modified which includes a target gene RAN sequence. After infection the plant will break down the viral RNA using siRNA, targeting simultaneously the plants' endogenous mRNA (Ruiz *et al*. 1998 and Baulcombe, 2004).

Grafting on GM Rootstock

Target gene may be silenced by silencing molecules delivered by graft transmission (Shaharuddin *et al.* 2006). Shoots of the plant in which genes are to be silenced would be grafted on transgenic rootstocks.

Suppression by Chemical Inhibitor

This deals with the exogenous application of compounds that cause inhibition or omission of recombination during meiosis e.g. DIDS (Ishida *et al.*, 2009), PSF (Morozumi *et al.*, 2009), Halenaquinone (Takaku *et al.*, 2011), Ri-1 (Budke *et al.*, 2012) inhibit RAD 51. Mirin inhibit MRN complex (Dupre *et al.*, 2008). The important feature of this technique is that the resultant RB products i.e. double haploids are free of transgene.

Transformants of crops that acquired a silencing construct are initially identified by their phenotype of resistance to the selective agent which has been used to obtain selective regeneration of transgenic cells expressing the selectable marker gene. Subsequently, the resistant transformants are further characterized molecularly to investigate the pattern of integration of the transformed DNA. Many techniques like polymerase chain reaction (PCR) or Southern blotting are available to carry out such an analysis.

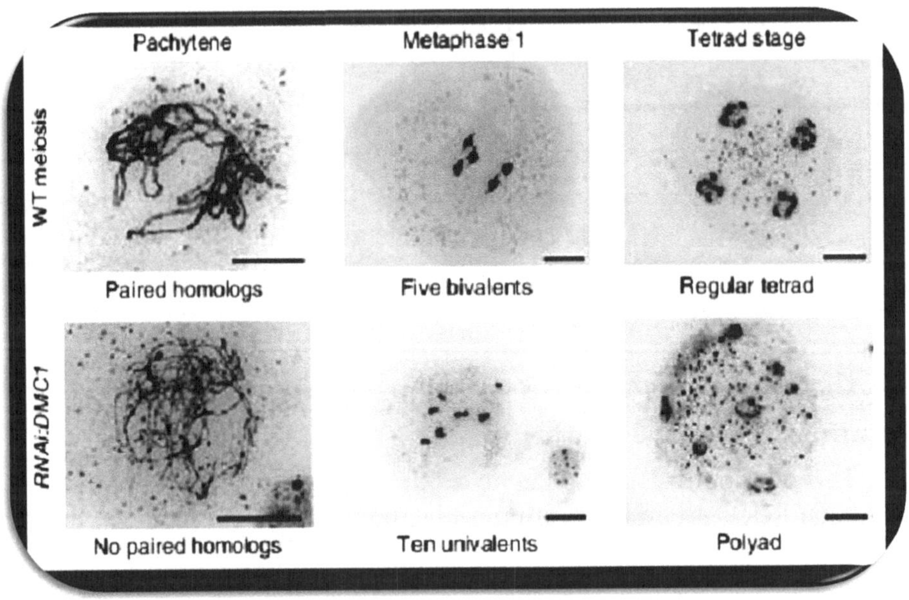

Fig. 9.3: **Meiosis in Wild-type and RNAi: DMC1 Transformants (Wijner *et al.* 2012)**

3. Production of haploid microspores

Recombination is prevented or suppressed before or while haploid cells are being formed, these cells are isolated and used for regeneration of a complete plant. Such plant is haploid and can become diploid either spontaneously or through other means, such as treatment with colchicine. Haploid cells can be derived from germ cells such as spore mother cells or somatic cells that have become haploid by means of a natural or induced process. Once the haploid plant is diploidized it is homozygous for all chromosomes and it can be used for reverse breeding (Dirks, *et al.*2009)

4 & 5. Use of double haploid

The production of diploid plants out of haploid spores is a tissue culture technique which is used widely in plant breeding to accelerate the production of plant which are completely homozygous. Usually this technology is referred to as doubled haploid or DH technology. The DHs made from spores produced from achiasmatic meiosis contain non-recombinant parental chromosomes. Achiasmatic meiosis leads to the production of both anuploide and euploide spores. Only euploide spores having complete set of chromosomes are important. Selection of the required euploid spores automatically achieved since only spores containing at least one copy of all chromosomes can pass through all developmental stages. Development of RB is limited to those crops in which double haploids are easily developed. The technique of double haploid is developed for many crops. (Maluszynski *et al.*, 2003 and Forster *et al.*, 2007). But still There are, some exceptions such as tomato, cotton, soybean in which doubled haploid plants are rarely formed or not available at all (Zhang *et al.*, 2008). Genotyping of DHs by molecular markers is indispensable for RB to ensure that final product should not contain any transgene.

6. Selection of plant pairs or parental lines

Among a collection of these homozygous diploid plants, parental pairs will be selected that together reconstitute the genetic composition of the original elite heterozygous elite line. Selection of homozygous parental plants that do not contain transgenes ensures that the resulting F_1-hybrids are non-genetically modified. This novel plant breeding approach offers clear advantages over existing techniques due to the fact that in principle any heterozygous plant can now be commercially exploited through re-synthesis of suitable parental lines.

(i) Chances of finding complementing parents

Assuming that each univalent has an equal chance of moving to either pole, the probability of a spore with a normal chromosome complement is ½ n, with n equaling the haploid chromosome number of the species. For plants with a basic chromosome number exceeding 12, the chances of finding balanced gametes get very small (with only one out of over 4000 spores being balanced).

If n is the basic chromosome number then maximum number of different DHs obtained from a heterozygous diploid in a RB experiment equals 2n, The probability that one randomly chosen pair of double haploid plants from this population, upon crossing, results in an F1 hybrid which has a genotype identical to genotype in which recombination has been suppressed (original genotype) is ½ n (because $2^n/(2^n)^2$)· The number of combinations between different DHs is n(n-1) D 2. and the probability of at least one complementary combination of two DHs is given by the formula $[(2^n\text{-}1)\ D\ 2^n]^{n(n-1)\ D\ 2} = 0.01$ (P = 99%) (Dirks *et al.* 2009)

Table 9.4: Probability of Number of DH Required in Different Species/Crops

Haploid Chromosome Number (X)	Probability of Number of DH Required	Model Species/Crop
5	18	Arabidopsis
6	25	Spinach, corn salad
7	35	Cucumber
8	49	Onion
9	69	Barley, carrot, sugarbeet,most vegetable Brassicas, lettuce
10	98	Maize, sorghum, asparagus, cocoa
11	138	Banana, watermelon, celery,fennel, common bean
12	195	Tomato, pepper,melon, rice, egg plant

(ii) Reconstruction of heterozygous germplasm

By the use of this technique superior heterozygous plants can be propagated without prior knowledge of their genetic constitution

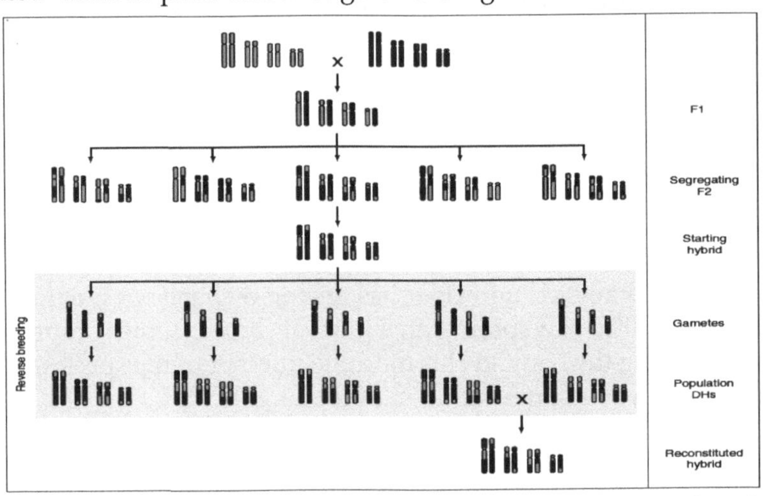

Fig. 9.4: **Reconstruction of Heterozygous Germplasm (Dirks, *et al.*2009)**

Figure 9.1 illustrates that crossing two homozygous parents (grey and black bars) creates a heterozygous F_1. Upon selfing the F_1 produces a segregating F_2 population. A F_2 plant of unknown genetic constitution but having desirable characters as per the objectives is selected as a starting material and subjected to the two steps of reverse breeding (grey box). Then meiotic crossing over is knockdown by down regulation of the target gene through a method referred to as RNA interference (RNAi). By knocking down meiotic crossing over, whole parental chromosomes are transmitted through spores without any change in their genetic information due to suppression of recombination. In this example the four chromosomes in the hybrid can generate 16 different combinations in the gametes–only five are shown for convenience. Using in vitro culture techniques the achiasmatic gametes (having complete set of parental chromosomes) are then used produce doubled haploid (DH) lines (not having any foreign modified DNA construct). From DHs lines, complementary parents are selected which, when crossed perfectly reconstitute the starting hybrid *i.e.* originally selected F_2 plant.

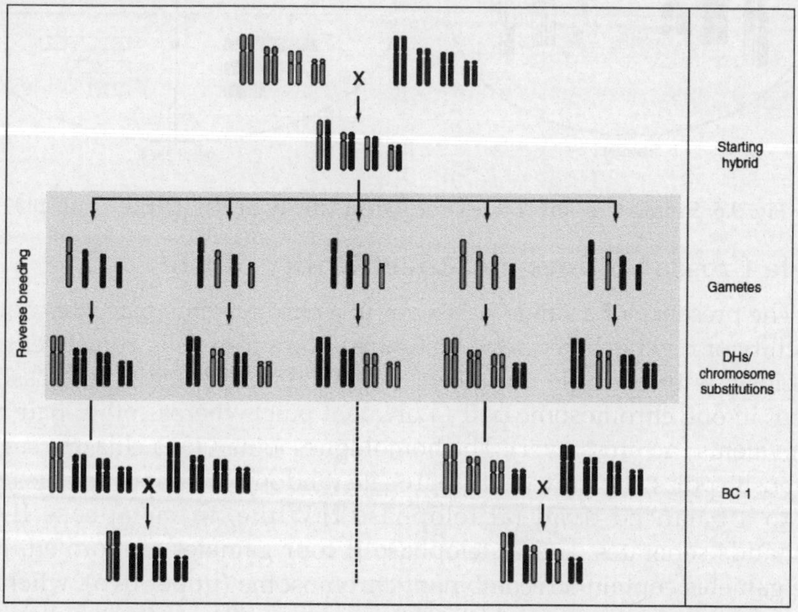

Fig. 9.5: **Development of Chromosome Substitution (Dirks, *et al.*, 2009)**

Development of Chromosome Substitution Lines to Study Gene Interaction

Figure explains how chromosome substitution lines can be obtained when RB is applied to an F1 hybrid of known parents. These homozygous chromosome substitution lines provide novel tools for the study of gene interactions. When crossed with one of the original parents, hybrids can be formed in which one of the chromosomes is homozygous (lower right), whereas it is also possible to produce hybrids in which just one chromosome is heterozygous (lower left).

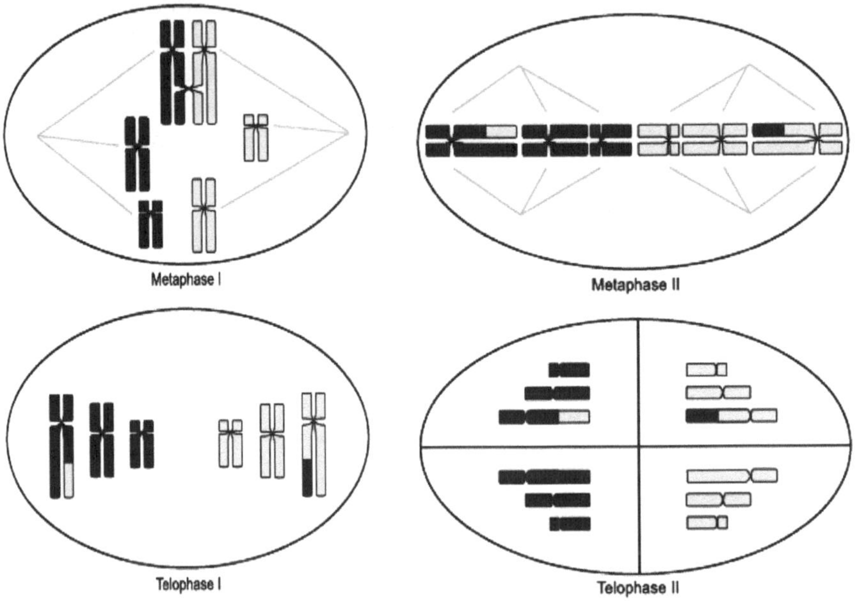

Fig. 9.6: **Single Crossover does not Affect Utility of RB (Dirks, *et al.* 2009)**

Single Crossover does not Affect Utility of RB

The presence of a single crossover in a chromosome pair does not affect the utility of reverse breeding. The ûgure shows four cells at different stages of meiosis with a single crossover. At metaphase I, a single crossover is present in one chromosome pair (a bivalent pair) whereas other pair remain as univalents (no cross over). The homologues joined by a chiasma segregate to opposite poles, the univalents segregate randomly to opposite poles, giving rise, to a balanced dyad (at telophase I).While, in metaphase II, sister chromatids seperates, and at telophase II four gametes are formed. Half of these gametes contain a recombinant chromosome (upper two), whereas the other half contain non-recombinant chromosomes (lower two) and are useful for reverse breeding.

Reverse Breeding for CMS Conversion

The CMS donor is made homozygous for a recessive mutation or a transgene that confers recombination suppression. The donor line is preferably genetically dissimilar from the line that has to be converted to male sterility for a large number of nuclear genetic markers so that the difference between the chromosomes of the CMS and the fertile donor can be more easily determined. In order to convert a desired inbred line or a pure line (homozygous or nearly homozygous) into a similar line but with a CMS background, a first cross is made by pollination of the said CMS homozygous recombination suppressed line with pollen of the desired line. The resulting F1 progeny contains CMS and 50% of the chromosomes of the desired line. In the meiosis of the resulting F1 plants, no recombination occurs as a result of the invention. This means that in the egg cells, independent chromosome assortment takes place. In the case of cabbage (*Brassica oleracea* L.) that has 9 chromosomes as a haploid set this means that 1 in 512 egg cells $((\frac{1}{2})^9)$ have the same (but haploid) genetic composition as the said desired line that was used for pollinating the recombination suppressed CMS line. This egg cell is again fertilized by pollen of the desired line and the resulting seed is genetically identical for the nuclear genes to the original desired line, but now has acquired the CMS plasma. So in the second cross with the desired line, 1 in 512 seeds is isogenic to the desired line but said having acquired the CMS plasma of the donor line. In the newly achieved CMS/nuclear composition, no transgenic genes/plants have to be retained due to segregation of the transgenic locus that is responsible for suppression of meiotic recombination and because the transgenic plants are not retained. Identification of the new CMS/desired nuclear line combination is very easy when DNA fingerprinting technology is used (Dirks, *et al.*, 2009).

Detection and Identification of Line Obtained by Reverse Breeding

Detection and Identification with Prior Knowledge

In some cases gene silencing using RNAi can lead to RNA-directed DNA methylation of the transcribed region. In such cases, like for the RdDM technique (see chapter 4), the following methods may be used for potential detection of methylation-related changes:

Methylation specific PCR-based techniques based on amplification of bisulphite-converted DNA

Methylation-sensitive/dependent restriction enzymes: Principle of methylation-sensitive restriction technique is that the methylation-sensitive restriction enzymes cannot cut the methylated DNA site

Methylation-Sensitive High-Resolution Melting (MS-HRM) analysis: High-resolution melting (HRM) analysis exploits the reduced thermal stability of DNA fragments that contain base mismatches to detect single nucleotide polymorphisms (SNPs)

However, it will in any case not be possible to identify the source of DNA methylation as resulting from a specific plant breeding technique since the DNA-methylation phenomenon also occurs in nature.

Note: standard PCR techniques are suitable to reliably confirm the absence of genetic modification-related DNA sequences into the lines selected for further breeding.

Detection and Identification without Prior Knowledge

Both detection and identification are not possible.

On that basis it was concluded that the end-products of reverse breeding are free of genetic modification-related DNA sequences since the homozygous parental lines are produced from double-haploid plants which are screened for the absence of RNAi construct during the breeding process.

It is therefore not possible to distinguish products resulting from the use of reverse breeding technique from products resulting from conventional breeding. Identification of products resulting from the use of reverse breeding technique is therefore not possible.

Potential Application in Current Breeding Programmes

Reverse breeding is still in its research phase, but is clearly a technique with high potential. The main advantage of reverse breeding is that using reverse breeding, elite heterozygous plants can be produced as F1 hybrids because of re-synthesis of parental lines.

Table 9.5: Comparison of End Products of New Breeding Techniques and Conventional Bred Crops

Reverse Bred Crop	Conventional Bred Crop
Parental line produced require less time	Parental line produced for further breeding require more time
Reconstitution of original parental line possible	Reconstitution of original parental line not possible in hybridization
Initial genetic modification involve but final product non-genetically modified	Final product is non genetically modified
End product not under GMO regulation	End Product not under GMO regulation

Environmental Consequences

For reverse breeding the consequences for the environment are similar to conventional breeding. Reason is that the parental lines and subsequent F1 produced by reverse breeding is devoid of any genetic and because a possible RNA-directed DNA methylation that is transmitted to the offspring will only have an effect on meiotic recombination. Such conventionally bred parental lines and F1-hybrids can serve as baseline.

Consequences for Food and Feed Safety

The F1 hybrids are usually used for food and feed production. Therefore, the F1-hybrids are considered for the consequences for food and feed safety, rather than the parental lines, which are the actual end products of reverse breeding. F1-hybrids obtained by crossing of reverse breeding-derived parental lines do not contain any genetic modification-related DNA sequences and a possible RNA-directed DNA methylation that is transmitted to the offspring will only have an effect on meiotic recombination. Therefore, products from these hybrids are as safe as products obtained from the original heterozygous line used for reverse breeding or as conventionally bred F1-hybrids. The original heterozygous line or conventionally bred F1- hybrids can serve as baseline.

Table 9.6: Findings on Food/Feed and Environmental Safety and on Regulatory Issues

Reverse breeding COGEM (2006)	It was concluded that risk analysis required for transgenic plants, is not needed for plants obtained through reverse breeding. This conclusion is based on the fact that hybrid plants obtained through reverse breeding do not contain recombinant DNA and do not have any new genetic characteristics. Therefore, no new open reading frames can be created through which toxic or allergenic products could be formed.The report also states that reverse breeding makes use of genetic modification and that therefore, according to the European legislation, a crop produced through reverse breeding would be recognised as a GMO. The authors recommend that plants that are acquired using the technique of reverse breeding should be handled as non-GMOs because they do not have any new characteristics compared to the starting heterozygous plant.
Schaart & Visser (2009)	Schaart & Visser (2009) conclude that food and feed of crops obtained through reverse breeding are as safe as products from the original heterozygous lines, because hybrids obtained by crossing of reverse breeding- derived parental lines do not contain any genetic modification-related DNA sequences and a possible RdDM that is transmitted to the offspring will only have an effect on meiotic recombination. For the same reasons the consequences for the environment will be similar to those of parental lines and F_1-hybrids obtained by conventional breeding.
Lammerts Van Bueren *et al.* (2007)	Lammerts Van Bueren et al. (2007) discuss cisgenesis and reverse breeding in the context of organic farming. They regard products obtained through these techniques as not acceptable for organic farming because of ethical reasons (respect of naturalness and integrity of all organisms).

Advantages of Reverse Breeding

1. This technique if used in vegetatively propagated species, it would be enable the propagation of an elite heterozygous line to be converted from vegetative to seed propagation (if feasible for that species).
2. Apomixis represent dead end as it could not be improved further by conventional hybrid breeding techniques.
3. Improvement of heterozygote through individual parental lines by conventional breeding methods possible.

Limitations of Reverse Breeding

1. Probably most suitable for vegetatively propagated crops where elite heterozygous varieties exist without inbred parents.
2. With this technique F1 Hybrids appears to be pointless because parents will already be known.
3. only considered workable for plants with a chromosome number less than 12 Require microspore derived DH technology to be available for particular crop species.
4. Requires molecular markers for all of the chromosomes.
5. Taken together these limitations point to a fairly narrow range of crops for which RB might be suitable.
6. On the basis of the available information, the technique did not have widespread application.

Future Prospects

1. Reverse Breeding is very young technique and therefore is still required to overcome technical problems and to fully exploit its potential.
2. The invention is suitable for use in agricultural, horticultural crops.
3. Crop plant may be subjected to the method of invention comprise maize, rice, sugar beet, oilseed rape, ryegrass, sunflower, soybean, tomato, cucumber, spinach, eggplant, onion, radish.

REFERENCES

Ahloowalia, B.S., Maluszynski, M., Nichterlein, K. (2004): Global Impact of Mutation-derived Varieties. *Euphytica*, 135: 187-204.

Baulcombe DC (1999) Fast Forward Genetics Based on Virus-induced Gene Silencing. *Current Opinion in Plant Biology*, 2: 109-113.

Budke, B., Logan, H.L., Kalin, J.H., Zelivianskaia, A.S., Cameron McGuire, W., Miller, L.L., Stark, J.M., Kozikowski, A.P., Bishop, D.K. and Connell, P.P. (2012): RI-1: A Chemical Inhibitor of RAD51 that Disrupts Homologous Recombination in Human Cells. *Nucleic Acids Res.*, 40(15): 7347-57.

Caryl, A.P., Armstrong, S.J., Jones, G.H. and Franklin, F.C.H. (2000) A Homologue of the Yeast HOP1 Gene is Inactivated in the Arabidopsis Meiotic Mutant Asy1. *Chromosoma*, 109: 62-71.

Chuang, C., and Meyerowitz, E. M.(2000): Specific and Heritable Genetic Interference by Double-stranded RNA in Arabidopsis Thaliana. Proc. Natl. Acad. Sci., 97(9): 4985-4990.

COGEM. (2006): New Techniques in Plant Biotechnology. COGEM Report CGM/061024-02. The Netherlands Commission on Genetic Modification (NL).

Comai L and Henikoff S (2006) TILLING: Practical Single-nucleotide Mutation Discovery. *Plant J*, 45: 684-694.

Couteau, F., Belzile, F., Horlow, C., Grandjean, O., Vezon, D. and Doutriaux, M.P. (1999) Random Chromosome Segregation without Meiotic Arrest in Both Male and Female Meiocytes of a dmc1 Mutant of Arabidopsis. *Plant Cell*, 11, 1623-1634.

Dirk,R., Kees van Dun, C. Bastiaan de Snoo, Mark van den Berg, Cilia L.C. Lelivelt, William Voermans, Leo Woudenberg, Jack P.C. de Wit, Kees Reinink, Johan W. Schut , Eveline van der Zeeuw, Aat Vogelaar, Gerald Freymark, Evert W. Gutteling, Marina N. Keppel, Paul van Drongelen, Matthieu Kieny, Philippe Ellul, Alisher Touraev, Hong Ma, Hans de Jong and Erik Wijnker. 2009. Reverse Breeding: a Novel Breeding Approach Based on Engineered Meiosis. *Plant Biotechnology Journal*, 7: 837-845.

Dirks, R.H.G., Van Dun, C.M.P. and Reinink, K. (2003) Rijk Zwaan Zaadteelt en Zaadhandel B.V. Reverse Breeding, WOD 2003D 017753.

Dupre, A., Boyer-Chatenet, L., Sattler, R.M., Modi, A.P., Lee, J.H., Nicolette, M. L., Kopelovich, L., Jasin, M., Baer, R., Paull, T.T. and Gautier J. (2008): A Forward Chemical Genetic Screen Reveals an Inhibitor of the Mre11-Rad50-Nbs1 Complex. *Nat Chem Biol.*, 4(2): 119-25.

Fire A. (1998) Potent and Specific Genetic Interference by Double-stranded RNA in Caenorhabditis Elegans. *Nature*, 391(6669): 806-11.

Forster, B.P., Heberle-Bors, E., Kasha, K.J. and Touraev, A. (2007) The Resurgence of Haploids in Higher Plants. *Trends Plant Sci.*, 12, 368-375.

Ishida, T., Yoshimasa Takizawa,Takashi Kainuma, Jin Inoue, Tsutomu Mikawa, Takehiko Shibata, Hidekazu Suzuki, Satoshi Tashiro and Hitoshi Kurumizaka (2009): DIDS, a Chemical Compound that Inhibits RAD51-mediated Homologous Pairing and Strand Exchange. *Nucleic Acids Res.*, 37(10): 3367-3376.

JRC (2011) New Plant Breeding Techniques. State-of-the-art and Prospects for Commercial Development. European Commission: Joint Research Center, (EUR 24760 EN): 1-219.

Lammerts Van Bueren, E.T., Verhoog, H., Tiemens-Hulscher, M., Struik, P.C., Haring, M.A. 2007: Organic Agriculture Requires Process Rather than Product Evaluation of Novel Breeding Techniques. *NJAS- Wageningen Journal of Life Sciences*, 54: 401-412.

Maluszynski, M., Kasha, K.J. and Szarejko, I. (2003) Published Protocols for Other Crop Plant Species. In Doubled Haploid Production in Crop Plants: A Manual (Maluszynski, M., Kasha, K.J., Forster, B.P. and Szarejko, I., eds), pp. 309-336, Dordrecht, the Netherlands: Kluwer Academic Publishers.

Morozumi, Y., Ino, R., Takaku, M., Hosokawa, M., Chuma, S. and Kurumizaka H. (2012): Human PSF concentrates DNA and Stimulates Duplex Capture in DMC1-mediated Homologous Pairing. *Nucleic Acids Res.*, 40(7): 3031-41.

Nonomura, K.I., Nakano, M., Murata, K., Miyoshi, K., Eiguchi, M., Iayao, A., Hirochika, H. and Kurata, N. (2004) An Insertional Mutation in the Rice PAIR2 Gene, the Ortholog of Arabidopsis ASY1, Results in a Defect in Homologous Chromosome Pairing during Meisosis. *Mol. Genet. Genomics*, 271, 121-129.

Noyes, R.D., Baker, R. and Mai, B. (2006) Mendelian Segregation for Two-factor Apomixis in Erigeron Annuus (Asteraceae).

Perotti, E., Grimanelli, D., John, P., Hoisington, D. and Leblanc, O. (2004) Why is Transferring Apomixis to Crops Still a Dream? In New Directions for a Diverse Planet: Proceedings for the 4th International Crop Science Congress (Fischer, T., Turner, N., Angus, J., McIntyre, L., Robertson, M., Borrell, A. and Lloyd, D., eds), Brisbane, Australia.

Roeder, G.S. (1990) Chromosome Synapsis and Genetic Recombination: Their Roles in Meiotic Chromosome Segregation. *Trends Genet.*, 6, 385-389.

Ruiz, J.M., Ríos, J.J., Rosales, M.A., Rivero, R.M. and Romero, L. (2006) Grafting Between Tobacco Plants to Enhance Salinity Tolerance. *Journal of Plant Physiology*, 163: 1229-1237.

Shaharuddin, N.A., Yuanhuai, H., Hongying, L. and Grierson, D. (2006) The Mechanism of Graft Transmission of Sense and Antisense Gene Silencing in Tomato Plants. *FEBS Lett.* 580: 6579-6586.

Schaart, J.G. 2009. Novel Plant Breeding Techniques.

Schaart, J.G., Visser, R.G.F. 2009: Novel Plant Breeding Techniques-Consequences of New Genetic Modification-based Plant Breeding Techniques in Comparison to Conventional Plant Breeding. COGEM Research Report Number 2009-02. The Netherlands Commission on Genetic Modification.

Takaku, M., Kainuma, T., Ishida-Takaku, T., Ishigami, S., Suzuki, H., Tashiro, S., van Soest, R. W., Nakao, Y. and Kurumizaka, H. (2011): Halenaquinone, a Chemical Compound that Specifically Inhibits the Secondary DNA Binding of RAD51. *Genes Cells*, 16(4): 427-36.

Ulker, B., Li, Y., Rosso, M. G., Logemann, E., Somssich, I. E. and Weisshaar, B. (2008) T-DNA – Mediated Transfer of *Agrobacterium* Tumefaciens Chromosomal DNA into Plants. *Nat. Biotechnol.* 26: 1015-1017.

Wesley, S.V., Helliwell, C.A., Smith, N.A., Wang, M.B., Rouse, D.T., Liu, Q., Gooding, P.S., Singh, S.P., Abbott, D., Stoutjesdijk, P.A., Robinson, S.P., Gleave, A.P., Green, A.G. and Waterhouse, P.M. (2001): Construct Design for Efficient, Effective and High-throughput Gene Silencing in Plants. Plant J., 27, 581-590.

Wijner Erik, Kees Van Dun, C., Bastian de Snoo, Cilia, L. C. lelivelt, Joost J.B. Keurentjes, Nazatul Shima Naharudin, maruthachalam Ravi, Simon W. L. Chan, Hans de Jong and Rob Dirks (2012) Reverse Breeding in Arabidopsis thaliana Generates Homozygous Parental Lines from a Heterozygous Plant. Nature Geneics, 44: 467-470.

Zhang, X., Jin, S., Liu, D., Lin, Z., Zeng, F., Zhu, L., Tu, L. and Guo, X. (2008) Cotton Biotechnology: Challenge the Future for Cotton Improvement. In Advances in Plant Biotechnology (Rao, G.P., Zhao, Y., Radchuk, V.V. and Bhatnagar, S.K., eds), pp. 241-301. Houston, Texas: Studium Press LLC.

Index

❑ ❑ ❑ ❑ ❑ ❑